READING MORE, READING BETTER

SOLVING PROBLEMS IN THE TEACHING OF LITERACY
Cathy Collins Block, Series Editor

Recent Volumes

READING MORE, READING BETTER

Edited by

ELFRIEDA H. HIEBERT

THE GUILFORD PRESS
New York   London

© 2009 The Guilford Press
A Division of Guilford Publications, Inc.
72 Spring Street, New York, NY 10012
www.guilford.com

Printed in the United States of America

This book is printed on acid-free paper.

Last digit is print number: 9 8 7 6 5 4 3 2 1

Library of Congress Cataloging-in-Publication Data

Hiebert, Elfrieda H.
  Reading more, reading better / edited by Elfrieda H. Hiebert.
    p. cm.—(Solving problems in the teaching of literacy)
  Includes bibliographical references and index.
  ISBN 978-1-60623-285-9 (pbk : alk. paper)
  ISBN 978-1-60623-286-6 (hardcover : alk. paper)
  1. Reading—United States. 2. Literacy—Study and teaching—United States.
I. Hiebert, Elfrieda H.
  LB1050.R4164 2009
  428.4071—dc22

                                        2009004702

About the Editor

Elfrieda H. Hiebert, PhD, is Adjunct Professor in the Graduate School of Education at the University of California, Berkeley. She is also a principal investigator at the National Center for Research on the Educational Achievement and Teaching of English Language Learners. Dr. Hiebert has worked in the field of early reading acquisition for 40 years as a classroom teacher, teacher educator, and researcher. Her research addresses methods for supporting students who depend on schools to become literate and for fostering students' reading fluency, vocabulary, and knowledge through appropriate texts. Dr. Hiebert's model of accessible texts for beginning and struggling readers—TExT (Text Elements by Task)—has been used to develop several reading programs that are widely used in schools. Dr. Hiebert was the 2008 recipient of the William S. Gray Citation of Merit, awarded by the International Reading Association, and is a member of the Reading Hall of Fame. Her publications, such as *Becoming a Nation of Readers* (Center for the Study of Reading, 1985), *Every Child a Reader* (Center for the Improvement of Early Reading Achievement, 1999), and *Finding the Right Texts* (Guilford Press, 2008), have contributed to making research accessible to educators. She is the author or editor of 10 books as well as numerous journal articles.

Contributors

Marilyn Jager Adams, PhD, Department of Cognitive and Linguistic Sciences, Brown University, Providence, Rhode Island

Richard L. Allington, PhD, College of Education, University of Tennessee, Knoxville, Tennessee

Elizabeth Bernhardt, PhD, Stanford Language Center, Stanford University, Stanford, California

Stergios Botzakis, PhD, Department of Reading Education, University of Tennessee, Knoxville, Tennessee

Devon Brenner, PhD, Department of Curriculum, Instruction and Special Education, Mississippi State University, Mississippi State, Mississippi

Gina N. Cervetti, PhD, School of Education, University of Colorado at Boulder, Boulder, Colorado

Barbara R. Foorman, PhD, Florida Center for Reading Research, Florida State University, Tallahassee, Florida

Linda B. Gambrell, PhD, Eugene T. Moore School of Education, Clemson University, Clemson, South Carolina

John T. Guthrie, PhD, Department of Human Development, University of Maryland, College Park, College Park, Maryland

Elfrieda H. Hiebert, PhD, Graduate School of Education, University of California, Berkeley, Berkeley, California

Carolyn A. Jaynes, PhD, Leap Frog Enterprises, Inc., Emeryville, California

Melanie R. Kuhn, PhD, Literacy, Language, Counseling, and Development Department, Boston University, Boston, Massachusetts

Leigh Ann Martin, MA, TextProject, Santa Cruz, California

Anne McGill-Franzen, PhD, Department of Reading Education, University of Tennessee, Knoxville, Tennessee

Angela McRae, MA, Department of Human Development, University of Maryland, College Park, College Park, Maryland

Paula J. Schwanenflugel, PhD, Department of Educational Psychology, University of Georgia, Athens, Georgia

Elizabeth A. Swanson, PhD, College of Education, University of Texas at Austin, Austin, Texas

Renarta Tompkins, PhD, Spadoni College of Education, Coastal Carolina University, Conway, South Carolina

Sharon Vaughn, PhD, College of Education, University of Texas at Austin, Austin, Texas

Jade Wexler, PhD, The Meadow Center for Preventing Educational Risk, University of Texas at Austin, Austin, Texas

PREFACE

To become a proficient reader, the adage "practice makes perfect" makes eminent sense (Gambrell, 2007). To read well requires that students spend time reading. Many Americans, particularly children and adolescents, are not spending a great deal of time reading (National Endowment of the Arts, 2007). While this pattern cannot be attributed to any one single factor, a premise underlying this volume is that one source of students' disinterest in reading can be traced to an insufficient amount of time spent reading in classrooms. Even in a time when policies mandate an increase in the amount of time spent on reading instruction, the time that students spend in reading texts has not increased substantially from earlier eras. Further, lessons in and practice on particular skills and subskills of reading do not necessarily translate into a habit of engaged reading over a lifetime.

Not one of the contributors to this volume argues that the answer is simply to give students more books and more time to read them, although they recognize that the availability of texts and time allocated to reading are factors that enter into the equation. However, the responses of the contributors are not simplistic ones. In particular, they do not rehash the debate on sustained silent reading, nor do they focus on students reading in home and community environments, even though such reading is essential and, it is anticipated, related to school reading. The focus instead is firmly on the opportunities provided for students to read in the school environment.

The responses of the contributors fall into three categories. Part I lays the groundwork for effective practice in schools by addressing frameworks and perspectives for productive reading experiences in classrooms. As evidenced by recent policies regarding instructional time devoted to reading, problems occur when allocation of time to reading is viewed without conceptual underpinnings. Chapter 1, by Elfrieda H. Hiebert and Leigh Ann Martin, demonstrates that the efficacy of policies on allocation of time, of recommendations in teachers' editions, and of teachers' choices of activities depends on informed frameworks of the critical components of productive reading opportunities. For example, a mandate that at least 90 minutes of a school day be spent on reading instruction in Reading First classrooms can be meaningless without conceptual grounding in what activities and texts are critical to reading proficiency and stamina.

In Chapter 2, Richard L. Allington asks again the question that he posed 30 years ago in a landmark article: If they don't read much, how they ever gonna get good? After reaching the conclusion that the evidence is even stronger today than it was when the original article was published, Allington asks the question: Why isn't this evidence being manifest in practice? For educators who struggle with the fact that many students who can read don't, Chapter 3, by Angela McRae and John T. Guthrie, is essential reading. In particular, the authors highlight the manner in which content and knowledge—the stuff of texts—is central to becoming engaged and proficient readers.

Part II builds on these models and frameworks to describe how reading opportunities can be designed and implemented in classrooms. In Chapter 4, Gina N. Cervetti, Carolyn A. Jaynes, and Elfrieda H. Hiebert describe the manner in which students' engagement in reading and their knowledge of science are facilitated through lessons that emphasize science content rather than the typical narrative texts of elementary classrooms. Anne McGill-Franzen and Stergios Botzakis, in Chapter 5, argue for recognizing the diverse forms of students' out-of-school reading in classroom settings, including books based on cartoon and fantasy figures such as Scooby-Doo and Superman. This content is not the be-all and end-all of a school curriculum but, by building on texts with which students are comfortable and familiar, the authors argue that students can be encouraged to ask questions, including ones about the content of popular culture.

The final chapters in this section contrast how time is currently allocated to reading instruction in classrooms and what happens when interventions are designed to increase students' opportunities to read. In Chapter 6, Devon Brenner, Elfrieda H. Hiebert, and Renarta Tompkins address how much time students are reading connected text in Reading First classrooms. In their study, students were receiving 90 minutes or more of reading instruction daily as mandated by federal policies, but they were spending only about 20% of this time with their eyes on text. In Chapter 7, Melanie R. Kuhn and Paula J. Schwanenflugel show that even a small reallocation of time to more reading of text can make a difference. In their study, students in classes that had the greatest growth read approximately 7 minutes more per day than did students in the least successful classrooms.

Part III addresses issues that merit additional attention in creating the opportunity to read—the needs of struggling readers, students with native languages other than English, and students with learning disabilities. As Marilyn Jager Adams demonstrates in Chapter 8, extensive reading opportunities need to include complex texts with new vocabulary and subject matter. Adams proposes that, by concentrating on the key words and concepts of particular disciplines, even struggling readers will become increasingly able to read texts of increasingly greater depth and complexity. Similarly, Elizabeth Bernhardt, in Chapter 9, recommends an abundance of informational text for a specific group of learners, English language learners (ELLs). Bernhardt explains that ELLs especially need informational text, not only for its positive effects on both literacy and content learning, but also because it contains content that is shared across cultures and is not culturally specific, as is the case with narrative text. As Elizabeth A. Swanson, Jade Wexler, and Sharon Vaughn show in Chapter 10, students with learning disabilities typically do not have extensive opportunities to read. However, when more extensive opportunities are provided, students with learning disabilities make significantly better progress. In Chapter 11, Barbara R. Foorman illustrates how students' reading of texts that match their proficiencies and interests can be increased through the use of assessments.

Part IV offers a summary of the volume's themes and a reflection on an ultimate goal of reading instruction—reading for pleasure—in Chapter 12, the last chapter. Linda B. Gambrell has been a consistent advocate over several decades for the need to create opportunities to read in classrooms. Ultimately what these opportunities in classrooms need to develop, Gambrell argues in this chapter, is wanting to read. In the end, the measure of whether we are successful as literacy educators is whether individuals turn to texts for information, restoration, inspiration, and enjoyment. The models and implementation projects of the contributors in this book can further support educators in reaching this goal by ensuring that students have opportunities to engage in the right kinds of reading with the right kinds of texts.

REFERENCES

Gambrell, L.B. (2007, June/July). Reading: Does practice make perfect? *Reading Today, 24*(6), 16.

National Endowment for the Arts. (2007). *To read or not to read: A question of national consequence* (Research Report No. 47). Washington, DC: Author.

CONTENTS

III. CRITICAL FACTORS IN SUPPORTING MORE AND BETTER READING

IV. SUMMARY

PART I

FRAMEWORKS ON READING MORE AND BETTER

1

OPPORTUNITY TO READ

A Critical but Neglected
Construct in Reading Instruction

ELFRIEDA H. HIEBERT
LEIGH ANN MARTIN

> A large amount of this time was spent in various forms of
> word study as distinguished from supplementary reading.
> It is advisable to investigate the widespread practice of
> confining the work to materials so loaded with new words
> as to force pupils to spend nearly half of their time in
> isolated word study instead of real reading.
> —GATES (1930, p. 12)

Gates (1930) came to this conclusion after extensive observations in U.S. first-grade classrooms. According to Gates, students spent approximately 37% of the reading period on text-level tasks and the remainder on word-level tasks. In 2007, students in classrooms where 90 minutes or more was devoted to reading/language arts instruction spent an average of 18 minutes reading text—20% of the reading period (Brenner, Hiebert, & Tompkins, Chapter 6, this volume). Teachers talked with students about reading strategies and skills, and, after lessons, students practiced aspects of reading. Their time in engaged reading, however, was limited.

In any domain that one can identify—whether it be medical diagnosis, flying an aircraft, or programming computers—it would be absurd to think that someone becomes proficient without participating extensively in the activity, whether it be diagnosing, flying, or programming. When it comes to teaching students to read in schools, however, little attention is paid to the amount that students read texts. Over the past 8 years, the five components of reading identified by the National Reading Panel (NRP; National Institute of Child Health and Human Development [NICHD], 2000) have been emphasized in instructional programs and policy mandates. These components (and likely several additional ones) merit attention. However, the manner in which these components combine into the act of reading text and the ratio between instruction in the components and the integrated act of reading text have been relegated to the background in discussion of these components.

The premise of this chapter—and indeed, the entire volume— is that one's opportunity to read (OtR) matters. OtR, as described by Guthrie, Schafer, and Huang (2001), refers to occasions when students encounter texts and have some form of responsibility (self- or other-imposed) for the encounter. The features of reading events, particularly over an extended period of time (school year, school career), determine the degree of engagement that students demonstrate in reading, which Guthrie et al. define as the bringing together of motivation, strategy use, and conceptual knowledge during reading. In this chapter, we review research on OtR and its relationship to reading development. But before we begin this review, we propose a framework for OtR. Without a framework, conclusions can be—and, in fact, have been—made about research on particular reading contexts such as sustained silent reading (SSR) and generalized to other contexts such as silent reading, independent reading, or reading of self-selected texts. Informed practices in classrooms and research that supports such practices depend on a complete view of appropriate OtRs.

A Framework of OtR

OtRs are influenced by numerous variables in classrooms. Teachers are central to classroom experiences (Darling-Hammond & Bransford, 2005). It is through teachers' choices about a particular set of variables that the students experience learning in school. These variables include time, text (both difficulty and genre), and task. There are also variables related to individual students that predicate teachers' choices, for example, engagement and reading proficiency.

All of these variables—time, text difficulty and genre, task, and students' engagement and reading proficiency—require attention in understanding the nature and efficacy of OtR. We are not claiming to present a complete framework of OtR. Substantial theory and research are needed before a comprehensive framework of OtR can be offered. Further, given that each of these variables has its own history and scholarship, we are not claiming to do a comprehensive review of the individual variables. By bringing these variables together under the rubric of OtR, however, we hope to draw attention to OtR and the complexity of this construct.

Time

Mandates regarding the allocation of time are frequently central to educational reforms, such as Reading First, where a 90-minute reading block has been identified as the minimum amount required for reading instruction (U.S. Department of Education, 2001). By itself, however, time is not a highly informative variable. As Jackson (1968) said of time as a variable, "It acquires value chiefly because it marks the expenditure of a precious commodity—human life" (p. 38). If, for example, 90 minutes or more are devoted to reading instruction but that instruction is consumed with trivial tasks, reading proficiency is not likely to increase. The mandates for longer reading periods could even, unintentionally, result in lower reading levels if students become increasingly disengaged by spending long periods of time in tedious or trivial practice tasks.

While by itself time may not be an informative variable, the construct of time sheds light on students' learning opportunities when it is included in descriptions of school experiences. Within Carroll's (1963) model of school learning, three of the five variables were time-related: time needed, time allowed, and time spent on in-school learning. Carroll's model was elaborated within the academic learning time (ALT) model (Fisher, Berliner, Filby, Marliave, Cahen, & Dishaw, 1980). One extension of Carroll's model within the ALT was to consider whether students were involved or engaged in a task. Second, the amounts of time that students spent performing tasks successfully and unsuccessfully were related to student performances. Third, allocation of time to academic tasks was distinguished from time spent in transitional or nonlearning tasks.

According to the ALT (Fisher et al., 1980), teachers support students' learning in a domain such as reading by the manner in which they expend the time available during a school day—whether that time is devoted to academic content, the features and structures of tasks that engage students, or the matchup between students' proficiency and the task's difficulty. Such complexity has been lacking within the studies of SSR on which the National Reading Panel (NICHD, 2000) based its conclusions about independent silent reading, where researchers often failed to report the amount of time spent on productive reading.

Text Difficulty and Genre

Text difficulty has not been a primary focus in practice, research, or theory over the past several decades. The reasons for this lack of attention reflect the fact that text difficulty has been associated with a behaviorist model of learning, and the educational community has been moving away from this model. While theoretical explanations for the role of text difficulty are rarely encountered, anyone who has ever read with a student will attest to the difference that text difficulty makes. When it comes to students' success with a text as well as students' stamina and persistence, text difficulty makes a difference.

Betts (1946) proposed particular guidelines for independent, instructional, and frustration levels of reading. While little research has been conducted that has validated precisely the percentages of familiar words identified by Betts, Anderson, Evertson, and Brophy (1979) documented that the success readers have with a text influences their ongoing engagement and proficiency. Anderson et al. concluded that students need to work with materials with which they are successful. Presumably there can be a range of different levels of texts that an individual can experience, depending on the support provided by such factors as other readers and the contexts of the text (e.g., voice recognition software, illustrations).

A recent perspective that has been prominent in pedagogical writing suggests that the difficulty of the text is a function of the level of scaffolding or support that students receive (Fountas & Pinnell, 1999). The perspective of text scaffolding has led to proposals that challenging text may be a more viable source for beginning and struggling readers than texts at the instructional and independent levels proposed by Betts (1946). This perspective underlies Kuhn and Stahl's (2003) conclusion that "some have argued that having children read easy text improves fluency ... but it seems that the most successful approaches involved children reading instructional-level text or even text at the frustration level with strong support" (pp. 17–18). Menon and Hiebert (in press) examined the studies reviewed by Kuhn and Stahl. In only two studies was text difficulty manipulated, one of which failed to find significant differences in text difficulty and the other reported that fluency was facilitated when texts had a high, rather than low, overlap of words. Of the remaining studies, 55% used texts at students' instructional levels (i.e., "easy" texts); 32% used texts at grade level or above (i.e., "hard" texts); and 13% did not report text level. The operative pattern in this group of studies was gains from the intervention, with 70% reporting significant gains for the treatment (with either easy or hard text). While Stahl's own intervention (Stahl & Heubach, 2005)—fluency oriented reading intervention (FORI)—used grade-level text, most students were rarely below 85% accuracy and often read texts in the 90–92% range. Further, those students who did not have a modicum of reading proficiency at the beginning of the intervention did not make substantial progress.

Menon and Hiebert (in press) located studies not included in the Kuhn and Stahl (2003) review. In one of these studies, Young and Bowers (1995) reported significant declines in reading rate, accuracy, and prosody with each increase in text difficulty. In another, O'Conner, Bell, Harty, Larkin, Sackor, and Zigmond (2002) compared the influence of text difficulty—reading-level matched or grade-level matched—on poor readers' reading growth. They found that students who read reading-level matched material had significantly greater oral reading fluency growth. These additional findings as well as their review of the studies in the Kuhn and Stahl (2003) sample led Menon and Hiebert (in press) to conclude that evidence is lacking that time spent with difficult texts can be profitable for low-performing students.

While Menon and Hiebert's (in press) conclusion suggests a general directive, the degree of discrepancy between students' reading levels and the requirements of a text is not understood. Learners benefit from at least a modicum of challenge to become more proficient (Miller & Meece, 1999). How great can the discrepancy be between students' reading levels and the task posed by a text before reading instruction is nonefficacious? Right now, for students in the bottom 40%, the discrepancy between their reading proficiencies and the difficulty of texts is substantial, particularly at the beginning levels (Hiebert, 2009). Already at the first-grade level the texts of core reading programs require proficiency with the 1,000 most-frequent words, something with which students at the 40th percentile are not automatic until the fourth grade (Hiebert, 2009).

Genre must also be considered in designing opportunities to read, for reasons that extend beyond the need for a balanced reading diet (Duke, 2000). Genres embody differences in the complexity of a text for students. Informational texts often have more complex text structures and require more specific background knowledge than narrative texts (Biber, 1988). At the same time, rarely occurring words tend to be repeated more in informational than narrative texts, thereby lessening text difficulty. Expository texts with information about the natural and physical world and narrative texts with their emphasis on the human experience also represent different functions. One prevalent argument has been that primary-level and struggling readers should be given narrative texts because these are more engaging to them than informational text. Cervetti, Bravo, Hiebert, Pearson, and Jaynes (in press), however, reported that third and fourth graders (many of whom were struggling readers) did not so much prefer narrative texts as they did informational and narrative texts equally well—a pattern that held true for both girls and boys. Students' preferences for genre may be reflected in their perseverance and engagement with texts.

Tasks

Tasks represent the "stuff" of learning and instruction—listening to the teacher read aloud a trade book, following along as other students read, and identifying a handful of unknown words from a story are each very different tasks. Students can read texts in different modes (silent, oral), in different social configurations (e.g., independently, dyads, small teacher-led groups, whole-class settings), and with different activities following or intermingled (e.g., discussion, worksheets).

These illustrations represent only a fraction of the many tasks that make up students' school days and school careers. We will not review the theories and models of task structures within the voluminous literature of various disciplines (e.g., business, economics, psychology) in addition to education (Blumenfeld, Mergendoller, & Swarthout, 1987; Fisher & Hiebert, 1990). Tasks are complex and interact with numerous other constructs, including the variables identified here. A task always occurs over a given time period, and texts are an essential part of reading tasks.

We will identify several dimensions of task structures that are not addressed directly among the other variables in this discussion. A particularly critical set of dimensions that requires consideration in the design of silent reading events has to do with the monitoring of and accountability of tasks (Santi & Vaughn, 2007). Unlike the situation in oral reading, students' processes and outcomes are not as tangible when they are reading silently. Explicitly setting expectations for students engaged in independent reading and follow-up to ensure that the expectations were met illustrates a dimension of task design that can increase the efficacy of silent reading (Manning & Manning, 1984).

One way in which time interacts with task is the relationship between the amount of time allocated for a task and students' proficiency with the task. Students at any grade differ substantially in their rates of reading (Hasbrouck & Tindal, 2006). Allocating the same time to all students for a reading task will have consequences for both above- and below-level students. The manner in which time is distributed to reading tasks illustrates another critical dimension of tasks. While laboratory studies have been conducted on the effects of massed and distributed time allocation to the learning of some reading skills (Bloom & Shuell, 1981), little is known about the consequences of short bursts of time devoted to many different texts over an extended reading period or to sustained time with the same text. Presumably, the massed or distributed allocations of time to reading text will differ in efficacy for students of different proficiencies.

Engagement

Numerous opportunities for reading can exist in students' classroom and out-of-school lives, but, if students do not read or read only half-heartedly, the opportunities have little value. Students' attention and involvement in a reading event determine whether the hoped-for outcomes occur. Often educators view students' interest in reading as a trait or a disposition that reflects students' motivation. Guthrie's work (see McRae & Guthrie, Chapter 3, this volume) demonstrates the manner in which engagement, while mediated in important ways by individual differences of students, is also a function of instructional features, particularly when viewed across a school year or school career (Fisher & Hiebert, 1990).

The recognition that reading is an important competency to acquire—and, hence, that available opportunities should be used well—initially lies with the adults in an environment. Eventually students are the ones who take responsibility for how they use available OtRs. Multiple techniques and pathways are needed to support students in taking on this ownership. It takes long periods of time to become proficient at complex processes—and reading is a complex process. The manner in which tasks and content interact with texts to develop and sustain student engagement in literacy is central to understanding OtR.

Reading Proficiency

For many students, developmental level and proficiency are inextricably interwoven. Young children are much more inexperienced in assessing the kinds of words that they can read and the complexity of ideas that they can process in text, as compared with older readers. Students in the middle grades typically can read texts with more complex ideas as well as words with more orthographically complex structures than students in the primary grades. However, proficiency and developmental level do not follow the same trajectory for all students. Some students within an age cohort read substantially less proficiently than their peers throughout their school careers.

In models of reading such as SSR, there has been a "one-size-fits-all" perspective. If a time was to be designated as silent reading for the students in a school, all students—whether 6 or 12 years of age—would read for the same length of time (Hunt, 1970). Application of the SSR model has not been the only place where the one-size-fits-all perspective has been applied. When a national panel recommends that elementary students' involvement in literature should be increased (Anderson, Hiebert, Scott, & Wilkinson, 1985), this recommendation is translated into policies that students of all grades, including first grade, should be reading authentic literature only (California English/Language Arts Committee, 1987). When a national panel concludes that SSR has not been shown to improve fluency (NICHD, 2000), this conclusion is translated into policies that students of all grades should be doing more oral reading and less silent reading (Hasbrouck, 2006).

A one-size-fits-all model can derail teachers from providing the focused instruction students require at particular levels. The developmental status and proficiency of students should be the basis for the selection of tasks and the choices about other variables such as the length of time spent on particular texts and tasks. To date, some models address developmental and proficiency trajectories of reading skills and strategies (e.g., Chall, 1983b), but these models—and others—are rarely as explicit and differentiated in the appropriateness of reading tasks and texts as a function of reader status. At present, even models of text differentiation at the word level are not taken into account in creating the core reading programs that govern American reading instruction (Hiebert, 2009).

Research on OtR

Research on the nature and effects of students' opportunities to read in classrooms can be described, at best, as sparse. Studies fall into one of two types, based on research design—descriptive research and quasi-experimental and experimental studies.

The first group of studies forms the foundation for understanding how much students are reading and the nature of tasks and texts that are part of these experiences. In some cases, researchers have analyzed students' reading proficiencies as a function of the quality and/or quantity of these experiences. When the proficiencies have been analyzed in relation to these classroom patterns, the conclusions are based on correlational analyses. While correlations cannot impute causality conclusively, they do point to the existence of potentially important relationships. In the complex arena of classrooms, correlations are often the initial—and sometimes the only—means of establishing and understanding the nature and influence of such critical factors as text difficulty and task design.

Often criticisms of the descriptive literature focus on the limitations of correlational data. An even greater deficit of this research paradigm, from the vantage point of creating the best possible OtRs, may be that most studies have examined the "enacted curriculum" (Rowan, Camburn, & Correnti, 2004), which refers to existing classroom patterns of what *is* being taught rather than what *could* or *should* be taught. Alternative paradigms describe practices and relationships in exemplary classrooms that show what is possible when best practices are put into effect. To date, much of the research on OtR emanates from descriptions of average classrooms rather than ones that have proven exceptional in engendering high levels of reading performance and interest among students.

Since 2000, the conclusions of the NRP (NICHD, 2000) have dominated discussions of the relationship between OtR and reading achievement. The decision of the NRP to report only findings based on experimental data meant that a particular form of opportunity to read has overshadowed any critical patterns from the descriptive research, namely, SSR and its effects specifically on fluency. Further, the existing experiments have considered only a particular form of SSR—a model where students read in self-selected texts with no accountability (Hunt, 1970). The experiments relating to this model were simplistic in their design. For example, most failed to report whether experimental students read more than control students, how much they read, or the match between student proficiency and texts. Such variables as time or tasks were rarely manipulated. We summarize the experimental studies on SSR separately from the descriptive evidence available on the five variables of time, text difficulty and genre, task, proficiency, and engagement. We do this because few, if any, of the studies on SSR considered the variables that we have proposed as central to effective opportunities to read.

Descriptive Research

Time Allocation

Following the suggestions of Carroll (1963) and Fisher et al. (1980), researchers have periodically considered how much of a reading instruction period is allocated to text reading. Kurth and Kurth (1987) observed that 36 first-, third-, and fifth-grade teachers spent an average of 29% of the reading period directing text reading (13% oral reading and 16% silent reading). McNinch, Schaffer, Campbell, and Rakes (1998) similarly observed that 20 third-through fifth-grade teachers allocated an average 35.5% of the reading period to reading connected text. However, they reported a large variance in terms of teacher allocations: one teacher allocated 100% of the lesson to text reading, while five teachers allocated no time for text reading. In a subsequent survey of 58 third-through fifth-grade teachers, McNinch, Schaffer, and Campbell (1999) reported that 76% of teachers believed that their students should spend 33–58% of daily reading instruction directly reading under their guidance. The teachers in the studies by Kurth and Kurth (1987) and McNinch et al. (1998) dedicated approximately one-third of the instructional period to text reading, the minimum of the specified range.

Studies at the levels of the student and classroom have reported similar findings on time allocated to text reading. Gambrell, Wilson, and Gantt (1981) reported that a sample of 70 fourth-grade boys read for an average of 46.5% of the time during reading periods. Juel and Minden-Cupp (2000) found that, across four first-grade classrooms that differed in instructional approaches, 26–43% of the reading period was devoted to text reading.

Implicit in these examinations of time spent reading is the assumption that the expertise gained while reading will influence achievement. One of the initial studies that considered the relationship between time spent reading and student achievement was the Beginning Teacher Effectiveness Study (BTES; Fisher et al., 1980). These researchers found that the amount of time allocated to instruction in a content area—including a specific skill area—was positively associated with student achievement in the content area. Differences in time allocations to reading and to particular reading processes were substantial across classrooms. For example, comprehension activities ranged from 1,000 to 5,000 minutes over a school year across fifth-grade classes.

The ALT model described earlier was used to make distinctions in success and engagement rates (Fisher et al., 1980). The proportion of time that students were engaged in the task was positively associated with learning, as was the level of success students experienced. Typical students spent approximately 50% of their time in tasks in which they were successful. Students who spent more time than the average in high-success activities had higher achievement scores at the end of the school year, while students who spent more time on excessively difficult material generally learned less than other students.

Using BTES-like procedures but comparing patterns in successful and less successful schools with similar demographics, Frederick, Easton, Muirhead, and Vanderwicken (1979) reported that "high-gain" schools allocated more time to reading instruction and students spent more of that time reading than in "low-gain" schools, where students spent more time in nonreading activities during reading periods. Differences were small but significant, even after controlling for the effects of poverty and initial academic achievement.

Recently an examination of time allocation factors was reported using the statistical technique of hierarchical linear modeling (HLM), which was not available 30 years ago, when most studies of time allocation were conducted. Foorman et al. (2006) observed 1,285 first- and second graders and their 107 teachers. Of 20 time allocation variables identified by Foorman et al. (2006), the amount of time allocated to text reading loaded highly onto its own factor, and time spent giving directions and preparation to teach loaded negatively. HLM was used to examine how the time allocation factors, along with teacher effectiveness ratings, grade level, and initial student reading ability, predicted end-of-year scores. Only time allocated for text reading significantly explained gains on any posttest measures (including word reading, decoding, and passage comprehension). No other time factors, including time spent on word, alphabetic, or phonemic awareness instruction, independently contributed to reading growth.

The effects of different amounts of reading have also been examined through the lenses of a particular program—Accelerated Reader (AR). AR is a computer program that provides students with comprehension quizzes on books that they have read from the AR list (which contains over 100,000 titles). Students' scores on the quizzes are based on the percentage of correct answers weighted by the number of words and the readability level of the book. Numerous studies of AR have been conducted, typically of existing implementation sites. This chapter is not the proper place for conducting an in-depth analysis of the literature on AR. In brief, however, students in AR classes typically have exhibited greater growth rates than those in control classrooms, with effect sizes ranging from 0.07 to 0.34 (Nunnery, Ross, & McDonald, 2006).

In several studies, researchers have compared the effects of students reading in school versus out of school on their achievement levels. Guthrie, Wigfield, Metsala, and Cox (1999) administered two questionnaires to 3rd- and 5th graders and 8th- and 10th graders, one about the amount of reading in school and the other about the amount of reading at home. The amount of in- and out-of-school reading significantly predicted text comprehension on two measures of reading, even when past reading achievement, prior topic knowledge, self-efficacy for reading, and reading motivation were controlled statistically.

In Taylor, Frye, and Maruyama's (1990) investigation, students spent an average of 15.8 minutes a day, or 31.6% of reading instructional time, in either assigned reading or SSR and a similar amount reading at home. However, in-school reading correlated to reading achievement at .37, while the correlation to home reading was half that size ($r = .16$). Even when differences in prior knowledge, prior reading ability, and time allowed for reading at school were controlled, reading time in school was a significant factor in reading growth.

Texts and Tasks

Fisher and Hiebert (1990) compared the tasks done with texts in literature- and skill-based classrooms. Students in literature-based classrooms engaged in more reading per instructional period (82% for grade 2 and 85% for grade 6) than skills-based classes (61% and 72%, respectively). Students in literature-based classes spent much of their time silently reading trade books of their own choosing. In contrast, students in the skills-based classes primarily read from teacher-selected materials during whole-class or ability group instruction. In terms of OtR, students in the two types of classes engaged in different amounts of reading, had access to different kinds of texts, and had different levels of control over what and how they read.

Surveys conducted over the past decade suggest that most teachers report using a balanced approach to text selection. Prior to the initiation of No Child Left Behind (NCLB), Baumann, Hoffman, Duffy-Hester, and Ro (2000) reported that 83% of teachers reported using both basal readers and trade books for instruction. Two percent of teachers reported using only basals, and 16% reported using only trade books. Teachers were also asked to rate how often they used different types of texts, including basals, fiction and nonfiction trade books, phonics workbooks, and magazines, using a five-point scale that ranged from exclusively = 5 to never = 1. Teachers gave the highest ratings to fiction trade books (3.4) and nonfiction trade books (3.0).

As the mandates of NCLB were beginning to be implemented, Chorzempa and Graham (2006) conducted a survey to establish the nature of text use across achievement levels. Teachers reported using basal reading series and workbooks more frequently with below-average groups than with average or higher groups. Student-selected materials and expository trade books were used most often with above-average groups and least often with below-average groups. These two surveys suggest that multiple kinds of texts are used in classrooms, although readers with higher proficiencies have access to a wider range of texts.

Socioeconomic status (SES) also seems to influence the kinds of texts and tasks in classrooms. Duke (2000) reported that low-SES class-rooms had significantly fewer extended books (i.e., texts longer than three related sentences) and magazines than high-SES classrooms (mean of 448.9 vs. 737.7 texts per classroom respectively, on visit 1). Students in low-SES classrooms spent an average of 34.9% with extended text, compared with 48.7% in the high-SES classrooms. The content of the extended texts differed as well. There were significantly fewer informa-tional texts in low-SES than high-SES classrooms (6.9% of books in low-SES and 12.7% in high-SES). In addition, the informational texts were rarely used: only 3.6 minutes a day of interaction with informational text (often in teacher read-aloud events).

Few studies have examined the effect of the match (or mismatch) between texts and students' proficiencies. One exception is Gambrell et al.'s (1981) analysis of the reading accuracy of low-achieving read-ers with their instructional texts. Approximately 61% read with 95% accuracy (i.e., easy texts), and 39% read with less than 95% accuracy (i.e., difficult texts). Students who had easy texts spent 42% of their time reading, while students who had difficult texts spent 22% of the time reading text.

Schumm, Moody, and Vaughn (2000) investigated the effect of a "one-size-fits-all" mode of reading instruction with 120 third-grade stu-dents from 21 classrooms where teachers used whole-class instruction and the same reading materials for all students. A group of students (two high-, average-, and low-achieving students and two students with learning disabilities) from each class was assessed on word recog-nition, decoding, comprehension, and reading self-concept and attitude in fall and spring. High-achieving students made the expected gain over the school year—one full grade. For the most challenged students, however, the gap between initial and ending performances increased. Low-achieving students had a gain of 3 months in comprehension, and learning-disabled students had a gain of 2 months.

Proficiency

One aspect of the allocation of time is whether readers of different proficiency levels are given comparable amounts of time for reading text. The practice called "ability grouping" was the most commonly used method of organizing reading instruction in American elementary schools until its use began to be questioned during the mid-1980s (Anderson et al., 1985). The rationale for ability grouping was that instruction could be tailored to meet the differing needs of students in order to narrow the achievement gap. However, some studies suggested that ability groups contributed to widening the gap between good and poor readers.

In Gambrell et al.'s (1981) observational study, high-achieving readers were on task 92% of the time as compared with 81% for low-achieving readers. Of this time, high-achieving readers spent 57% of the time reading text, while low-achieving readers spent only 33% of the time reading text. The remainder of time was spent on letter and word work (7% vs. 13% for high- and low-achieving readers, respectively) and nonreading activities such as listening to the teacher (36%, compared with 54%). While these differences are small in terms of a single instructional period, they can lead to large differences when viewed over time.

Allington (1982) used the amount of text read by students to consider differences in reading experiences. Based on surveys of 60 teachers of first-, third-, and fifth-grade classes, Allington (1982) reported that high-achieving first graders read 261 words per day in the same time that students in the lowest group read 90 words. Similarly, the high-achieving groups daily read 1.9 and 1.8 times more words than the low-achieving ones in the third and fifth grades, respectively. The amounts of text read orally versus silently differed significantly, with low-performing students reading orally more than high-performing ones. These findings led Allington (1983) to recommend that low-performing readers should spend more time reading silently since more text can be read silently than orally during the same time period. Allington also argued that low-performing students needed to spend *more* instructional time doing text reading than higher-performing students if the achievement gap was to be reduced or eliminated. Surveys of teachers' practices (Baumann et al., 2000; Chorzempa & Graham,

2006) suggest that this recommendation was not applied in many classrooms.

Engagement

Fisher et al. (1980) defined engagement as the degree of student participation in tasks. Leinhardt, Zigmond, and Cooley (1981) used this definition in studying learning-disabled students, two-thirds of whom read near grade level and one-third 1 year or more below grade level. Leinhardt et al. documented the amount of time engaged in direct reading (oral or silent), indirect reading (i.e., discussion, listening, worksheets, etc.), and nonreading activities. They found that the amount of time that students spent reading was approximately 15% of the time allocated to reading instruction. The correlation between reading achievement and time spent reading was +.63. They reported on a regression equation that revealed a dramatic relationship: an increase of one minute of daily silent reading by students resulted in a 1-point increase in their reading improvement scores. A second regression indicated that an increase of 1 minute in teacher instruction resulted in a 1-minute increase in student reading time. Teachers' affective behaviors such as encouraging a student to stay on task or positive feedback were also significant in contributing to increases in the amount of time students engaged in reading. These equations suggested that increasing a teacher's allocation of instructional time and supportive behaviors could result in students' spending more time reading, which in turn could result in improved reading. In a reanalysis of the data from the Leinhardt et al. study, however, Wilkinson, Wardrop, and Anderson (1988) concluded that pretest ability influenced the amount of time students spent reading. While time as a factor had a positive effect on reading achievement, this effect was not significant. Preexisting reading ability, Wilkinson et al. concluded, is more predictive of reading achievement.

In a study similar to Leinhardt et al.'s (1981), Stallings (1980) explored the relationship between how 87 middle school remedial reading teachers allocated time during reading instruction and their students' reading growth. In the classes where students had the lowest pretest scores but the highest posttest gain scores, teachers allocated the most time for oral reading, instruction, discussion, praise and support, and feedback. In classes that experienced no posttest gains, teachers allocated the most time to what Stallings termed "noninteractive" activities (i.e., classroom management, silent reading, and written assignments). In classes where teachers spent large amounts of time in activities such as grading papers and making lesson plans while students read silently and independently, silent reading did not positively influence reading achievement.

Guthrie et al. (2001) created a measure of engaged reading based on students' answers to questions about the frequency of (1) reading for enjoyment, (2) reading self-selected books in class, (3) silent reading, and (4) checking out books from public or school libraries. From questionnaires answered by teachers, Guthrie et al. created measures of OtR in classrooms: frequency of class visits to the school library, frequency of student reading in self-selected texts, frequency of silent reading during reading instruction, and diversity of text types. Measures of reading achievement and student engagement (the amount of text read by students) were constructed from available National Assessment of Educational Progress (NAEP) data. Highly engaged readers had higher achievement scores than moderately engaged students, who, in turn, had scored higher than students with low engagement. Further, the more OtR in a classroom, the more highly students were engaged. While OtR did not directly predict reading achievement, it significantly predicted student engagement, which, in turn, significantly predicted reading achievement.

Experimental Investigations of OtR

We give a brief overview of reviews and meta-analyses of reading, typically SSR, and then move to several experimental or quasi-experimental studies that have been conducted on aspects of OtR since the NRP's (NICHD, 2000) report.

Reviews and Meta-Analyses

When Lewis (2002) combed the literature for reviews of SSR prior to that of the NRP, she located seven. Three reviews reported generally positive effects on reading attitudes, general performance, and reading attitudes and reading comprehension when combined with a program of instruction. Two reviews reported generally positive results for long-term projects, and two studies reported inconclusive or mixed results.

All of the analyses reviewed by Lewis (2002) had been conducted prior to the NRP (NICHD, 2000) except for one (Chow & Chou, 2000), although none was cited in the report. Further, many of the individual studies in these seven reviews were not included in the NRP database because they did not meet the criteria for research design (experimental or quasi-experimental) or publication in peer-reviewed national research journals. The NRP's application of these criteria resulted in the identification of 10 studies, 5 of which reported no statistically significant effect for SSR on students' reading achievement. Of the 5 studies that favored SSR, effect estimates were relatively small and were of a noneducationally significant size or were mixed in terms of effects on outcome assessments. The NRP concluded that "even though encouraging students to read more is intuitively appealing, there is still not sufficient research evidence obtained from studies of high methodological quality to support the idea that such efforts reliably increase how much students read or that such programs result in improved reading skills" (NICHD, 2000, p. 13).

Because data from descriptive studies were not included in the review, the conclusions of the NRP were not highly nuanced. For example, factors that characterized effective SSR were not considered, such as Manning and Manning's (1984) observation that reading scores improved somewhat when SSR included peer discussion or teacher conferencing. Since the NRP's criteria had eliminated studies such as this, Lewis (2002) conducted a follow-up analysis with broader criteria of research design and measures than those of the NRP. In all, Lewis identified 92 studies, of which 49 were used in a meta-analysis and 43 in a directional analysis.

The 49 studies in the meta-analysis were by no means homogeneous, as evident in Lewis's further categorization of the focus of the studies as: (1) independent reading, mostly SSR (26); (2) students' reading on their own (including home reading) (11); (3) print exposure (5); and (4) miscellaneous factors that considered variations of reading in instructional programs rather than in independent reading (7). Similar to the studies examined by the NRP, the majority of the studies pertained to independent reading (i.e., 37 in the first two categories). Of the 49 studies, 8 were true experiments with random assignment of students, 24 were quasi-experiments (using preexisting groups), and 17 used correlational analyses. The studies included 106 student samples with 192 comparisons that, when analyzed individually, had an average z of .10 under fixed assumptions and .194 under random assumptions, converting to r values of .10 and .192, respectively—indices that fall in the low range. By contrast, the overall d-index effect size was 0.422 for the eight experiments and 0.534 when averaged across separate student samples; the d-index was 0.534 and 0.612 when averaged across studies. Lewis felt that these high to medium d-index values justified the conclusion that some sorts of reading experiences lead to significantly higher achievement than not having this exposure.

The studies in the directional analysis reported whether results were positive or negative but provided insufficient data for inclusion in a meta-analysis. Of a total of 108 separate student samples from these 43 studies, 85 reported positive effects on reading achievement from reading practice and exposure, 9 reported negative results, and 14 reported no effect. Thus, the proportion of positive sample results was .79%. The samples in most of the studies that reported no effects or negative growth from reading experiences consisted of fourth graders or higher. Lewis (2002) speculated that, because these students are fairly proficient readers already, 10- to 15-minute reading periods—as was typical in these studies—may have been insufficient to significantly influence performance. For students who were less proficient readers (e.g., beginning readers, learning-disabled, second-language), even such short periods typically produced benefits.

Recent Experimental Studies

Since the NRP (NICHD, 2000), several experimental studies with more rigorous designs and theoretical frameworks than studies from earlier eras have examined the effects of different reading opportunities on students' achievement. Reutzel, Fawson, and Smith (2008) reconfigured SSR into scaffolded silent reading (ScSR), where students read widely in independent-level texts that cover a range of genres and with periodic teacher monitoring and accountability through completed book response assignments. SsSR was compared to *guided repeated oral reading* (GROR), the approach that the NRP (NICHD, 2000) identified as effective. In GROR, students orally read a single text repeatedly, typically at grade level or instructional level, while receiving feedback from a teacher or other students. Reutzel et al. (2008) conducted a randomized year-long experiment of third-grade students' fluency and comprehension but also gathered qualitative data such as interviews and surveys to establish trends and themes. No significant differences were found between these two forms of reading in affecting third-grade students' fluency and comprehension development, with the exception of one significant difference favoring ScSR on expression of a single passage. The qualitative data showed that exclusive use of either reading approach tended toward tedium and reduced overall student enjoyment and motivation. Reutzel et al. suggested that the optimal approach may be to combine the two forms of reading.

Kuhn and Schwanenflugel (Chapter 7, this volume) led a research team that examined the effects of different text experiences on students' reading. One treatment was FORI (Stahl & Heubach, 2005), where during a week of instruction students used a single text from the basal anthology but with guided and repeated oral reading. In the second approach, wide reading, students read two grade-level trade books in addition to the week's basal selection. In the first year, both intervention groups had higher performances on word reading and comprehension than comparison students who read the basal anthology texts without repeated reading. The wide-reading but not the FORI group significantly outperformed comparison students on fluency. The pattern for the second year was similar. A year later, fluency was similar for all three groups, but students in the FORI and wide-reading groups had better comprehension than control students. The investigators chose to scale up FORI in the third year because wide reading, though initially more beneficial, was perceived as prohibitive in cost. At the end of 6 months, students in FORI classes performed no differently in word reading or reading comprehension and more poorly on words correct per minute than those in control classrooms. Data from the seven classes most successful in increasing reading rate were compared to the seven least successful classes, regardless of condition. This analysis showed that students in successful classes read 7 minutes more daily than students in the least successful classes.

Wu and Samuels (2004) implemented a quasi-experimental study in third- and fifth-grade classes where the amount of time devoted to AR differed. With the exception of time spent in independent reading (one group, 15 minutes; the other group, 40 minutes), other factors were controlled (e.g., teacher experience, reading program). The group that read more had significantly higher reading achievement than the group that read less. Further, while poor readers showed significantly greater gains in word recognition and vocabulary than good readers even after 15 minutes, reading comprehension gains occurred only with 40 minutes of reading.

Toward a Comprehensive View of OtR

Research on the association between reading opportunity and achievement has languished in the case of SSR. The topic is much broader, as the review in this chapter and the contributions throughout this volume illustrate. We have proposed a framework in which the developmental and proficiency levels of readers are considered in relation to tasks, texts, engagement, and time. Individually, each feature is complex. When considered together, research designs can be expected to be highly complex. Such work is needed, however, if the effects of opportunity to read are to be understood. In the remainder of this chapter, we identify particular questions that need to be addressed.

Ratio of Time Devoted to Reading of Different Types

We began the chapter with a quote about the amount of time that students were reading—observations that appear to be as pertinent in 2009 as they were in 1929, when Gates (1930) was observing in American classrooms. While recommendations have been made as to amounts of time that should be spent reading (see, e.g., Allington, Chapter 2, this volume), research on the efficacy of different configurations of the contexts and types of reading, particularly with students at different performance and developmental levels, is needed before policies and mandates can claim to be based on evidence. The distinctions in the ratio of oral and silent reading, in particular, would benefit from research attention. In a kindergarten and first-grade classroom, much of students' reading will be oral (even when they are reading independently, most will vocalize). As students move into second grade, the ratio of silent to oral reading would be expected to change, with much more reading in the form of silent reading. Silent reading does not equate with SSR. As demonstrated by Reutzel et al. (2008), repeated reading of texts that includes silent reading can be effective. Except for students who are struggling with fluency, middle-grade and middle school students will primarily be reading silently. For those middle-grade students who are struggling with fluency, the inclusion of silent reading within a fluency intervention is likely critical. Oral reading does have a place with proficient readers insofar as they are preparing for performances or presentations.

OtR and Reading-Related Tasks

There is a substantial amount of apparatus related to reading. Chall (1967/1983a) found that the size of the teachers' guides had at least doubled over a 15-year period. A comparable analysis has not been conducted recently, but, in eyeballing a stack of 1983 teachers' manuals and one for 2008, the amount of information in the basic teachers' manual appears to have roughly doubled again.

What should the ratio be of reading text to instruction about and practice in the skills of reading, including time spent in discussion of the text? At present, this question cannot be answered with strong evidence, but we are willing to state with considerable confidence that the ratio will not be the same across developmental and proficiency levels (as is the case in current core reading programs). The one-size-fits-all perspective is evident in core reading programs in the lengthy discussions that are recommended, regardless of the complexity of the text. An illustration of such a perspective is an anthology selection for first graders of 185 words about a young rabbit who is trying to catch a fish and, in the same core reading program, an anthology selection for sixth graders of 2,011 words about an immigrant girl adjusting to life in the United States (Afflerbach et al., 2007). The former has 11 comprehension questions on predicting, inferential, literal, and critical character evaluation; the latter has 13 that cover the same proficiencies. The content of these two texts differs remarkably in its complexity, and yet the instructional apparatus is almost identical.

The Level of Difficulty in Students' Success and Engagement as Readers

As evident in the review in the first section of this chapter, text difficulty has not been a priority among scholars, either in theory or in empirical investigations. With the dramatic shift in the model of text that dominates current core reading programs, texts have become substantially harder for a particular segment of an age cohort (Hiebert, 2009). Even with a substantial amount of scaffolding (including read-alouds of the text by the teacher, as recommended in core reading programs), it is unlikely that many students will be able to read the texts independently. While the discrepancy between the features of text does not escalate greatly beyond this point, there are few venues for students to get the foundation they need to become proficient readers. By the fourth grade, most students in a grade cohort can read a majority of the words in texts, but those in the bottom 40%, in particular, read slowly (Daane, Campbell, Grigg, Goodman, & Oranje, 2005). Even when given OtRs, these students may not be highly engaged with text and have little stamina for reading. The manner in which consistent experiences with accessible texts, starting from kindergarten entry, support students' engagement in reading should be one of the foremost research questions on the national research agenda.

The Role of Content within a Reading Program

The mandates of Reading First have meant increased time in reading/ language arts and mathematics and less time in science and social studies (Dorph, Goldstein, Lee, Lepori, Schneider, & Venkatesan, 2007). We can identify at least three reasons why the study of how students perform as a function of greater opportunities to read content-area text should be part of the design of curriculum and research on OtR. First, students require critical bodies of background knowledge to read well. Reading is a primary means whereby individuals extend their background knowledge after a certain point, and background knowledge is the biggest predictor of how students do as readers (and also as thinkers in other domains). If the bulk of school time is spent reading stories that mimic the experiences of students' daily lives, it is unlikely that they will develop extensive knowledge about content.

McRae and Guthrie (Chapter 3, this volume) and Cervetti, Jaynes, and Hiebert (Chapter 4, this volume) underscore the second reason, namely, that reading to learn something is engaging. We are not talking about a superficial nod to content. Knowledge needs to be at the center of the literacy curriculum in a way it is not now (Walsh, 2003). Third, content-area texts may be a source for greater cultural access for linguistically and culturally diverse students. As Bernhardt (Chapter 9, this volume) argues, narrative texts represent the experiences of particular cultural groups. This cultural peculiarity can create challenges for English language learners who may not have the wide-ranging knowledge required for particular narratives. With informational text, the content is independent of students' cultures.

Developing Reading Preferences as a Skill

One element that was not recognized in the original SSR scheme (Hunt, 1970) is the degree to which individuals who read extensively have developed expertise in finding appropriate texts. Marino and Moylan's (1994) examination of the characteristics of voracious readers established the centrality of a network of information and people in their reading, including friends, bookstores (and now websites), and book reviews in newspapers and magazines. As one reader studied by Marino and Moylan observed, "I'm always thinking of the next book" (p. 22).

Attending to preferences may be the most neglected of all reading strategies in the current curriculum. When the selections are constrained and fail to offer a broad set of choices of topics and genres, nothing supports students in becoming more skillful in their selections of text. To become truly engaged readers, students need to be exposed to a wide range of genres and topics over the course of their school careers. When teachers conduct lessons on authors, illustrators, and the features of high-quality texts, even children as young as second graders were able to employ thoughtful strategies in selecting texts in a library (Mervar & Hiebert, 1989). Students in these classes could explain why they chose particular texts, through knowledge of illustrators, authors, or topics. For classes without such lessons, students simply pulled books off of the shelf and gave few reasons for their choices. Every topic and genre will not be a match for every student, but, over time, students develop preferences and areas of expertise.

Conclusion

The digital age provides unprecedented availability of knowledge and communication. To participate in this digital world necessitates high levels of literacy proficiencies. Even in a time when policies mandate an increase in the amount of time spent on reading instruction (and the entire school day, it appears, consists of reading instruction), the time that students spend in reading texts has not increased substantially from earlier eras. A framework has been presented in this chapter that highlights the constructs that require consideration in designing classroom experiences where students are reading more and more of the "right stuff." The chapters within this volume elaborate upon this framework to support educators in creating classroom opportunities that engage students in reading more of the right kinds of text—and, as a result, enable them to read more critically and proficiently.

References

Afflerbach, P., Blachowicz, C. L. Z., Boyd, C. D., Cheyney, W., Juel, C., Kame'enui, E. J., et al. (2007). *Reading Street*. Glenview, IL: Scott Foresman.

Allington, R. L. (1982). *Content coverage and contextual reading in reading groups*. Paper presented at the annual meeting of the National Council of Teachers of English, Denver, CO.

Allington, R. L. (1983). The reading instruction provided readers of differing reading abilities. *The Elementary School Journal, 83*(5), 547–559.

Anderson, L., Evertson, C., & Brophy, J. (1979). An experimental study of effective teaching in first grade reading groups. *Elementary School Journal, 79*, 193–222.

Anderson, R. C., Hiebert, E. H., Scott, J. A., & Wilkinson, I. A. G. (1985). *Becoming a nation of readers: The report of the Commission on Reading.* Washington, DC: National Institute of Education.

Baumann, J. F., Hoffman, J. V., Duffy-Hester, A. M., & Ro, J. M. (2000). *The First R* yesterday and today: U.S. elementary reading instruction practices reported by teachers and administrators. *Reading Research Quarterly, 35*(3), 338–377.

Betts, E. A. (1946). *Foundations of reading instruction.* New York: American Book Co.

Biber, D. (1988). *Variation across speech and writing.* New York: Cambridge University Press.

Bloom, K. C., & Shuell, T. J. (1981). Effects of massed and distributed practice on the learning and retention of second-language vocabulary. *Journal of Educational Research, 74,* 245–248.

Blumenfeld, P. C., Mergendoller, J., & Swarthout, D. (1987). Task as an heuristic for understanding student learning and motivation. *Journal of Curriculum Studies, 19,* 135–148.

California English/Language Arts Committee. (1987). *English-language arts framework for California public schools (kindergarten through grade twelve).* Sacramento: California Department of Education.

Carroll, J. (1963). A model for school learning. *Teachers College Record, 64,* 723–733.

Cervetti, G. N., Bravo, M. A., Hiebert, E. H., Pearson, P. D., & Jaynes, C. (in press). Text genre and science content: Ease of reading, comprehension and reader preference. *Reading Psychology.*

Chall, J. S. (1983a). *Learning to read: The great debate* (3rd ed.). Fort Worth, TX: Harcourt Brace. (Original work published 1967)

Chall, J. S. (1983b). *Stages of reading development.* New York: McGraw-Hill.

Chorzempa, B. F., & Graham, S. (2006). Primary-grade teachers' use of within-class ability grouping in reading. *Journal of Educational Psychology, 98*(3), 529–541.

Chow, P., & Chou, C. (2000). Evaluating sustained silent reading in reading classes. *The Internet TESOL Journal, 6*(11). Retrieved September 17, 2008, from *iteslj.org/Articles/Chow-SSR.html.*

Daane, M. C., Campbell, J. R., Grigg, W. S., Goodman, M. J., & Oranje, A. (2005). *Fourth-grade students reading aloud: NAEP 2002 special study of oral reading.* Washington, DC: U.S. Department of Education, Institute of Education Sciences.

Darling-Hammond, L., & Bransford, J. (Eds.). (2005). *Preparing teachers for a changing world: What teachers should learn and be able to do.* Hoboken, NJ: Jossey-Bass.

Dorph, R., Goldstein, D., Lee, S., Lepori, K., Schneider, S., & Venkatesan, S. (2007). *The status of science education in the Bay Area.* Berkeley, CA: Lawrence Hall of Science, UC-Berkeley.

Duke, N. K. (2000). 3.6 minutes per day: The scarcity of informational texts in first grade. *Reading Research Quarterly, 35*(2), 202-224.

Fisher, C. W., Berliner, D. C., Filby, N. N., Marliave, R., Cahen, L. S., & Dishaw,

M. M. (1980). Teaching behaviors, academic learning time, and student achievement: An overview. In C. Denham & A. Lieberman (Eds.), *Time to learn* (pp. 7–32). *Washington, DC: U.S. Department of Education.*

Fisher, C. W., & Hiebert, E. H. (1990). Characteristics of tasks in two approaches to literacy instruction. *The Elementary School Journal, 91*(1), 3–18.

Foorman, B. R., Schatschneider, C., Eakin, M. N., Fletcher, J. M., Moats, L. C., & Francis, D. J. (2006). The impact of instructional practices in grades 1 and 2 on reading and spelling achievement in high poverty schools. *Contemporary Educational Psychology, 31*, 1–29.

Fountas, I. C., & Pinnell, G. S. (1999). *Matching books to readers: Using leveled books in guided reading, K–3.* Portsmouth, NH: Heinemann.

Frederick, W., Easton, J., Muirhead, S., & Vanderwicken, S. (1979, April). *Procedures and use of time in reading classes in high-gain and low-gain elementary schools in Chicago.* Paper presented at the annual meeting of the American Educational Research Association, San Francisco, CA. (ERIC Document Reproduction Services No. ED 176237)

Gambrell, L. B., Wilson, R. M., & Gantt, W. N. (1981). Classroom observations of task-attending behaviors of good and poor readers. *Journal of Educational Research, 74*(6), 400–404.

Gates, A. I. (1930). *Interest and ability in reading.* New York: Macmillan Co.

Guthrie, J. T., Schafer, W. D., & Huang, C. W. (2001). Benefits of opportunity to read and balanced instruction on the NAEP. *Journal of Educational Research, 94*(3), 145–162.

Guthrie, J. T., Wigfield, A., Metsala, J. L., & Cox, K. E. (1999). Motivational and cognitive predictors of text comprehension and reading amount. *Scientific Studies of Reading, 3*, 231–256.

Hasbrouck, J. (2006). Drop every and read—but how? *American Educator* (summer). Retrieved September 11, 2008, from *www.aft.org/pubs-reports/american_educator/issues/summer06/fluency.htm.*

Hasbrouck, J., & Tindal, G. A. (2006). Oral reading fluency norms: A valuable assessment tool for reading teachers. *The Reading Teacher, 59*, 636–644.

Hiebert, E. H. (2009). The (mis)match between texts and students who depend on schools to become literate. In E. H. Hiebert & M. Sailors (Eds.), *Finding the right texts: What works for beginning and struggling readers* (pp. 1–20). New York: Guilford Press.

Hunt, L. C. (1970). Effects of self-selection, interest, and motivation on independent, instructional, and frustration levels. *The Reading Teacher, 24*, 146–151.

Jackson, P. W. (1968). *Life in classrooms.* New York: Holt, Rinehart & Winston.

Juel, C., & Minden-Cupp, C. (2000). Learning to read words: Linguistic units and instructional strategies. *Reading Research Quarterly, 35*(4), 458–492.

Kuhn, M. R., & Stahl, S. A. (2003). Fluency: A review of developmental and remedial practices. *Journal of Educational Psychology, 95*, 3–21.

Kurth, R. J., & Kurth, L. M. (1987). *The use of time in formal reading instruction in elementary schools.* Paper presented at the annual meeting of the American Educational Research Association, Washington, DC.

Leinhardt, G., Zigmond, N., & Cooley, W. W. (1981). Reading instruction and its effects. *American Educational Research Journal, 18*(3), 343–361.

Lewis, M. (2002). *Read more—read better?: A meta-analysis of the literature on the relationship between exposure to reading and reading achievement.* Unpublished dissertation, University of Minnesota.

Manning, G. L., & Manning, M. (1984). What models of recreational reading make a difference? *Reading World, 23*(4), 375–380.

Marino, M., & Moylan, M. E. (1994). *The self actualized reader.* (ERIC Document Reproduction Services No. ED 375394)

McNinch, G. H., Schaffer, G. L., & Campbell, P. (1999). What do teachers perceive as the most important use of reading time? *Reading Improvement, 36*(2), 90–96.

McNinch, G. H., Schaffer, G. L., Campbell, P., & Rakes, S. (1998). Allocation of time in reading. *Reading Horizons, 39*(2), 123–130.

Menon, S., & Hiebert, E. H. (in press). Instructional texts and the fluency of learning disabled readers. In A. McGill-Franzen & R. L. Allington (Eds.), *Handbook of reading disabilities research.* Mahwah, NJ: Erlbaum.

Mervar, K., & Hiebert, E. H. (1989). Literature selection strategies and amount of reading in two literacy approaches. In S. McCormick & J. Zutell (Eds.), *Cognitive and social perspectives for literacy research and instruction* (38th Yearbook of the National Reading Conference) (pp. 529–535). Chicago: National Reading Conference.

Miller, S. D., & Meece, J. L. (1999). Third graders' motivational preferences for reading and writing tasks. *The Elementary School Journal, 100,* 19–35.

National Institute of Child Health and Human Development. (2000). *Report of the National Reading Panel. Teaching children to read: An evidence-based assessment of the scientific research literature on reading and its implications for reading instruction* (NIH Publication No. 00-4769). Washington, DC: U.S. Government Printing Office.

Nunnery, J. A., Ross, S. M., & McDonald, A. (2006). A randomized experimental evaluation of the impact of Accelerated Reader/Reading Renaissance implementation on reading achievement in grades 3 to 6. *Journal of Education for Students Placed at Risk, 11*(1), 1–18.

O'Conner, R. E., Bell, K. M., Harty, K. R., Larkin, L. K., Sackor, S. M., & Zigmond, N. (2002). Teaching reading to poor readers in the intermediate grades: A comparison of text difficulty. *Journal of Educational Psychology, 94*(3), 474–485.

Reutzel, D. R., Fawson, P. C., & Smith, J. A. (2008). Reconsidering silent sustained reading (SSR): An exploratory study of scaffolded silent reading (ScRC). *Journal of Educational Research, 102*(1), 37–50.

Rowan, B., Camburn, E., & Correnti, R. (2004). Using teacher logs to measure the enacted curriculum: A study of literacy teaching in third-grade classrooms. *The Elementary School Journal, 105*(1), 75–101.

Santi, K., & Vaughn, S. R. (2007). Progress monitoring: An integral part of instruction. *Reading and Writing Quarterly, 20,* 535–537.

Schumm, J. S., Moody, S. W., & Vaughn, S. (2000). Grouping for reading instruction: Does one size fit all? *Journal of Learning Disabilities, 33*(5), 477–488.

Stahl, S. A., & Heubach, K. (2005). Fluency-oriented reading instruction. *Journal of Literacy Research, 37*, 25–60.

Stallings, J. (1980). Allocated academic learning time revisited, or beyond time on task. *Educational Researcher, 9*(11), 11–16.

Taylor, B. M., Frye, B. J., & Maruyama, G. (1990). Time spent reading and reading growth. *American Educational Research Journal, 27*(2), 351–362.

U.S. Department of Education. (2001). *No Child Left Behind.* Retrieved September 16, 2008, from *www.ed.gov/policy/elsec/leg/esea02/index.html.*

Walsh, K. (2003). Basal readers: The lost opportunity to build the knowledge that propels comprehension. *American Educator, 27*(1), 24–27.

Wilkinson, I. A. G., Wardrop, J. L., & Anderson, R. C. (1988). Silent reading reconsidered: Reinterpreting reading instruction and its effects. *American Educational Research Journal, 25*(1), 127–144.

Wu, Y., & Samuels, S. J. (2004, May). *How the amount of time spent on independent reading affects reading achievement.* Paper presented at the annual meeting of the International Reading Association, Reno, NV.

Young, A., & Bowers, P. (1995). Individual differences and text difficulty determinants of reading fluency and expressiveness. *Journal of Experimental Child Psychology, 60*, 428–454.

2

IF THEY DON'T READ MUCH
... 30 YEARS LATER

RICHARD L. ALLINGTON

Over 30 years ago (Allington, 1977) I published a paper, "If They Don't Read Much, How They Ever Gonna Get Good?" That paper has become one of the most frequently cited papers I've ever written. The paper appeared during the last heyday of skills instruction. It followed on the heels of another paper that challenged the prevailing view that learning to read primarily involved the sequential mastery of a hierarchical set of subskills (Johnson & Pearson, 1975). Given the return to an emphasis on mastery of reading subskills in the design of federally funded reading interventions, it seems time to revisit the question raised in my original paper.

My original paper reported on some not very rigorous observations of reading instruction in elementary schools (later, more rigorous studies verified the original findings: Allington, 1980, 1983, 1984; Gambrell, 1984; Hiebert, 1983; Knapp. 1995; Thurlow, Gaden, Ysseldyke, & Algozzine, 1984; Vaughn, Moody, & Schumm, 1998). I noted that struggling readers read very little during either classroom or remedial reading lessons. My question was a simple one: *Should reading lessons for struggling readers include greater opportunities to engage in reading connected text?* The tenor of my argument, however, was that volume did matter—if only because practice is associated with improved performance in virtually every human proficiency.

For a decade or two, it appeared that my original article had struck a nerve, and both researchers and educators began to consider a role for reading volume in the design of both classroom and remedial reading programs and lessons (see Stanovich, 1986, 2000, for his discussion of reading volume and reading development). At the turn of the 21st century, however, the relationship between reading volume and reading achievement was challenged in the report of the National Reading Panel (NRP; National Institute of Child Health and Human Development [NICHD], 2000).

Translations of Research on Volume: Consensus or Conflict?

The NRP (NICHD, 2000) examined the research on reading volume and concluded: "Even though encouraging students to read more is intuitively appealing, there is still not sufficient research evidence obtained from studies of high methodological quality to support the idea that such efforts reliably increase how much students read or that such programs result in improved reading skills" (pp. 12–13). NRP member Tim Shanahan interpreted the findings thusly: "Of course, the NRP did not actually oppose encouraging children to read. ... Unfortunately, the panel found very few studies of these schemes and, overall, the quality of these studies was not particularly high. Given this, the panel had no findings with regard to such plans, though it did recommend that researchers turn their attention to this issue" (Shanahan, 2004, p. 245). Another NRP member, S. Jay Samuels (2002), noted: "Having advocated extensive reading as a way to increase fluency, in fairness, I should point out that the fluency section of the NRP report neither endorses nor condemns independent silent reading. Failure to endorse should not be interpreted as a criticism of this technique, however" (p. 174).

While both the NRP report and these comments from two NRP members suggest that few well-designed studies of the effect of the volume of reading activity are available, none suggest-no role for reading volume in the development of reading proficiencies. However, in a widely distributed "plain language" guide for teachers, the National Institute for Literacy (NIFL) seemed to broach that interpretation: "Rather than allocating instructional time for independent reading in the classroom, encourage your students to read more outside of school" (Armbruster, Lehr, & Osborn, 2001, p. 29).

According to the introduction of this booklet, this advice was drawn from the NRP findings. This advice by the NIFL to limit in-school reading and to read after school is not just a misrepresentation of the NRP findings, it is also bad advice. Why? The students most in need of independent reading will not do it outside of school. One puzzling aspect of the NIFL statement is that it seems to suggest that there is evidence indicating that independent reading outside of the school day is causally related to reading achievement, while no such evidence exists for independent reading during the school day. There are research-based recommendations indicating that increasing reading volume improves achievement. However, such advice rarely differentiates between increasing reading in school or out of school. For instance, in their review of the research on vocabulary acquisition, Kuhn and Stahl (1998) concluded: "Ultimately, increasing the amount of reading children do seems to be the most reliable approach to improving their knowledge of word meanings, with or without additional training in learning words from context" (pp. 135–136). Oddly, perhaps, the NIFL document reaches the same conclusion while also recommending against allocating time during the school day for independent reading.

Krashen (2001) took a different stance on the NIFL advice in his interpretation of the NRP (NICHD, 2000) analyses, arguing that, since the NRP analyses found no significant differences when traditional reading instructional time was replaced with independent reading time, this finding in itself was reason to reject the NIFL interpretation. Following the release of the NRP report, Lewis and Samuels (n.d.) conducted a meta-analysis of 49 studies of reading volume and concluded that there was a moderately strong positive relationship between reading exposure and reading outcomes. They reported that separate analysis of d-index effect sizes from experimental studies provided causal evidence that students who have in-school independent reading time, in addition to regular reading instruction, do significantly better on measures of reading achievement than peers who have not had reading time (an effect size of $d = 0.42$). The d statistic reported by Lewis and Samuels is almost identical to that reported by the NRP for the effect of adding systematic phonics as an instructional feature ($d = 0.44$). Lewis and Samuels also identify several variables that influence the efficacy of independent reading (e.g., text difficulty, role of teacher-directed reading) that I will address later in this chapter.

The most recent challenge to those who would deny the value of extensive independent reading comes from a series of studies led by Kuhn and Schwanenflugel (Kuhn & Schwanenflugel, Chapter 7, this volume; Kuhn et al., 2006). These studies were prompted by a question raised in a review of fluency research where Kuhn and Stahl (2003) noted that few studies in which repeated reading of texts was compared with comparable amounts of independent reading produced comparable benefits for reading development. Noting that involving students in repeated reading activity typically increased the volume of reading for these students, they asked: *Is it simply the case that when poor readers read more extensively, which occurred in both conditions, reading proficiency improves?*

Kuhn and Schwanenflugel (Chapter 7, this volume) compare repeated-reading fluency-oriented reading instruction (FORI) with a condition labeled "wide reading." In FORI, pupils repeatedly read a single text over a week. In wide reading, pupils read and reread one text for 2 days and then moved on to read multiple texts on the remaining days. The amount of time spent reading text was equivalent for the two groups. The results indicated that the wide-reading condition improved fluency and text reading more quickly than the repeated-reading condition and that at the end of 1 year the two conditions produced comparable growth on standardized achievement measures.

The issue of repeated reading versus wide reading is complicated. One advantage of repeated reading for struggling readers is that after about four rereadings they can experience what it is like to be a fluent reader, at least with the text they are practicing repeatedly. Word repetition is one of the factors that contribute to word learning, and repeated reading accomplishes this. Thus, the blended model in the wide-reading condition seems a way to take advantage of the strengths of both procedures. While the NRP endorsed repeated reading as an instructional strategy for fostering both fluency and general reading development, the findings from Kuhn and Schwanenflugel indicate that it is increased reading practice that perhaps matters more than which technique is used to foster expanded reading activity.

At this point in time, then, the issue of the role of reading volume, and especially student-directed independent reading, in reading development is contested. Almost everyone with a stake in the issue, however, indicates that the research currently available includes experimental evidence for a causal role for reading volume in fostering improved reading proficiency.

In this chapter I revisit the original question posed 30 years ago and argue that the question may be more complicated than either I or most other researchers recognized. Complicated in that the nature of the reading activity (teacher-directed vs. student-directed) seems to play an important role in determining the relative progress made by young good and poor readers. Complicated because there exists too little useful research on the issue of the appropriate level of text difficulty in fostering reading growth in teacher-directed or student-directed reading activity. Complicated, especially, because the role of intrinsically motivated and deliberate reading activity (Guthrie, 2004; Guthrie & Humenick, 2004) needs to be better delineated in accounting for the effects of reading practice.

The Relationship between Reading Volume and Reading Proficiency

The answer to the question of whether reading volume affects reading proficiency is a pretty straightforward "yes." Numerous studies have delineated the positive correlation between reading volume and reading achievement (see Anderson, Wilson, & Fielding, 1988; Cunningham & Stanovich, 1998; Knapp. 1995; Krashen, 2004a; Meyer & Wardrop. 1994; NICHD, 2000; Stanovich, 2000; Stanovich, West, Cunningham, Cipielewski, & Siddiqui, 1996; Wu & Samuels, 2004). Unavailable in the current research, however, is clear experimental support for answering the real questions of interest: How much reading practice and what sorts of practice are required to foster proficient reading? Before I address these questions, I examine the various ways reading practice has been conceptualized in research and theory.

Conceptualizations of Reading Volume

I (Allington, 2006) have used the term *reading volume* (or *volume of reading*) to describe, literally, how much reading practice students experience over a certain time period. Volume, in my definition, could be captured by measures of time spent reading connected text, by measures of the number of words, pages, or books a student has read, and by estimates of print exposure, as opposed to observed or recorded measurements of these same factors. Thus, I have largely collapsed various terms (e.g., *reading practice, reading time, independent reading, voluntary reading, print exposure, amount of reading,* and so on) into the single term *reading volume.* I draw upon a variety of research using one or more of these operational definitions of reading activity and include each of them under the broader term *reading volume.*

At the same time, my use of *reading volume* as a primary descriptor may be too simplistic. For instance, evidence indicates that certain types of reading practice are far more strongly related to reading growth than other types. Additionally, there seems to be increasing evidence that the nature and role of reading practice vary developmentally. Thus, my general call for greater attention to the role of the volume of reading that students do—especially struggling readers—is not wrong but may be underspecified and therefore misunderstood. When misunderstood as a simple call that students do more reading, in and out of school, the potential in enhancing reading volume may not be fully realized.

Deliberate Practice/Engaged Reading

One concern is well expressed by Guthrie (2004) in his detailed discussion of reading volume. He uses the term *engaged reading* in his argument for the critical nature of the role of extended reading practice. But he defines engaged reading multidimensionally and as much more than the simple passing of eyes over words in a text. For him, engaged reading requires students who are actively using cognitive processes while reading, with an emphasis on the use of cognitive strategies or the development of conceptual knowledge, or both. Guthrie's engaged reading is reading that is purposeful, intrinsically motivated, and socially interactive. This characterization of engaged reading extends well beyond the older and more prominent notion of engaged reading in the time-on-task studies of the 1970s and 1980s (e.g., Fisher & Berliner, 1985; Kiesling, 1978; Leinhardt, Zigmond, & Cooley, 1981) that influenced my original thinking on the topic of reading volume.

Guthrie's specifications for engaged reading are similar to the description of "deliberate practice" advanced by Ericsson, Krampe, and Tesch-Romer (1993) in their review of the development of high levels of competence across a variety of human domains (e.g., physical and athletic skills, musical and artistic proficiencies, and game playing abilities). Ericsson et al. consider practice to be deliberate when it involves intrinsically motivated activity intended to improve performance (note the similarities to Guthrie's definition of engaged reading). They note that "natural ability" has been commonly invoked to explain superior performance in a variety of human skill areas, but much research indicates that "deliberate" and extended practice is a more likely explanation for the wide variations in performances. In other words, it is the amount (volume) of deliberate practice that explains exceptional levels of skilled performances rather than some innate characteristic of particular high-performing individuals.

However, currently, the "natural-ability" hypothesis still seems widely held in explaining reading acquisition and the difficulties that some children experience in learning to read. Conventional wisdom asserts that for roughly 60% of students the nature of reading instruction matters little, but for roughly 40% the nature of that instruction is a critical factor in determining reading success (Lyon, 1998). In other words, some children's natural ability enables them to acquire reading proficiencies even in the face of weak or mediocre instruction and, perhaps, little deliberate practice.

On the other hand, a vast research base exists indicating that this natural-ability hypothesis is largely wrong—in other words, high levels of human proficiency in any domain are largely attributable to the time spent in deliberate practice. But determining what is "sufficient" practice or the nature of the structure of "optimal" practice is more problematic. "Just practicing may not be sufficient since studies show that individuals often reached a plateau in skill level that could not be improved without restructuring practicing activity" (Ericsson et al., 1993, p. 366). Ericsson et al. noted that the available research typically shows only a weak to moderate effect on performance from the amount of practice, but this ambiguity is due, they argue, to the vague notion of what constitutes "practice." I will suggest that the same is true for studies of the effects of reading volume.

I believe that Guthrie (2004) largely has it right when he argues for the critical importance of "engaged reading" in stimulating reading development. As Ericsson et al. (1993) concluded, intentional and active, intrinsically motivated reading—deliberate practice—appears to be what really matters in furthering reading development. However, reading researchers have used quite wide-ranging notions of practice, more often equating reading practice with observed time on connected reading tasks or estimated time reading drawn from personal reading logs or author or title recognition tests. In other words, the available evidence provides little useful information on the role of extended engaged reading, or deliberate reading practice. Similarly, in studies where volume of reading is manipulated experimentally, there has been almost no explicit recognition that time spent in coerced reading (e.g., Carver & Liebert, 1995) may not produce the effects associated with the same amount of voluntary reading.

At the same time, there seems to be widespread awareness that many struggling readers do not engage in such deliberate practice when provided the opportunity to do so. Tovani (2001) describes the "fake reading" that many struggling readers engage in, and McIntyre, Rightmeyer, Powell, Powers, and Petrosko (2006) describe just how frequently struggling early readers avoid reading during independent reading time.

Thus, one way to improve the research we have on the effects of reading activity would be to use a more refined or specific definition of reading volume. If we can gather data on voluntary engaged reading, or deliberate reading practice, we can begin to assess the effects of increasing reading activity in a manner more consistent with the research on practice in other domains. But gathering such data will be far more labor-intensive than simply surveying the room and noting which pupils have their eyes focused on a text.

Intrinsic Motivation

Central to both the Guthrie (2004) and Ericsson et al. (1993) conceptualizations of engaged or deliberate practice is intrinsic motivation to learn or to acquire new skills or improve them. However, intrinsic motivation seems typically to play no significant role when we plan either research studies or instruction. In the available research—with but a few notable exceptions, such as the line of research Guthrie and his colleagues (see McRae & Guthrie, Chapter 3, this volume) and Schraw and his colleagues (Schraw & Bruning, 1999; Schraw, Flowerday, & Reisletter, 1998) have pursued—intrinsic motivation is largely omitted from the variables that are studied. Instructional planning, when using the typical core reading program, largely ignores any concern with intrinsic motivation. In schools, attempts to foster extrinsic motivation are far more commonly seen than efforts to build intrinsic motivation for reading. Thus, we more often see points or pizzas awarded for "voluntary" reading activity or grades awarded for reading proficiency than we see focused attempts to build intrinsic motivation for reading into lessons and activities.

Guthrie and Humenick (2004) provide strong evidence for the importance of classroom factors that are linked to intrinsic motivation using a meta-analysis of studies of classroom factors that enhance reading motivation and comprehension. They report that easy access to interesting books, regular opportunities for students to choose what they will read, and routine opportunities for students to collaborate on their work all produced significant gains in reading motivation and achievement. In fact, the effect sizes were two to four times as large as those reported by the NRP (NICHD, 2000) for including systematic phonics in reading lessons.

The current emphasis on using a commercial core reading program—something deemed research-based, or scientific, by federal regulations—runs counter to the research Guthrie and Humenick (2004) summarize.

That is, the core reading programs developed by the largest and most successful publishers offer only an identical set of texts to be read by every student, and thus individual choice of reading materials is not an option.

These programs do not provide a rich array of interesting texts but, instead, a small sample of texts whose content meets the various criteria for political correctness and grade-level appropriateness. And collaborative learning activities are far less common in these materials than are activities where each student will be working alone. A recent report on the nature of fifth-grade reading instruction (Pianta, Belsky, Houts, & Morrison, 2007) indicated that students were working on whole-group assignments alone at their desks over 90% of their reading instructional time. While Pianta et al. describe this level of commitment to instructional collaboration as, at best, "mediocre," I would suggest that these data indicate that few classrooms have instruction organized around the scientific principles of conducting effective reading lessons. Given the widespread use of these core reading programs, these "proven programs" (although not a single rigorous study actually supports their use—see *www.whatworks.ed.gov* for a report on the lack of research) may be largely responsible for recent damning data on the nature of reading instruction in the upper elementary grades and the complete lack of any changes in reading proficiency in the middle and high school grades for over 30 years (National Center for Educational Statistics [NCES], 2006).

We have good research available on how to foster intrinsic motivation for reading and learning to read (see Guthrie, 2004; Pressley, Dolezal Kersey, Bogaert, Mohan, Roehrig, & Bogner Warzon, 2003; Schraw & Bruning, 1999). However, much of that research is ignored in designing federal and state reading curriculum mandates, creating core reading programs, and improving professional practices in classroom and remedial reading lessons.

In studying exemplary teachers, we found that they typically implemented a multisource/multilevel curriculum across the school day (Allington & Johnston, 2002; Pressley, Allington, Wharton-MacDonald, Collins-Block, & Morrow, 2001). Within this increased access to interesting texts, students were typically provided opportunities to choose the texts they would read and the topics they would write about. We argued that these classroom conditions alone seem to account largely for the high levels of engaged reading and writing we observed and the dramatic growth in the proficiencies of both achieving and struggling readers. I also noted that these exemplary teachers typically had to ignore state and district curriculum mandates and teach "against the organizational grain" in order to produce the achievement growth we observed (Allington, 2002).

However, providing easy access to interesting books and giving students the opportunity to select much of their reading lesson material are necessary but not sufficient to ensure engaged reading practice. Furthermore, while both are empirically linked to greater intrinsic motivation and increased engaged reading and improved reading achievement, attempting to partial out the effects of these environmental variables and their links to engaged reading and achievement increases will be a daunting task that will require substantially different data collection methods than those previously deemed sufficient.

Task/Text Difficulty

Adding to the complexity of investigating the role of reading volume is the question of task difficulty. In this case we might focus only on text difficulty, but there are many ways a text might be difficult. Additionally, expectations of what the teacher and reader are to do before, during, and after reading the text present another set of issues.

We can think of text difficulty in various ways (Hiebert, 2002), but even the most seemingly straightforward method of estimating text difficulty, the use of readability formulas, offers no easy solution. As Hiebert noted, there is little agreement in difficulty ratings when one compares the estimates from different established readability procedures. Given these findings, the most appropriate method of establishing the difficulty of various texts might be to use item response theory (Paris et al., 2004). But this scaling procedure requires that large numbers of students be engaged with each text.

Probably the most direct method of establishing text difficulty is to record individual student responses, as in collecting oral reading accuracy, reading rate, and comprehension data. But that method presumes an accurate oral rendition of the text is the goal of reading, and there is extensive evidence that many students can accomplish the accurate oral rendition with little understanding of what was read (see Allington & McGill-Franzen, 2009, for a review). Further, there is little agreement at the moment as to what level of accuracy is deemed appropriate and optimal. Researchers have used 90% and 95% oral reading accuracy as the standard for appropriateness in recent studies (Kuhn, 2005; McIntyre et al., 2006), while Betts (1949) recommended 99% accuracy for independent reading (i.e., reading done alone, with little or no teacher guidance). So, what accuracy standard should research-ers use? Does it depend on the nature of the reading activity? Are the more liberal accuracy standards appropriate for guided reading activ-ity and the more stringent criteria Betts set to be used when estimating the difficulty of texts for independent reading? How does the level of a student's interest in the topic of the text influence the issue of appropri-ate text difficulty? Does a student's reading developmental level matter when we discuss appropriate levels of text difficulty?

There is some evidence that reading texts with higher levels of accuracy promotes reading engagement and development to a greater extent than does reading harder texts (Ehri, Dreyer, Flugman, & Gross, 2007; Fisher & Berliner, 1985; Gambrell, Wilson, & Gantt, 1981; Jorgen-son, 1977; Jorgenson, Klein, & Kumar, 1977). But Stahl and Heubach (2005) found that lessons could be adapted such that texts initially read with an accuracy as low as 80% could foster substantial reading growth when lessons were redesigned to provide substantially increased teacher support and multiple readings of those difficult texts. So, where does this leave us as researchers and as teachers?

I suggest that there are many reasons for using texts that can be read at the higher levels of accuracy. The first reason, as both Stanovich (2000) and Torgesen and Hudson (2006) have argued, is that it takes multiple successful recognitions of a word before readers recognize that word "at a glance." This is precisely why repeated reading can be a useful routine for fostering fluent reading. Adams (1990) pointed to the same conclusion concerning accurate text reading as she developed the notion of orthographic processing as the stage that follows alphabetic decoding.

I have argued (Allington, 2006, 2009) that a steady diet of difficult texts—text read at an accuracy level below 95–98%—that many strug-gling readers encounter day after day—may be one important reason that these readers never become fluent readers. That is, these readers too frequently misread words and thereby fail to construct a large store-house of words that are recognized with little effort. Accordingly, I have argued that increasing the amount of "high-success" reading (99%-plus accuracy) activities for struggling readers is likely necessary to foster such development. Torgesen and Hudson (2006) offer the same hypoth-esis.

Ehri et al. (2007) provided strong evidence of the importance of high-success reading (98% accuracy or better) in the development of younger struggling readers. But we still have too little evidence to make definitive statements about the optimal levels of text difficulty for readers of any age or developmental level for either instructional or independent practice activities. However, I agree with Torgesen and Hudson (2006) that "this difficulty in recovering the 'lost ground' in the development of sight-word vocabulary that results from several years of minimal and inaccurate reading is the simplest current explanation for the enduring reading-fluency problems of students even after they become more accurate readers through strong reading interventions" (pp. 152–153). In other words, too little reading practice and, especially, too little high-success reading practice produce too many children with huge gaps that are difficult to overcome.

We can, then, confidently conclude that text difficulty will play an important role in explaining reading development while acknowledging that we actually have very little research that provides clear guidelines for either estimating the difficulty of texts or for selecting appropriate texts for instruction. And there is little research on how these variables interact with intrinsic motivation (or with variables that have been shown to affect intrinsic motivation). The question that remains largely unexplored is: What is the optimum text difficulty for promoting reading growth?

A larger and equally unexplored question is: How do we create instructional environments where readers self-select texts of appropriate difficulty such that intrinsic motivation for reading is enhanced and reading growth is accelerated?

Task Difficulty Reconsidered

Perhaps we should go beyond the sheer accuracy of an oral reading of a text in establishing the difficulty of the text. I will call this *task difficulty* just to try to keep the two notions separate and distinct. The concept of *task difficulty* is not yet well understood. What if we wanted students to do something specific during or after (orally or silently) reading a text? We might want students to comprehend the ideas in the text that was read, for instance. But even this begs the question of what we mean by "comprehending." Will simply recalling the key aspects of a narrative text suffice (basically, remembering what was read)? Even that task can vary in complexity, depending on how we decide to assess recall (Francis, Fletcher, Catts, & Tomblin, 2005).

And what if we wanted the reader to be able to make connections between the text just read and texts read earlier (Keene & Zimmerman, 1997)? What if we wanted to assess understanding by evaluating the reader's ability to synthesize the new information with existing information? And, given this new requirement, how does personal prior knowledge of and interest in the topic presented impact the difficulty of the task? There is much concerning just this one variable set—task/ text difficulty—that we know little about, especially as that variable set affects learning to read over the longer term.

The Efficacy of Three Types of Reading Practice

Thus far, I have not differentiated between guided reading practice (teacher-directed activity), assigned independent reading practice (student directed activity), and free voluntary reading (student directed deliberate activity). It is time to consider whether one of these three types of reading practice is more important in fostering reading growth than the others and whether each is necessary.

A continuum of teacher-directed to student-directed reading activities could be created. Likewise, a continuum of voluntariness could be created with a mandatory "read this" on one end of the continuum and "read something" on the other. But for now I will stay with this three-category system.

Defining Types of Reading Practice

By *teacher-directed* reading activities, I refer to the traditional guided reading activity. Here the teacher typically selects the texts to be read, offers guidance before the students read, monitors student performance while reading, and follows up after reading with additional guidance or assessment activities.

Student-directed refers to the traditional independent reading activity as observed typically in both assigned and voluntary reading activity. *Assigned independent reading* is the traditional drop-everything-and-read activity, for instance, or the daily 15-minute read-at-home assignment. In most cases students have the opportunity to select the text to be read, but often within teacher-monitored constraints (such as texts deemed "appropriate in content and difficulty" by the teacher), and the reading activity is required. However, the voluntary aspect of engaging in reading is not usually an option. *Free voluntary reading* (FVR; Krashen, 2004b) refers to students' selection of texts when students read for and to themselves. Central to FVR is intrinsic motivation, choice, and access to interesting texts.

No research study has yet attempted to measure the amount of each of these three types of reading activity that people typically engage in. The usual study examining the impact of reading volume has simply included any type of reading activity in the calculation of volume. In a few studies there has been a focus on out-of-school reading, which could be construed as either assigned independent reading or FVR (e.g., Anderson et al., 1988; Taylor, Frye, & Maruyama, 1990). But such distinctions are rarely made in studies of reading volume.

FVR must be considered, if for no other reason than that available studies indicate substantial variance in measures of reading volume, especially in comparisons of more and less proficient readers (Guthrie, 2004). Some of that variance can likely be explained by differences in the reading lessons experienced by more and less proficient readers (Allington, 1984), but it is very difficult to imagine that huge differences in reading volume such as those depicted in Figure 2.1 (and reported by Anderson et al., 1988) could be explained solely by curricular differences.

The role of reading volume is inconsistently depicted in the research if only because we have not developed or utilized characterizations of reading activity that reflect the very different motivations, strategies used, and cognitive activities that we most certainly would find if we gathered better and richer information on reading in different situations (e.g., reading a poorly written test preparation paragraph on soil as part of a mandated activity versus voluntarily reading the most recent title in the Junie B. Jones series, your favorite trade series). In addition, few studies have differentiated the various teacher-directed, assigned student-directed, or FVR activities. However, if the research on how practice affects other human proficiencies can be extrapolated to reading development, some types of reading activity appear to be more powerful than others, and some sort of guidance is important.

The Nature of Developmental Differences

A further issue is whether the ratio, for lack of a better word, of teacher directed, assigned independent reading, or FVR varies developmentally. It seems obvious, perhaps, that at the very initial stages of reading development there would be little FVR because at that stage students have developed few of the necessary skills to read independently. But what about the memorized reading associated with frequently recited teacher-read books? Or the picture reading of both wordless and worded books? What about rereading texts introduced earlier in a shared reading session? Or reading one's own writing? Are these potentially intrin-

90th percentile	4,180,000 words
70th percentile	1,790,000 words
50th percentile	883,000 words
30th percentile	357,000 words
10th percentile	59,000 words

FIGURE 2.1. Estimated annual reading volume of fifth-grade students by reading volume percentile rank. Data from Anderson, Wilson, and Fielding (1988).

sically motivated reading activities important for early literacy development?

While there are only a handful of studies examining the possibility of developmental differences in the most powerful blend of the three types of reading, the evidence from these studies seems to converge around the assertion that developmental differences exist and must be considered when designing reading instruction and learning environments. For instance, McIntyre et al. (2006) report on a qualitative study of 66 first-grade struggling readers in 26 classrooms. Classrooms were classified as either "reads-little" or "reads-much," based on observational analyses of classroom reading lessons. McIntyre et al. found no significant differences in achievement gains on broad measures of reading achievement between the two types of classrooms. However, students in the reads-little classrooms showed more gains on end-year tests on measures of isolated word recognition than children in the reads-much classes. The authors hypothesize that the students in the reads-little classrooms may have been at a stage where more basic skills instruction was appropriate since their beginning first-grade performance means were significantly lower than those of children in the reads-much classrooms. The authors also note that much of the reading in the reads-much classrooms was not mediated by the teacher (i.e., there was more student-directed activity) and suggests that that may account for what seemed to be the limited effects of different classroom instruction on reading achievement.

Connor, Morrison, and Katch (2004) found the effectiveness of particular decoding lessons on end-of year achievement levels depended on first-grade students' entering vocabulary and decoding skills. Children with low decoding skills and vocabulary benefited from greater amounts of teacher-managed explicit decoding instruction with increasing amounts of child-managed instruction across the year. If the amount of time spent in child-managed reading activity did not increase, then decoding skills did not develop as quickly. Students with stronger vocabulary and decoding skills benefited more from greater child-managed implicit instruction all year long.

In a similar vein, Connor, Morrison, Fishman, Schatschneider, and Underwood (2007) report on a randomized field trial involving teachers who used computer-generated daily lesson plans. These lessons were individually targeted to different levels of early literacy development. The general model is based on findings from the earlier study suggesting that high- and low-readiness first graders benefited from different sorts of instructional emphases. Low-readiness children benefited more from teacher-directed and skills-emphasis activities, while high-readiness children benefited from more self-directed and meaning-emphasis activities. Teachers used either Open Court or SRA Reading Mastery as the core curriculum in 90-minute daily lessons. One group of teachers was trained in the use of computer-guided reading lesson design, and the other was not. The authors also report that the use of algorithmic-guided individualized instruction improved student reading outcomes, and teachers who used it more frequently had higher student achievement levels than those who used it less frequently.

Scanlon, Vellutino, Small, Fanuele, and Sweeney (2005) contrasted a "text-emphasis" intervention with a "phonological skills" tutoring intervention for at-risk first-grade students. The text emphasis intervention featured 15 minutes of reading and rereading texts in each 30-minute tutorial and 15 minutes on skills work. The phonological skills intervention featured just 5 minutes of reading and rereading texts and 25 minutes of skills work in the 30-minute daily sessions. Both intervention models produced significantly better reading achievement than the no-intervention control group. The phonological skills emphasis intervention produced better results for the lowest-achieving first graders, but the text-emphasis approach produced the better results on both word recognition and reading comprehension measures overall.

Vadasy, Sanders, and Peyton (2005) also contrasted expanded text reading versus expanded decoding activities with struggling first-grade readers. They also found that the intervention that expanded reading activity produced greater gains on reading rate, text reading accuracy, and a standardized measure of reading comprehension. They summarized their findings in this way: "Scaffolded oral text reading practice produced significantly higher fluency than word study only" (p. 378).

Finally, Wu and Samuels (2004) assigned third- and fifth-grade classes to one of two conditions. In the reads-much classrooms, students read independently for 40 minutes each day. In the control classrooms, students read independently for 15 minutes daily, and the teacher read to them for 25 minutes, thus equating time spent in reading/listening activities beyond the core reading instruction. After 6 months of experimental treatment, student reading skills were assessed on a variety of measures, including reading rate and accuracy, comprehension, and word recognition.

The findings indicated a mixed effect. Better readers benefited more from the additional (i.e., 40-minute) independent reading time than the poor readers on all measures, but the poor readers benefited more and had greater gains on all measures from the 15 minutes of independent reading than the better readers did. The authors concluded that the appropriate distribution of independent reading may vary, depending on a student's level of reading development. While independent reading was beneficial to all students, because attention span is related to reading skill, longer periods of independent reading were most useful for the more highly skilled readers and shorter periods for the less skilled.

The findings of these studies should hardly be surprising. First, expanding reading volume typically produced greater benefits as compared to having students spend the same amount of time engaged in skill activities. Second, and in general, struggling readers exhibiting stronger development of reading skills benefited more from increasing the volume of teacher-directed and/or self-directed reading than did struggling readers with less well developed reading proficiencies.

There are several possible explanations for this latter finding. First, it may be that stronger readers have greater intrinsic motivation for engaging in reading than less skilled readers. Thus, the weakest readers may simply not be involved in as much "deliberate" or "engaged" reading practice even when a standard time is set aside for such purposes.

Second, the weakest readers may simply not have developed the stamina for reading for longer periods. Thus, even when the time is allocated for teacher- or self-directed reading, they simply cannot read for the longer period of time. Consider the analogy to running. Runners may become adept at running shorter distances (i.e., a half-mile or 1 or 2 miles) but be unable to run a full 26-mile marathon.

Third, the weakest readers may move their eyes across the pages for the period of time but be unable to maintain effective strategy use for the extended self-directed reading period. In this case, the whole process, especially in the comprehension domain, breaks down after a few minutes of reading. Then, once comprehensibility falls apart, the motivation to continue reading declines. The weakest poor readers will likely need both guided reading instruction and extended practice in maintaining effective strategy use when encountering longer texts.

Finally, it may be that the weakest readers are simply less likely to select a text appropriate to their level of development (or have their teachers select texts that are appropriate for them; see McGill-Franzen, Zmach, Solic, & Zeig, 2006). If these readers are asked to read texts that are harder for them than the texts good readers are asked (or select) to read, then they may be required to exert a level of effort in reading those texts that exceeds the effort required of better readers. In such a case, they would be more likely to tire of reading after a shorter period than would better readers.

However, there is little evidence to support any of these hypotheses at the moment. Additionally, five of the six studies undertaken involved first-grade students, while the remaining study involved third- and fifth-grade students, and this study (Wu & Samuels, 2004) did not include teacher-directed reading as a variable of interest. So, while these studies suggest that a balancing of reading activity and skill work produced gains superior to a regimen solely focused on skill work, several of the studies also suggest that different ratios of teacher-directed and student-directed reading activities optimize one's reading growth, depending on a student's initial proficiency level. Needless to say, much yet remains to be learned about how to best distribute teacher- versus student-directed reading activity across a school day. And none of these studies, unfortunately, addresses the issue of intrinsically motivated FVR versus assigned but self-selected reading.

Summary and a Review of Questions Yet to Be Answered

As with many questions about the optimal design of reading instruction, the available research on reading volume and its impact on reading achievement remains incomplete. The federal mandate for using research in making instructional decisions seems to acknowledge this situation in defining *evidence-based education* as "the integration of professional wisdom with the best available empirical evidence in making decisions about how to deliver instruction" (Whitehurst, 2002). Recommendations of the role that reading volume should play in the design of reading instruction will necessarily require relying on professional wisdom at least as much as we rely on the research.

My stance is that the available research points to an important, if not well understood, role for extensive reading activity in the development of proficient readers. For me, then, the evidence pointing to the very modest volume of reading accomplished by struggling readers suggests a design feature of lessons that should still be of some concern (Allington, 2006). The evidence from the numerous correlational studies stands out in this regard. While correlation does not necessarily equate with causation, such consistent and positive correlations (Stanovich, 2000) between reading volume and achievement cannot be ignored.

The evidence from Krashen's review (2004b) that 8 of 10 studies of extensive reading treatments showed significant positive effects (while the outcomes of studies of shorter duration were less compelling) and meta-analyses (Lewis & Samuels, n.d.) demonstrating positive achievement effects for experimental comparisons of more extensive reading treatments, when combined with the significant positive effects that more extensive reading had in the studies led by Kuhn and Schwanenflugel (see Kuhn & Schwanenflugel, Chapter 7, this volume; Kuhn et al., 2006) and the Kuhn and Stahl (1998) review of vocabulary growth converge in demonstrating the potential of expanding reading volume as a strategy for enhancing reading development. Finally, the evidence from a small set of early intervention studies (Connor et al., 2007; Scanlon et al., 2005; Vadasy et al., 2005) provide consistent evidence of the benefits of expanding reading volume with early readers who struggle with acquiring reading proficiency.

So, for me, the 30-year-old question "If they don't read much, how they ever gonna get good?" remains a key concern. That said, I am also convinced that we have not sufficiently spelled out the nature of the most effective forms of reading practice. While a few analyses (e.g., Guthrie, 2004; Guthrie & Humenick, 2004; Krashen, 2004a) have seriously addressed the issue of intrinsically motivated practice, and while others (e.g., Connor et al., 2007) have differentiated between teacher-directed and student-directed reading activity, we remain largely ignorant of how either of these variables might impact the role that reading volume would have on reading development.

My working hypothesis is that all pupils need explicit teacher-directed instruction along with teacher-directed reading practice, teacher-assigned but self-directed reading practice, and large amounts of FVR practice. It is my sense that in many, if not most, classrooms today, the distribution of these activity types is skewed toward teacher-directed, with less emphasis on teacher-assigned independent reading and with little attention given to fostering FVR.

The meta-analysis by Guthrie and Humenick (2004) that shows the enormous influence on reading motivation and achievement of providing students with easy access to a wide range of texts that vary by genre, topic, and difficulty suggests that we can create classrooms where achievement is high because FVR has a significant presence. Their findings on the influence of student opportunities to choose at least some the texts they read similarly supports my thinking. As Vellutino (2003) concludes, "Instruction that capitalizes on children's inherent interests and surrounds them with high-interest reading materials at their level of proficiency is more effective than instruction that does less" (p. 77).

Finally, concerning the most appropriate decision on text difficulty, I am convinced that developing readers need an enormous volume of high-success reading experience. And, at least from the second grade onward, I will continue to recommend a daily dosage of text reading with something at or near the 99% accuracy level. I will suggest that 85–90% of all texts students read in or for school for should be at what Betts (1949) originally identified as the independent level.

Here again I have to rely more on professional wisdom than experimental data (although some small studies support my argument). If beginning readers are to develop a vast storehouse of words they can recognize at a glance, they must be engaged in high-accuracy reading. Likewise, if readers are to develop into fluent readers who read accurately with expression and comprehension, a steady diet of high-accuracy reading is essential. And if older readers are to acquire new vocabulary and content, they too must have texts in their hands they can read accurately and fluently.

Finally, success fosters intrinsic motivation. If substantial amounts of FVR are essential in developing high levels of reading proficiency, then ensuring high levels of success when reading in and for school seems absolutely critical.

There remains much research that yet needs to be completed before we can reduce our reliance on professional wisdom and base decisions primarily on experimentally derived evidence. But the evidence available, I believe, supports my 30-year-old argument that reading volume matters. I hope that it will not take another 30 years to gather the critical evidence needed to finally support or refute that hypothesis convincingly.

References

Adams, M. J. (1990). *Beginning to read: Thinking and learning about print.* Cambridge, MA: MIT Press.

Allington, R. L. (1977). If they don't read much, how they ever gonna get good? *Journal of Reading, 21,* 57–61.

Allington, R. L. (1980). Poor readers don't get to read much in reading groups. *Language Arts, 57*(8), 872–877.

Allington, R. L. (1983). The reading instruction provided readers of differing abilities. *Elementary School Journal, 83,* 548–559.

Allington, R. L. (1984). Content coverage and contextual reading in reading groups. *Journal of Reading Behavior, 16*(1), 85–96.

Allington, R. L. (2002). What I've learned about effective reading instruction from a decade of studying exemplary elementary classroom teachers. *Phi Delta Kappan, 83*(10), 740–747.

Allington, R. L. (2006). *What really matters for struggling readers: Designing research-based programs* (2nd ed.). Boston: Allyn & Bacon.

Allington, R. L. (2009). *What really matters in fluency.* Boston: Allyn & Bacon.

Allington, R. L., & Johnston, P. H. (Eds.). (2002). *Reading to learn: Lessons from exemplary fourth-grade classrooms.* New York: Guilford Press.

Allington, R. L., & McGill-Franzen, A. (2009). Comprehension difficulties of struggling readers. In S. Israel & G. G. Duffy (Eds.), *Handbook of research on reading comprehension* (pp. 551–568). Mahwah, NJ: Erlbaum.

Anderson, R. C., Wilson, P., & Fielding, L. (1988). Growth in reading and how children spend their time outside of school. *Reading Research Quarterly, 23,* 285–303.

Armbruster, B., Lehr, F., & Osborn, J. (2001). *Put reading first.* Washington, DC: National Institute for Literacy.

Betts, E. A. (1949). Adjusting instruction to individual needs. In N. B. Henry (Ed.), *The forty-eighth yearbook of the National Society for the Study of Education: Part II. Reading in the elementary school* (pp. 266–283). Chicago: University of Chicago Press.

Carver, R. P., & Liebert, R. E. (1995). The effect of reading library books at different levels of difficulty upon gain in reading ability. *Reading Research Quarterly, 30*(1), 26–48.

Connor, C. M., Morrison, F. J., Fishman, B. J., Schatschneider, C., & Underwood, P. (2007, January). Algorithm-guided individualized reading instruction. *Science, 315,* 464–465.

Connor, C. M., Morrison, F. J., & Katch, E. L. (2004). Beyond the reading wars: The effect of classroom instruction by child interactions on early reading. *Scientific Studies of Reading, 8,* 305–336.

Cunningham, A. E., & Stanovich, K. E. (1998). The impact of print exposure on word recognition. In J. Metsala & L. Ehri (Eds.), *Word recognition in beginning literacy* (pp. 235–262). Mahwah, NJ: Erlbaum.

Ehri, L. C., Dreyer, L. G., Flugman, B., & Gross, A. (2007). Reading rescue: An effective tutoring intervention model for language minority students who are struggling readers in first grade. *American Educational Research Journal,* *44*(2), 414–448.

Ericsson, K. A., Krampe, R. T., & Tesch-Romer, C. (1993). The role of deliberate practice in the acquisition of expert performance. *Psychological Review,* *100*(3), 363–406.

Fisher, C. W., & Berliner, D. C. (1985). *Perspectives on instructional time.* New York: Longmans.

Francis, D. J., Fletcher, J. M., Catts, H. W., & Tomblin, J. B. (2005). Dimensions affecting the assessment of comprehension. In S. G. Paris & S. A. Stahl (Eds.), *Children's reading comprehension and assessment* (pp. 369–394). Mahwah, NJ: Erlbaum.

Gambrell, L. (1984). How much time do children spend reading during reading instruction? In J. A. Niles & L. A. Harris (Eds.), *Changing perspectives on research in reading/language processing and instruction* (pp. 127–135). Rochester, NY: National Reading Conference.

Gambrell, L. B., Wilson, R. M., & Gantt, W. N. (1981). Classroom observations of task-attending behaviors of good and poor readers. *Journal of Educational Research, 74*(6), 400–404.

Guthrie, J. T. (2004). Teaching for literacy engagement. *Journal of Literacy Research, 36*(1), 1–28.

Guthrie, J. T., & Humenick, N. M. (2004). Motivating students to read: Evidence for classroom practices that increase motivation and achievement. In P. McCardle & V. Chhabra (Eds.), *The voice of evidence in reading research* (pp. 329–354). Baltimore, MD: Brookes.

Hiebert, E. H. (1983). An examination of ability grouping for reading instruction. *Reading Research Quarterly, 18,* 231–255.

Hiebert, E. H. (2002). Standards, assessments, and text difficulty. In A. Farstrup & S. J. Samuels (Eds.), *What research has to say about reading instruction* (pp. 337–369). Newark, DE: International Reading Association.

Johnson, D. D., & Pearson, P. D. (1975). Skills management systems: A critique. *Reading Teacher, 28*(8), 757–764.

Jorgenson, G. W. (1977). Relationship of classroom behavior to the accuracy of the match between material difficulty and student ability. *Journal of Educational Psychology, 69*(1), 24–32.

Jorgenson, G. W., Klein, N., & Kumar, V. K. (1977). Achievement and behavioral correlates of matched levels of student ability and materials difficulty. *Journal of Educational Research, 71,* 100–103.

Keene, E. L., & Zimmerman, S. (1997). *Mosaic of thought: Teaching comprehension in a reader's workshop.* Portsmouth, NH: Heinemann.

Kiesling, H. (1978). Productivity of instructional time by mode of instruction for students at varying levels of reading skill. *Reading Research Quarterly, 13*(4), 554–582.

Knapp, M. S. (1995). *Teaching for meaning in high-poverty classrooms.* New York: Teachers College Press.

Krashen, S. (2001, October). More smoke and mirrors: A critique of the National Reading Panel report on fluency. *Phi Delta Kappan, 83,* 119–123.

Krashen, S. (2004a). False claims about literacy development. *Educational Leadership, 61*(6), 18–21.

Krashen, S. (2004b). *The power of reading: Insights from the research* (2nd ed.). Portsmouth, NH: Heinemann.

Kuhn, M. R. (2005). A comparative study of small group fluency instruction. *Reading Psychology, 26,* 127–146.

Kuhn, M. R., Schwanenflugel, P. J., Morris, R. D., Morrow, L. M., Woo, D., Meisinger, B., et al. (2006). Teaching children to become fluent and automatic readers. *Journal of Literacy Research, 38,* 357–387.

Kuhn, M. R., & Stahl, S. A. (1998). Teaching children to learn word meanings from context: A synthesis and some questions. *Journal of Literacy Research, 30*(1), 119–138.

Kuhn, M. R., & Stahl, S. A. (2003). Fluency: A review of developmental and remedial practices. *Journal of Educational Psychology, 95*(1), 3–21.

Leinhardt, G., Zigmond, N., & Cooley, W. (1981). Reading instruction and its effects. *American Educational Research Journal, 18*(3), 343–361.

Lewis, M., & Samuels, S. J. (n.d.). *Read more, read better? A meta-analysis of the literature on the relationship between exposure to reading and reading achievement.* Unpublished paper, University of Minnesota.

Lyon, G. R. (1998, April 28). Overview of reading and literacy initiatives. Retrieved May 1, 2007, from *www.educationnews.org/Curriculum/Reading/ Overview_of_Reading_and_Literacy_Initiatives.htm.*

McGill-Franzen, A., Zmach, C., Solic, K., & Zeig, J. L. (2006). The confluence of two policy mandates: Core reading programs and third-grade retention in Florida. *Elementary School Journal, 107*(1), 67–91.

McIntyre, E., Rightmeyer, E., Powell, R., Powers, S., & Petrosko, J. (2006). How much should young children read? A study of the relationship between development and instruction. *Literacy Teaching and Learning, 11*(1), 51–72.

Meyer, L. M., & Wardrop, J. L. (1994). Home and school influences on learning to read in kindergarten through second grade. In F. Lehr & J. Osborn (Eds.), *Reading, language, and literacy: Instruction for the twenty-first century* (pp. 165–184). Hillsdale, NJ: Erlbaum.

National Center for Education Statistics. (2006). *National Assessment of Educational Progress, selected years, 1971–2004 long-term trend reading assessments.* Retrieved April 17, 2008, from *nces.ed.gov/nationsreportcard/ltt/results2004/ nat-reading-scalescore.asp.*

National Institute of Child Health and Human Development. (2000). *Report of the National Reading Panel. Teaching children to read: An evidence-based assessment of the scientific research literature on reading and its implications for reading instruction* (NIH Publication No. 00-4769). Washington, DC: U.S. Government Printing Office.

Paris, S. G., Pearson, P. D., Cervetti, G., Carpenter, R., Paris, A. H., DeGroot, J., et al. (2004). Assessing the effectiveness of summer reading programs. In G. D. Borman & M. Boulay (Ed.), *Summer learning: Research, policies, and programs* (pp. 121–161). Mahwah, NJ: Erlbaum.

Pianta, R. C., Belsky, J., Houts, R., & Morrison, F. E. (2007). Opportunities to learn in America's elementary classrooms. *Science, 315*(5820), 1795–1796.

Pressley, M., Allington, R. L., Wharton-MacDonald, R., Collins-Block, C., & Morrow, L. (2001). *Learning to read: Lessons from exemplary first-grade classrooms.* New York: Guilford Press.

Pressley, M., Dolezal Kersey, S. E., Bogaert, L. R., Mohan, L., Roehrig, A. D., & Bogner Warzon, K. (2003). *Motivating primary grade students.* New York: Guilford Press.

Samuels, S. J. (2002). Reading fluency: Its development and assessment. In A. Farstrup & S. J. Samuels (Eds.), *What research has to say about reading instruction* (3rd ed., pp. 166–183). Newark, DE: International Reading Association.

Scanlon, D. M., Vellutino, F. R., Small, S. G., Fanuele, D. P., & Sweeney, J. M. (2005). Severe reading difficulties—can they be prevented?: A comparison of prevention and intervention approaches. *Exceptionality, 13*(4), 209–227.

Schraw, G., & Bruning, R. (1999). How implicit models of reading affect motivation to read and engagement. *Scientific Studies of Reading, 3*(3), 281–302.

Schraw, G., Flowerday, T., & Reisletter, M. F. (1998). The role of choice in reader engagement. *Journal of Educational Psychology, 90,* 705–714.

Shanahan, T. (2004). Critiques of the National Reading Panel report: Their implications for research, policy, and practice. In P. McCardle & V. Chhabra (Eds.), *The voice of evidence in reading research* (pp. 235–265). Baltimore, MD: Brookes.

Stahl, S. A., & Heubach, K. (2005). Fluency oriented reading instruction. *Journal of Literacy Research, 37*(1), 25–60.

Stanovich, K. E. (1986). Matthew effects in reading: Some consequences of individual differences in the acquisition of literacy. *Reading Research Quarterly, 21,* 360–407.

Stanovich, K. E. (2000). *Progress in understanding reading: Scientific foundations and new frontiers.* New York: Guilford Press.

Stanovich, K. E., West, R. F., Cunningham, A. E., Cipielewski, J., & Siddiqui, S. (1996). The role of inadequate print exposure as a determinant of reading comprehension problems. In C. Cornoldi & J. Oakhill (Eds.), *Reading comprehension difficulties: Processes and intervention* (pp. 15–32). Mahwah, NJ: Erlbaum.

Taylor, B. M., Frye, B. J., & Maruyama, G. M. (1990). Time spent reading and reading growth. *American Educational Research Journal, 27*(2), 351–362.

Thurlow, M., Gaden, J., Ysseldyke, J., & Algozzine, R. (1984). Student reading during reading class: The lost activity in reading instruction. *Journal of Educational Research, 77*(5), 267–272.

Torgesen, J. K., & Hudson, R. F. (2006). Reading fluency: Critical issues for struggling readers. In S. J. Samuels & A. E. Farstrup (Eds.), *What research has to say about fluency instruction* (pp. 130–158). Newark, DE: International Reading Association.

Tovani, C. (2001). *I read it, but I don't get it: Comprehension strategies for adolescent readers.* Portland, ME: Stenhouse.

Vadasy, P. F., Sanders, E. A., & Peyton, J. A. (2005). Relative effectiveness of reading practice or word-level instruction in supplemental tutoring: How text matters. *Journal of Learning Disabilities, 38*(4), 364–380.

Vaughn, S., Moody, S. W., & Schumm, J. S. (1998). Broken promises: Reading instruction in the resource room. *Exceptional Children, 64,* 211–225.

Vellutino, F. R. (2003). Individual differences as sources of variability in reading comprehension in elementary school children. In A. P. Sweet & C. E. Snow (Eds.), *Rethinking reading comprehension* (pp. 51–81). New York: Guilford Press.

Whitehurst, G. J. (2002, October). *Evidence-based education.* Presentation at the Student Achievement and School Accountability Conference. Washington, DC: U.S. Department of Education, Institute for Education Sciences. Retrieved from *www.ed.gov/nclb/methods/whatworks/eb/edlite-slide003.html.*

Wu, Y., & Samuels, S. J. (2004, May). *How the amount of time spent on independent reading affects reading achievement.* Paper presented at the annual meeting of the International Reading Association, Reno, NV.

3

PROMOTING REASONS FOR READING

Teacher Practices
That Impact Motivation

ANGELA McRAE
JOHN T. GUTHRIE

Almost all agree that some specific amount of reading practice is vital to becoming a good reader. Expertise does not arise without active participation. Some educators maintain that the best way to become a proficient reader is by reading widely and frequently. But other educators suggest that gaining proficiency may not be so simple for many students, who may need more contextual support. Contextual support is extremely important in attaining reading proficiency, but we are suggesting that, while explicit instruction and appropriate texts are valuable, an often overlooked factor is motivational support. We maintain that when classroom practices help engender powerful motivations for reading, students acquire proficiency steadily and predictably.

When students read a passage or a book, they usually have a reason for doing it. Likewise when they avoid reading a text that they may be expected to read, they usually have a reason for their resistance. The most prominent reason for recreational reading is "I enjoy it." This reason refers to interest or intrinsic motivation, which means doing something for its own sake, and these motivations are internal to the student. Students who consistently read for their own interest are often quite competent and are usually highly achieving readers. Wigfield and Guthrie (1997) documented that students who are intrinsically motivated spend 300% more time reading than students who have low intrinsic motivation for reading. Compared to 10 other motivations, intrinsic motivation for reading was most highly correlated with whether or not students read widely and frequently on their own.

Another reason students read in school is external pressure. Often students say that their reason for reading is that "the teacher assigned it" or "I'll get in trouble if I don't." In this case, the reason for reading is external motivation (Ryan & Connell, 1989). This reason is not chosen by the student, and this reading will be avoided if possible. An extremely widespread research finding is that internal motivations (interest, intrinsic motivation) are positively correlated with reading achievement, and external motivations (pressure, requirements, rules) are not correlated with reading achievement (Guthrie & Coddington, in press). In elementary school external motivations are usually not negatively correlated with reading competence, but in secondary school the external reasons for reading become negatively related to achievement. By secondary school, students who read only for the reason of avoiding getting in trouble or only to avoid feeling ashamed for failing show low and declining achievement (Otis, Frederick, & Pelletier, 2005).

The reasons for reading, then, are crucial, while the simple act of reading is insufficient for analysis. When internal motivations such as intrinsic motivation and interest energize students' reading, students interact with text deeply and gain relatively large amounts of knowledge or experience aesthetic benefits (Schiefele, 1999). If students' reading interests are weak or indefinite, their competency grows little and their quality as readers diminishes (Guthrie, Hoa, et al., 2007).

In this chapter we present five motivations that have been widely found to foster achievement. Tables 3.1 and 3.2 cite classroom practices that, respectively, affirm and undermine motivation as it relates to interest (or intrinsic motivation), ownership, self-efficacy, social interaction, and mastery. In further explicating these five types of motivation, we discuss the reasons for reading when the motivation is affirming (positive) and the reasons for avoiding reading when the motivation is undermining (negative).

Most important, there are classroom practices that encourage these five reasons for reading, and each practice can be implemented

TABLE 3.1. Classroom Practices That Affirm Motivation

Teacher practices	Motivations	Reasons to read when practice is affirming
Relevance	Interest/intrinsic motivation	"I enjoy it." "It's fun."
Choice	Ownership	"I chose it." "It belongs to me."
Success	Self-efficacy	"I can do it well." "I like to be successful."
Collaboration	Social interaction with peers	"I can do it with others." "I enjoy relating to my peers."
Thematic units	Mastery	"I want to understand." "I like to learn new things."

in the short term or the long term. We present classroom practices that impact internal reasons for reading, according to empirical studies. We draw on a variety of research, including studies of Concept-Oriented Reading Instruction (CORI) (Guthrie, McRae, & Klauda, 2007) and a meta-analysis of 22 studies (Guthrie & Humenick, 2004). What makes CORI and other motivational programs different from traditional reading instruction is the focus on increasing not only reading comprehension but also reading engagement for students at all reading levels. This focus is achieved through the explicit inclusion of motivational support in the classroom. In CORI, for example, teachers are trained

TABLE 3.2. Classroom Practices That Undermine Motivation

Teacher practices	Student outcomes	Reasons to avoid reading when practice is undermining
Nonrelevance	Avoidance	"I do not enjoy it." "It is not fun."
Excessive control	Low ownership	"I did not choose it." "It does not belong to me."
Difficult lessons	Perceived difficulty	"I cannot do it." "I am not capable."
Frequent individual work	Isolation	"I cannot do it with others." "I am not able to relate to my peers."
Disconnected units	Mastery avoidance	"I do not care about understanding." "I cannot create meaning."

to implement five motivational practices that are embedded in the curriculum.

Intrinsic Motivation

Students who read for the sheer enjoyment of reading are intrinsically motivated. They are not reading for the external rewards sometimes offered by teachers, such as toys, food, candy, or grades. These students also choose to read during their free time both in and out of school, initiating reading without promises of either reward or punishment. Teachers can implement practices in the classroom that either support or undermine student intrinsic motivation.

Relevance Builds Intrinsic Motivation

When reading material is made relevant for students, they are more likely to become engaged and competent readers (Vansteenkiste, Lens, & Deci, 2006). When teachers encourage intrinsic motivation in students by making the reading activity in class relevant, students more readily initiate and persist in the reading tasks. To assure relevance, text and activities should be linked to real-life experiences, hands-on activities, or a conceptual theme and should be culturally relevant. This emphasis on relevance is the purpose of hands-on science activities in CORI that we have examined extensively (Guthrie, Hoa, et al., 2007). Activating the background knowledge of students before, during, and after reading helps them to make connections between their own lives, their interests, and the text. For example, having a discussion about recent trips students have taken to the city may help get their minds acclimated to an upcoming text about urban architecture.

For situations in which students have little or no existing background knowledge, hands-on activities help to bring personal experience of a new concept to the class. Dissecting an owl pellet and observing the animal bones, skull fragments, and hair found within it is a good way to bring quick personal experience to bear on a text about the survival mechanisms of the owl. These are some of the activities used in grade 3 implementations of CORI (Guthrie et al., 2004). Students are much more likely to pick up a book about owls and read it with engagement after such a hands-on activity, resulting in effective practice of cognitive reading strategies and gained conceptual knowledge (Guthrie, McRae, & Klauda, 2007). The power of hands-on experiences that are tightly linked to book reading activities was shown in one investigation by Guthrie et al. (2006). Reading growth was higher for students in classrooms where there were a large number of hands-on science activities tightly linked to books than in classrooms where fewer activities of this kind occurred.

In addition to selecting texts that connect to students' interests and backgrounds, teachers encourage students' intrinsic motivation by making the reading activity in class maximally relevant to them. Relevance gives them reason to both initiate and persist in completing the reading task. Students are also more likely to be engaged in reading if there is an ongoing relevant conceptual theme. Teachers who create units of study that focus on some conceptual theme based on student interest are encouraging students to read the expository and narrative texts with greater enthusiasm over an extended period of time, thereby sustaining engagement. In various versions of CORI, we have used the conceptual themes of survival of life in wetlands, plant and animal communities, or habitats for birds around the world. For third graders, the concepts of survival were explored by means of such subconcepts as feeding, locomotion, predation, defense, reproduction, respiration, communication, niche, competition, and adaptation to habitat (Barbosa & Alexander, 2004).

While providing experiences for students that activate and add to their background knowledge centered on a conceptual theme, teachers must be aware of and attentive to the cultural backgrounds of their students. This is especially important since studies have found differences in levels of intrinsic motivation among ethnic groups. Unrau and Schlackman (2006) studied urban middle school students' intrinsic motivations for reading. The middle school was located in Los Angeles, and the majority of the students (about 75%) were Hispanic, while about 20% were Asian. The authors found that intrinsic motivation positively related to and predicted reading achievement for the Asian students, but they did not find this result for Hispanic students. It is, therefore, important to consider what cultural values and opportunities students are often presented with within the context of their home environments and communities.

Including themes and texts from various parts of the world enriches students' appreciation for and understanding of their culture as well as cultures outside their own. Teachers who include texts and references to the specific cultures represented in the classroom are more likely to engage students, especially those who do not normally see their backgrounds reflected in mainstream instruction and texts. This helps to bring some of their own personal background knowledge to the reading activity, thereby increasing comprehension. With repeated experiences of relevance in the classroom, students increase their interest, and their reasons for reading increasingly become enjoyment rather than external pressure.

Nonrelevance Undermines Intrinsic Motivation

When teachers do not assure the relevance of text or reading activity, students tend to avoid reading (Assor, Kaplan, & Roth, 2002). For example, students may experience low relevance when there are multiple unrelated topics within one lesson with few or no links to background knowledge. Teaching texts and topics that have no basis or connection to students' background knowledge has the effect of disengaging them, and gives them an additional reason not to read the text. If students are consistently given texts and reading activities that are outside of their own experiences or that disregard their interests and preferences, there is little reason for them to initiate reading the text and even less chance that they will become immersed in the reading. Over time, students come to regard the readings as tedious chores, and, given their dislike of the texts, they will tend to avoid reading (Oldfather, 2002).

Ownership

Too often, teachers create an environment in the classroom that emphasizes the teacher's authority and ownership of the space, the materials, the curriculum, and, by extension, the learning that takes place. However, once students are placed at the center of the learning experience and are encouraged to think of reading as their own personal asset, they see the value of investing their time and energy in reading.

Affording Choices Strengthens Ownership

There are opportunities throughout the school day to offer meaningful choices to students. These choices can be manifested in several ways that effectively give students a sense of ownership that becomes one of the reasons to read. The main factors to consider when providing choices are whether the choice is meaningful, whether it is relevant to the activity, and whether the level of choice is appropriate for the student. If the choices provided by the teacher meet these criteria, the result is an increased sense of ownership that the student feels toward reading as well as increased self-regulation and investment in the acquisition of reading strategies. Experiments show that giving choices of what to read or how long to spend on specific texts increases students' sense of being "in charge" and their time spent reading (Reynolds & Symons, 2001).

For choices to be meaningful, they should be based on students' personal goals and interests (Assor et al., 2002). A simple but impactful choice is that of text selection. Students have individual interests and preferences when it comes to text genre, format, and topic. Even if the topic has been set by the teacher, a variety of texts can be offered that appeal to students, giving them a sense of responsibility; once they choose a particular text, there is now a responsibility to read and follow through with that choice. One research team (Reeve & Jang, 2006) observed teachers in a brief 10-minute lesson on how to solve a problem. Afterward, they asked students about their motivations and their sense of being in charge of their learning. Students were not motivated to participate in tasks when the teacher talked constantly, gave detailed directions, asked controlling questions, gave deadlines, criticized students, and gave answers before students finished talking. In contrast, students reported feeling engaged and motivated for tasks when their teachers listened, asked what students wanted, provided a rationale for work, picked up on student questions, gave encouraging feedback, and recognized challenges (Reeve & Jang, 2006).

In another study, Vansteenkiste et al. (2006) presented a text on nutrition to students who were moderately or highly obese. One group was asked to read it for their own interest and personal benefit. Another group was asked to read quickly to get a high score on a test. The former group, whose personal needs were addressed in the reading, felt a sense of ownership of the text. They comprehended deeply and understood the implications of the text for them. The second group, who read for external goals only, gained superficial knowledge of a few facts but missed the central messages of the text.

Effective teachers scaffold choices so that at first there are limited options, and eventually students are making multiple choices within a lesson such as topic and text selection, partner or group selection, or the character of the end product. It is vital, however, that students not be given choices that are overwhelming either in breadth or depth. If students have a particularly hard time with decoding text, for example, an appropriate approach would be for the teacher to select the topic and provide two texts from which the students can make a choice. Students who are more independent could choose from five texts, and especially proficient students might have a choice of topic as well as text. The goal is to move students gradually to the point where they are making multiple choices within a lesson, such as topic and text selection, partner or group selection, and decisions about the end product. If students are forced to make multiple choices initially, they might be overwhelmed and perhaps unlikely to accomplish the desired goals of the lessons.

In discussion of scaffolding for student choice, Antonio and Guthrie (2008) suggested that teachers consider (1) offering simple choices at first, (2) helping students practice making good choices, (3) providing feedback about their choices, (4) using team choices for younger students, (5) offering information that clarifies good choices, and (6) affording students choices within a task (e.g., ordering, sequence, topic). In effective scaffolding for choice, a teacher initially shares responsibility with the students and gradually shifts the decision making into the students' hands. In an interview study, Flowerday and Schraw (2000) found that secondary teachers offered choices on (1) the topic of study, (2) reading materials, (3) methods of assessment, (4) the order of activities, (5) social arrangements, and (6) procedural sequences. These teachers said that their purpose was to increase students' interest in and commitment to the learning and reading activities.

In an environment such as CORI, where students are consistently given meaningful options and then guided to make appropriate choices, students subsequently experience an increase in reading comprehension and increased self-regulation (Guthrie et al., 2004). This success contributes to greater attention to reading tasks and a commitment to the completion of these tasks. Throughout the process of reading, and once it is complete, students emerge with a sense of ownership of the reading strategies they have learned and practiced, ownership of the knowledge they have attained, and accountability for the further development of the strategies and knowledge that have been developed through their choices.

Excessive Control Undermines Ownership

A teacher who controls every aspect of reading instruction is sending the clear message to students that their opinions and preferences do not matter. When students do not have any options in designing their learning, they become passive spectators to the teacher's agenda. As a result, students have no sense of ownership of the strategies being taught, the text used, or the knowledge presented, and have no reason to read that text. When it comes time to share the results of the learning experience, students feel no accountability. For many students, this lack of accountability is reflected in a failure to complete tasks and the likelihood that information will be forgotten as soon as the experience is over. Based on observing classrooms, Assor, Kaplan, Kanat-Maymon, and Roth (2005) found that frequent directives, interfering with the preferred pace of learning, and suppressing critical thinking were ways of exerting excessive control. Such overcontrol resulted in the expression of anger, anxiety, and resentment toward the teacher among fourth- and fifth-grade students.

Readers need to establish and maintain a state of flow, or engagement, while reading. If readers are constantly interrupted or made to start and stop at the teacher's command, there is no feeling of ownership or personal responsibility for the reading assignment (Assor et al., 2005). Students who sense that their opinions and preferences are not heard and not valued are made to feel unimportant and powerless in the classroom. This impression can lead to the view that the reading activity itself is unimportant (Seifert & O'Keefe, 2001). There is no need for one to self-regulate if the teacher is making all of the decisions. Students may follow along passively without any decision-making processes taking place and without the benefit of the trial and error involved in developing effective learning processes.

Lack of ownership also diminishes the selection and use of reading strategies (Reynolds & Symons, 2001). When teachers give students only a trivial choice such as which pen color to use, they know the choice is irrelevant to their learning and that it provides no connection between them and the reading task. Students who are not allowed to make choices about which strategy to use or how to use it are being taught to view reading in a very limited manner, where there is only one way to approach a problem and no alternatives are presented. With little ownership, students' reasons for reading become external. They may say, "The teacher wants it done" or "I'm only reading because I have to." These strictly external reasons are likely to lead to only superficial use of strategies and to lower proficiency in challenging tasks.

Self-Efficacy

Students who believe they can read well are going to read often. When students have high self-efficacy in reading, the potentially daunting task of reading a text that is challenging becomes surmountable. They work toward goals and frequently enjoy the feeling of success that comes with tackling a difficult passage. Self-efficacy in students is related to cognitive engagement and persistence at challenging tasks (Pintrich & De Groot, 1990).

Maintaining Success Improves Self-Efficacy

Teachers who support their students' perception that they are capable of reading well are setting the students up for success as a major reason to become engaged in reading (Wigfield, Guthrie, Tonks, & Perencevich, 2004). When teachers guide students to repeat tasks until they are proficient, students enjoy increases in self-efficacy. Teachers who support student self-efficacy also evaluate student work based on effort and accuracy. This process promotes students' willingness to place greater efforts into challenging texts and reading tasks, which then has a reciprocal effect, enabling the students to experience meaningful success.

In classrooms that promote student self-efficacy, the students' success is linked to challenging tasks. Miller and Meece (1999) reported that third-grade students preferred challenging reading and writing tasks. The students were interviewed after completing tasks such as essays, research papers, and the analysis of characters in a class-read novel. The interviews revealed that, even when students found a task easy, they did not necessarily have an interest in completing the task, often finding it boring. When presented with a challenging task, however, they stated that they especially enjoyed creating their responses and preferred these types of tasks.

To allow for sufficient challenge in their lessons, teachers should identify the current level of the student in decoding, comprehension, and writing and then create tasks that build upon and extend the student's current capacities. This means providing decodable text for students that is slightly above their reading level but within a level of comfort where the student is able to become engaged and read fluently with little interruption. The focus here should be on solidifying existing decoding skills while building vocabulary and conceptual knowledge, giving the student a sense of accomplishing a meaningful task that is challenging. Once the student has successfully attained the reading strategy or concept at hand and has shown proficiency in decoding that text, the difficulty of the text may be increased, always challenging the student but never overwhelming him or her. This approach fosters self-efficacy and encourages reading engagement (Linnenbrink & Pintrich, 2003).

The assessment of the student should be based on effort and persistence with challenging text. Text that is well below the level of the student has already been mastered, and the student gains very little if there is no additional conceptual knowledge to be gained. Evaluating reading ability with this kind of text does not accurately represent the student's reading level or growth, even though the student appears successful. On the other hand, a student who is applying effort to the reading task and who experiences some element of challenge is more likely to experience growth in reading ability, and the assessment of student success should be grounded in this context of appropriate challenge.

Allowing Frequent Failure Undermines Self-Efficacy

When students perceive that reading tasks are insurmountable, they are less likely to put forth effort or even to attempt new and challenging reading tasks (Schunk, 2003). This reluctance leads to teacher evaluations that rate the students as poor readers, which in turn further discourages them from attempting similarly difficult reading activities.

A focus on task completion rather than students' learning accomplishments lies at the heart of practices that undermine self-efficacy, as shown by Schunk (2003) in a review of studies designed to increase self-efficacy in reading and learning. Such a task focus occurs most often when students are expected to read a textbook that is too difficult. For example, many textbooks in content areas contain excessively difficult vocabulary, are poorly organized, and are connected with students' background knowledge only remotely if at all. For secondary students, this threat to self-efficacy prevents them from believing that school is worthwhile (Otis et al., 2005). Focusing on content coverage and the completion of the tasks enumerated in a lesson plan or teachers' guide can hinder the self-efficacy of students who are developing readers as well as those who are proficient readers. In the case of developing readers, students who are given tasks that are too difficult and asked to repeat the tasks repeatedly, without additional instruction, are likely to be disengaged (Chapman & Tunmer, 1995). Whatever vestige of students' self-efficacy for reading that exists to that point drops even more. This experience of repeated failure causes the students to detach themselves mentally from the reading task and, in a broader sense, from reading altogether (Coddington & Guthrie, in press). The most frequently cited reason for not reading a particular text is the belief that "I cannot read it." Repeated experiences of excessive difficulty humiliate students, and naturally they become avoidant.

Teachers may unintentionally undermine self-efficacy when reading lessons are focused on a task, such as a skill exercise, with no consideration given to whether students are gaining success and competence. Students who do not feel challenged are less motivated and have lower self-efficacy (Miller & Meece, 1999). When nothing but completion of the task is required, and students are given the message that their success in comprehending or appreciating the material is irrelevant, they may complete the task to the teacher's specifications, but it is possible that neither permanent knowledge nor an ongoing strategy has been acquired. Students then learn to go through the motions of completing tasks without any purpose or benefit, translating success as merely finishing a task rather than mastering a goal.

Social Motivation

Sharing reading is a social experience, whether students are reading in unison, discussing a novel, or working together to decode and define a new word. One of the aspects of school that children enjoy is spending time with friends. When given the opportunity to interact with friends during class time, students will approach the given task with more enthusiasm.

Arranging for Collaboration Fosters Social Motivation

Students are social beings, and this is apparent both in and out of the classroom. Just as they crave social interaction on the playground, when in the classroom, discussion and collaboration are natural parts of a student's learning and development, and students will readily embrace collaboration with peers as a reason to read. When teachers support this need for collaboration by allowing students to share ideas and build knowledge together, a sense of belongingness to the classroom community is established, and the extension and elaboration of existing knowledge is facilitated (Wentzel, 2005). Students gain the perspective of others while debating topics in the classroom, broadening their own views. Students who work together on a reading task are combining their background knowledge and skill sets, learning from one another, and building a shared understanding of the material (Chinn, Anderson, & Waggoner, 2001).

In a study by Almasi (1995), fourth-grade average and below-average readers were observed and interviewed while engaging in the discussion of stories during reading class. Students were placed in either peer-led or teacher-led groups and were given stories to read based on their interest and reading level. The resulting text-related discussions among students in the peer-led groups were more elaborate than the discussions that were teacher-led. In the peer-led groups, students shared their opinions and background knowledge, leading to new interpretations of the text. The students in the teacher-led groups were not nearly so actively engaged in discussing incongruities in the text, as the teacher was the dominant member of the group and posed explicit questions, guiding students through the analysis of the text. Student engagement is supported when students are encouraged to read aloud together, create questions together, and extract meaning from text together (Chinn et al., 2001).

In a literature review of motivation and engagement among Caucasian and African American students, several experimental studies found that African American students benefit from collaborative structures for interacting with text more than Caucasian students. Not only do African American students prefer collaborative to individual learning, but also their text comprehension is much enhanced in collaborative learning activities that are well structured (Guthrie, Rueda, Gambrell, & Morrison, 2009). Even sharing prior knowledge helps to motivate students when they are allowed to find common experiences with their peers, making them feel a sense of belonging within the classroom community. When they learn that a classmate has experienced something that they have never seen or even thought of before, this discovery creates a respect for and curiosity about fellow students. Once this kind of rapport is established and dialogue has been devoted to the given topic, students are more likely to engage in reading text communally and subsequently recall the resulting knowledge much better, as demonstrated in a study of African American fifth graders (Dill & Boykin, 2000).

Grouping students of varying reading levels can also be motivating, as the struggling students gain the perspective of more experienced readers, and the advanced readers clarify their own understanding through explaining concepts and reading strategies to their peers (Sikorski, 2004). For example, modeling and scaffolding students to say appropriately "I disagree with you" or "I want to add two points to what you are saying" enables learners to become more interactively effective. Students working individually may be more likely to fall prey to misconceptions and adopt errant perspectives on a text than students in an open discussion. Working individually, students also miss the chance for verbal give-and-take. This approach also lessens the dependence or overreliance on the teacher, and students come to feel a greater sense of independence when creating meaning with peers instead of always having to receive help from the presumed authority figure.

This extension of knowledge and perceptions leads to the greater elaboration of text. The initial concepts are read and decoded by the students, but then these concepts are extended beyond the boundaries of the text to include multiple interpretations and a complex structure of prior knowledge, perspectives, and emerging knowledge that has been built collaboratively. It is important for teachers to model and facilitate elaborative speech in their lessons in order for students to develop their collaborating skills (Webb & Farivar, 1994).

Individual Work Undermines Social Motivation

Some teachers believe that a quiet classroom where students work individually and independently when not in whole-group instruction is a controlled and well-maintained class. The silence in the room is not an indicator of student engagement, nor is it necessarily conducive to complex learning processes such as building an argument or combining multifaceted knowledge to form new knowledge links. Students in this environment tend to feel isolated and do not sense a connection between themselves and a greater community of scholars. Isolated learners may adhere to faulty logic or inaccurate interpretations without realizing the alternatives or may focus exclusively on one "correct" interpretation or conclusion (Applebee, Langer, Nystrand, & Gamoran, 2003). These students also miss the chance to build social skills that include negotiation, persuasion, and synthesis of one's perspectives with those of peers, which is something researchers have found students enjoy when given the opportunity (Clark et al., 2003).

Mastery Motivation

Students' goals in the classroom vary from wanting to perform well to earn a grade to wanting to master and become experts in some new reading strategy, concept, or topic. The quest for deep understanding through enhanced reading skills is made possible by mastery motivation.

Thematic Units Cultivate Mastery Motivation

By emphasizing mastery goals as an explicit reason to read, teachers contribute to both student motivation and reading comprehension

(Grolnick & Ryan, 1987; Pintrich, 2000). Teachers who provide concepts that are both complex and persist over an extended period of time do much to support the acquisition of deep-seated conceptual knowledge. Goal orientation has been shown to be related to reading achievement (Guthrie et al., 2006). One way to scaffold mastery goals is to place large conceptual learning goals on the blackboard, a bulletin board, or a chart. As the lessons progress, key information is added and additional concepts are linked to the visible display. A teacher might scaffold mastery goal learning by beginning a large concept map and adding to it during the course of a thematic unit. This approach focuses students on deep understanding rather than test scores or the number of pages covered in a text.

Placing an emphasis on mastery of new material, not just the performance of tasks, typifies the teacher who is focused on mastery goal orientation. In the classroom, concepts are introduced and then related to one another to form a complex web of knowledge. Students are able to explore topics in depth and at length, and they come away with a more nuanced understanding of the text that can then enhance future reading experiences.

Even at the lower elementary grades, students are capable of learning multiple concepts and making connections among those concepts. Although at first they may appear more challenging, decodable texts that include conceptual knowledge are more likely to sustain student interest and foster curiosity, thereby creating engaged readers. Addressing additional teacher attention to mastery goals for students facilitates this conceptual learning (Meece, Anderman, & Anderman, 2006). Making a lesson conceptual also helps to integrate domains such as science and social studies.

The concepts within reading lessons should also be focal points for several days or even weeks. This focus on concepts enables students to gain a sense of becoming experts in a given topic or subject area. Introducing the concept in a way that takes into account students' prior knowledge can in itself take multiple lessons to accomplish. Then, providing students with hands-on experiences and exposure to multiple texts should be the core piece of the unit, and again may extend over several days or weeks. Teachers can conclude with a culminating project that lets students express their accumulated conceptual knowledge.

There is also a connection between other motivational practices and mastery orientation. In a study by Meece and Miller (1999), teachers who supported student choice, intrinsic motivation, collaboration, and self-efficacy were effective in promoting mastery goals in their third-grade classrooms. These findings were based on an intervention study that increased opportunities for students to complete challenging assignments in a small-group setting. Ratings of work-avoidant goals decreased, but mastery goals remained stable for the students in classrooms where teachers were rated as demonstrating effective implementation of the intervention.

Disconnected Units Undermine Mastery Motivation

When lessons emphasize the factual knowledge of disparate topics, students tend to avoid a mastery orientation and focus instead on short-term gains that do not result in the meaningful building of learning strategies or permanent knowledge (Seifert & O'Keefe, 2001). Teachers need to be attentive to the goal orientation of whole classes, especially as students move into the upper elementary grades when their goal orientations can fluctuate widely (Meece & Miller, 1999).

Student engagement is diminished whenever the topics change so rapidly that students are left with no clear conceptual reason to read the text. Teachers who switch quickly from one unrelated topic to another are not giving students a chance to reflect on or digest new information. Even if the teacher is choosing appropriate conceptual themes, this is not an effective approach unless students are given the time to manipulate these concepts and integrate them with their existing knowledge. When students are made to read unrelated texts and then are questioned in an oversimplified manner—such as asking them to recite dates that have been memorized or other surface knowledge without any connection to larger systems—their inclination to seek deeper understanding is effectively rebuffed.

Finally, students may learn new reading strategies while reading text just for factual information or to receive a grade for their performance. This level of accomplishment does not mean that they are engaged readers or that they are mastering anything more than a skill set to be used within a specific context. Teachers who emphasize performance instead of mastery tend to stress formal assessments and grades rather than engagement (Patrick, Anderman, Ryan, Edelin, & Midgley, 2001). Limiting the use of reading strategy to shallow themes teaches students to think in a very restricted way about reading and its purpose. Once a strategy has been employed and comprehension gained from text, if that meaning is trivial, then students are not compelled to initiate use of the strategy in the future, nor are they excited about beginning a new text, since there is no meaningful knowledge to be gained.

Reading Identity

The variables that we have discussed to this point affect reading identity. Reading identity refers to the extent that an individual values reading as personally important, and it views success in reading as an important goal. Regrettably, very little is known about educational conditions that foster the development of reading identity. However, it is well established that high achievers tend to identify with school and feel a sense of belonging in the classroom (Voelkl, 1997). Students who identify themselves as readers are the ones who are more likely to read and to gain knowledge from reading. Teachers support this by explaining that texts are important and functional and that reading is relevant for students' long-term interests and personal development. Under the best conditions, students connect reading skill and life outcomes such as career attainment and personal success.

Although there is little research on this issue, we maintain that when teachers model their own personal identification as readers and make explicit the fact that they value reading, students perceive reading as beneficial and worthwhile. When teachers support students' identity as readers, students have a commitment to complete the act of reading, not just to the satisfaction of the teacher but to their own personal standard of excellence. This level of commitment may result in a sense of accomplishment once a reading task is mastered that goes beyond the teacher and lesson, as the student is fulfilling his own personal sense of responsibility to excel at reading.

As students progress through school, their identity as learners and readers can progressively deteriorate. Young children typically give high ratings to reading and learning (Coddington & Guthrie, in press). However, as students approach the end of the elementary grades, many students cease to aspire to higher achievement or proficiency in tasks such as reading in any subject matter (Wigfield & Eccles, 2002). As they enter middle school, some students detach their sense of self-worth from school success. This is especially true for African American and Hispanic students. Beginning in grades seven and eight, many of these minority students reject reading achievement and view it as unimportant. Taylor and Graham (2007) showed that African American and Hispanic students cease to value achievement in middle school.

As Osborne (1997) documented for a national sample, African American males increasingly disidentify with academics through middle and high school. Their sense of self-worth progressively detaches from their level of achievement. They do not experience any benefit that justifies putting effort into reading. School is viewed not as an avenue for advancement or success but rather as merely a requirement imposed on them. Nussbaum and Steele (2007) found that African American students often disengage themselves from evaluations in order to prevent unfavorable appraisals of their achievements.

Although there is little evidence on this issue, it is likely that when teachers encourage students to make connections with reading and to apply their personal experiences in the classroom, they may increase their engagement with text. Teachers' interpersonal relationships with students are also likely to impact their engagement favorably, which may foster their process of identification in the long term.

Next Steps for Educators

One remarkable quality about the motivations presented here—consisting of interest, ownership, self-efficacy, social interaction, and mastery goals—is that they are associated with more and better reading at all grade levels, K–12. These motivations are also associated with more and better reading in classroom contexts that are created both in the short term and in the long term. If a teacher supports students' ownership by giving many choices in one lesson, the students are likely to respond positively with more motivation for reading. More profoundly, however, if a curriculum embeds choices across the school year and daily instruction underscores students' self-directed learning, students' ownership of reading will grow substantially and drive achievement upward.

As a first step in short-term planning, educators can take stock of their current teaching practices. For each of the motivations presented in this chapter, educators can ask:

1. "Do I support this motivation already?"
2. "How often do I do this?"
3. "When do I support this motivation?"
4. "How well does my support work?"
5. "How can I support this motivation more?"
6. "How can I support this motivation more effectively?"
7. "How can I connect this practice to my current teaching more deeply?"

Many teachers are already connecting reading to students' real-world experiences and background knowledge to some degree. However, using these questions to reflect on teaching and to expand teachers' support for relevance will improve the amount and depth of students' reading.

For an entire course or a discipline in school such as reading instruction, educators can ask:

1. "How does the course increase students' motivations already?"
2. "How often does the course support these motivations explicitly?"
3. "When does the course do this?"
4. "How well do the instructional supports for motivation work?"
5. "How can we support motivation more frequently?"
6. "How can we support motivation better?"
7. "How can the course connect to the motivation practices described here more thoroughly?"

The first step in thinking about supporting motivation more fully is self-appraisal. One starting point for self-appraisal is to use conversational questionnaires about motivation in the classroom. Useful inquiries can be made into the students' viewpoint (through a student questionnaire). Educators can also explore the teachers' viewpoint (through a teacher questionnaire). One exemplary set of questionnaires is available in *Engaging Adolescents in Reading* by Guthrie (2008). Regardless of which tools for self-improvement are used, the implications of this chapter are that educators can advance the breadth and depth of students' reading by explicitly and systematically nourishing their practices that affirm students' motivations as readers.

References

Almasi, J. F. (1995). The nature of fourth graders' sociocognitive conflicts in peer-led and teacher-led discussions of literature. *Reading Research Quarterly, 30,* 314–351.

Antonio, D., & Guthrie, J. T. (2008). Reading is social: Bringing peer interaction to the text. In J. T. Guthrie (Ed.), *Engaging adolescents in reading* (pp. 49–63). Thousand Oaks, CA: Corwin Press.

Applebee, A. N., Langer, J. A., Nystrand, M., & Gamoran, A. (2003). Discussion-based approaches to developing understanding: Classroom instruction and student performance in middle and high school English. *American Educational Research Journal, 40,* 685–730.

Assor, A., Kaplan, H., Kanat-Maymon, Y., & Roth, G. (2005). Directly controlling teacher behaviors as predictors of poor motivation and engagement
in girls and boys: The role of anger and anxiety. *Learning and Instruction,
15*, 397–413.

Assor, A., Kaplan, H., & Roth, G. (2002). Choice is good, but relevance is excellent: Autonomy-enhancing and suppressing teacher behaviours predicting students' engagement in schoolwork. *British Journal of Educational Psychology, 72*, 261–278.

Barbosa, P., & Alexander, L. (2004). Science inquiry in the CORI framework. In
J. T. Guthrie, A. Wigfield, & K. C. Perencevich (Eds.), *Motivating reading
comprehension: Concept-Oriented Reading Instruction* (pp. 113–141). Mahwah, NJ: Erlbaum.

Chapman, J. W., & Tunmer, W. E. (1995). Development of young children's
reading self-concepts: An examination of emerging subcomponents and
their relationship with reading achievement. *Journal of Educational Psychology, 87*, 154–167.

Chinn, C. A., Anderson, R. C., & Waggoner, M. A. (2001). Patterns of discourse in
two kinds of literature discussion. *Reading Research Quarterly, 36*, 378–412.

Clark, A., Anderson, R. C., Kuo, L., Kim, I., Archodidou, A., & Nguyen-Jahiel,
K. (2003). Collaborative reasoning: Expanding ways for children to talk
and think in school. *Educational Psychology Review, 15*, 181–198.

Coddington, C. S., & Guthrie, J. T. (in press). Teacher and student perceptions of
boys' and girls' reading motivation. *Reading Psychology*.

Dill, E. M., & Boykin, A. W. (2000). The comparative influence of individual,
peer tutoring, and communal learning contexts on the text recall of African American children. *Journal of Black Psychology, 26*, 65–78.

Flowerday, T., & Schraw, G. (2000). Teacher beliefs about instructional choice: A
phenomenological study. *Journal of Educational Psychology, 92*, 634–645.

Grolnick, W. S., & Ryan, R. M. (1987). Autonomy in children's learning: An
experimental and individual difference investigation. *Journal of Personality
and Social Psychology, 52*, 890–898.

Guthrie, J. T. (Ed.). (2008). *Engaging adolescents in reading*. Thousand Oaks, CA:
Corwin Press.

Guthrie, J. T., & Coddington, C. S. (in press). Reading motivation. In K. Wentzel
& A. Wigfield (Eds.), *Handbook of motivation at school*. Mahwah, NJ: Erlbaum.

Guthrie, J. T., Hoa, L. W., Wigfield, A., Tonks, S. M., Humenick, N. M., & Littles,
E. (2007). Reading motivation and reading comprehension growth in the
later elementary years. *Contemporary Educational Psychology, 32*, 282–313.

Guthrie, J. T., & Humenick, N. M. (2004). Motivating students to read: Evidence
for classroom practices that increase reading motivation and achievement.
In P. McCardle & V. Chhabra (Eds.), *The voice of evidence in reading research*
(pp. 329–354). Baltimore, MD: Brookes.

Guthrie, J. T., McRae, A., & Klauda, S. L. (2007). Contributions of Concept-Oriented Reading Instruction to knowledge about interventions for motivations in reading. *Educational Psychologist, 42*, 237–250.

Guthrie, J. T., Rueda, R., Gambrell, L. B. & Morrison, D. A. (2009). Roles of engagement, valuing, and identification in reading development of students from diverse backgrounds. In L. Morrow, R. S. Rueda, & D. Lapp (Eds.), *Handbook of research on literacy and diversity*. New York: Guilford Press.

Guthrie, J. T., Wigfield, A., Barbosa, P., Perencevich, K. C., Taboada, A., Davis, M. H., et al. (2004). Increasing reading comprehension and engagement through Concept-Oriented Reading Instruction. *Journal of Educational Psychology, 96*, 403–423.

Guthrie, J. T., Wigfield, A., Humenick, N. M., Perencevich, K. C., Taboada, A., & Barbosa, P. (2006). Influences of stimulating tasks on reading motivation and comprehension. *Journal of Educational Research, 99*, 232–245.

Linnenbrink, E. A., & Pintrich, P. R. (2003). The role of self-efficacy beliefs in student engagement and learning in the classroom. *Reading and Writing Quarterly, 19*, 119–137.

Meece, J. L., Anderman, E. M., & Anderman, L. H. (2006). Classroom goal structure, student motivation, and academic achievement. *Annual Review of Psychology, 57*, 487–503.

Meece, J. L., & Miller, S. D. (1999). Changes in elementary school children's achievement goals for reading and writing: Results of a longitudinal and an intervention study. *Scientific Studies of Reading, 3*, 207–229.

Miller, S. D., & Meece, J. L. (1999). Third graders' motivational preferences for reading and writing tasks. *The Elementary School Journal, 100*, 19–35.

Nussbaum, A. D., & Steele, C. M. (2007). Situational disengagement and persistence in the face of adversity. *Journal of Experimental Social Psychology, 43*, 127–134.

Oldfather, P. (2002). Students' experiences when not initially motivated for literacy learning. *Reading and Writing Quarterly, 18*, 231–256.

Osborne, J. W. (1997). Race and academic disidentification. *Journal of Educational Psychology, 89*, 728–735.

Otis, N., Frederick, M. E. G., & Pelletier, L. G. (2005). Latent motivational change in an academic setting: A 3-year longitudinal study. *Journal of Educational Psychology, 97*, 170–183.

Patrick, H., Anderman, L. H., Ryan, A. M., Edelin, K. C., & Midgley, C. (2001). Teachers' communication of goal orientations in four fifth-grade classrooms. *The Elementary School Journal, 102*, 35–58.

Pintrich, P. R. (2000). Multiple goals, multiple pathways: The role of goal orientation in learning and achievement. *Journal of Educational Psychology, 92*, 544–555.

Pintrich, P. R., & De Groot, E. V. (1990). Motivational and self-regulated learning components of classroom academic performance. *Journal of Educational Psychology, 82*, 33–40.

Reeve, J., & Jang, H. (2006). What teachers say and do to support students' autonomy during a learning activity. *Journal of Educational Psychology, 98*, 209–218.

Reynolds, P. L., & Symons, S. (2001). Motivational variables and children's text search. *Journal of Educational Psychology, 93*, 14–23.

Ryan, R. M., & Connell, J. P. (1989). Perceived locus of causality and internalization: Examining reasons for acting in two domains. *Journal of Personality and Social Psychology, 57,* 749–761.

Schiefele, U. (1999). Interest and learning from text. *Scientific Studies of Reading, 3,* 257–279.

Schunk, D. H. (2003). Self-efficacy for reading and writing: Influence of modeling, goal setting, and self-evaluation. *Reading and Writing Quarterly, 19,* 159–172.

Seifert, T. L., & O'Keefe, B. A. (2001). The relationship of work avoidance and learning goals to perceived competence, externality and meaning. *British Journal of Educational Psychology, 71,* 81–92.

Sikorski, M. P. (2004). Inside Mrs. O'Hara's classroom. In J. T. Guthrie, A. Wigfield, & K. C. Perencevich (Eds.), *Motivating reading comprehension: Concept-Oriented Reading Instruction* (pp. 195–223). Mahwah, NJ: Erlbaum.

Taylor, A. Z., & Graham, S. (2007). An examination of the relationship between achievement values and perceptions of barriers among low-SES African American and Latino students. *Journal of Educational Psychology, 99,* 52–64.

Unrau, N., & Schlackman, J. (2006). Motivation and its relationship with reading achievement in an urban middle school. *Journal of Educational Research, 100,* 81–101.

Vansteenkiste, M., Lens, W., & Deci, E. L. (2006). Intrinsic versus extrinsic goal contents in self-determination theory: Another look at the quality of academic motivation. *Educational Psychologist, 41,* 19–31.

Voelkl, K. E. (1997). Identification with school. *American Journal of Education, 105,* 294–318.

Webb, N. M., & Farivar, S. (1994). Promoting helping behavior in cooperative small groups in middle school mathematics. *American Educational Research Journal, 31,* 369–395.

Wentzel, K. R. (2005). Peer relationships, motivation, and academic performance at school. In A. J. Elliot & C. S. Dweck (Eds.), *Handbook of competence and motivation* (pp. 279–296). New York: Guilford Press.

Wigfield, A., & Eccles, J. S. (Eds.). (2002). *Development of achievement motivation.* San Diego, CA: Academic Press.

Wigfield, A., & Guthrie, J. T. (1997). Relations of children's motivation for reading to the amount and breadth of their reading. *Journal of Educational Psychology, 89,* 420–432.

Wigfield, A., Guthrie, J. T., Tonks, S., & Perencevich, K. C. (2004). Children's motivation for reading: Domain specificity and instructional influences. *Journal of Educational Research, 97,* 299–309.

PART II

⌒

INSTRUCTION THAT SUPPORTS MORE AND BETTER READING

4

INCREASING OPPORTUNITIES TO ACQUIRE KNOWLEDGE THROUGH READING

Gina N. Cervetti
Carolyn A. Jaynes
Elfrieda H. Hiebert

The way in which students spend their time in American elementary classrooms has changed substantially over the past decade as a result of new educational policies (No Child Left Behind [NCLB], U.S. Department of Education, 2001). The nature and magnitude of these changes is evident in the findings of two recent studies that report that students are spending more time in reading/language arts and mathematics instruction than was the case a decade ago (Dorph et al., 2007; McMurrer, 2008). Whereas elementary teachers had previously been devoting an average of 2 hours a week to science instruction, 80% of the teachers studied by Dorph et al. (2007) reported allocating an hour a week to science, and another 16% reported spending no time in science. The gap between the literacy proficiencies of many American students and the complex literacy demands of the information age has resulted in a decade of policies that require that more time be spent in reading/language arts instruction for students not meeting standards. If students aren't reading well, policymakers reason, they should be spending more time learning to read. The phase of learning to read has been conceptualized as primarily a narrative experience that focuses on the learning of linguistic content (e.g., phonemes) and of reading strategies (e.g., summarizing main ideas).

The perspective that we will develop in this chapter is counter to this commonplace interpretation of what beginning and struggling readers need. We will argue that an important part of the reading experience for all students—but particularly struggling readers—is to read to acquire knowledge. We are not suggesting that beginning and struggling readers do not require exposure to and experiences with information about the alphabetic system; nor are we suggesting that narratives have no place in the early reading curriculum. But we will argue that acquiring knowledge is an important and currently neglected part of reading development. Acquiring information through text, we will demonstrate, serves as a powerful incentive for reading and writing. Increasing the amount of instructional time devoted to reading skills while decreasing opportunities to use reading and writing to learn about the physical and social world may serve to decrease involvement and expertise in reading. In addition, knowledge is critically important for continued reading, learning, and school achievement, and so reading instruction should be viewed as one context in which to build this knowledge. Delaying involvement with the compelling information of science and the social studies until students can "read well" may have the unintended consequence of making the poor even poorer while the rich get richer (Stanovich, 1986). We suggest that the integration of literacy and content-area instruction is a potentially effective way to create an engaging knowledge-supportive context for learning to read as well as necessary for students' acquisition of critical bodies of knowledge.

In this chapter, we develop a model of integrated content-area and literacy learning in three phases. First, we review scholarship to establish how knowledge acquisition affects comprehension and how it is affected, in turn, by reading experiences. The second section of the chapter presents prior efforts in which language and literacy processes have been integrated or combined with content-area learning goals. Finally, we present theory and research for integrated instruction where knowledge acquisition is in the foreground and reading processes are developed in the service of that knowledge acquisition.

Knowledge Building as a Goal of Literacy Instruction

The model in Figure 4.1 demonstrates the cyclical relationship between knowledge and comprehension. Comprehension depends on background knowledge. Since knowledge begets more knowledge, comprehending the information in texts serves as the context for obtaining and elaborating upon knowledge. This section of the chapter describes the research on the processes depicted in this model—the manner in which knowledge is developed through literacy and the manner in which knowledge supports comprehension. Underlying these processes is the relevance or authenticity of knowledge acquisition in students' learning.

Developing Knowledge

In the context of discussing the relationship between school funding and educational opportunity, Neuman and Celano (2006) argue the significance of the knowledge gap between low-income and middle-income children. They suggest not only that knowledge leads to more knowledge—those who have access to information read more, have higher-level conversations, and more continued educational opportunities—but also that the knowledge gap is associated with quality-of-life differences, including health and crime prevention.

We know a great deal about the strong relationship between background knowledge and school learning (e.g., Alao & Guthrie, 1999; Hailikari, Nevgi, & Komulainen, 2008): the more people know about something, the more likely they will learn something new about it. This work also suggests that learning that is not connected to existing knowledge is more likely to be forgotten. Dochy, Segers, and Buehl (1999) reported that more than 90% of the studies examining the contribution of prior knowledge to learning have found a positive effect and that prior knowledge generally explains 30–60% of the variance in performance on outcome measures of learning.

Given this relationship between background knowledge and aca-

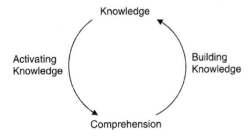

FIGURE 4.1. Model of reciprocity between knowledge and comprehension.

demic achievement, Marzano (2004) suggests that enhancing knowledge should be at the top of any list of interventions to support students' academic achievement. The most obvious way to enhance students' world knowledge is to provide knowledge-enriching experiences in school; yet, literacy programs have long missed the opportunity to use reading, writing, and speaking as tools for developing knowledge (Marzano, 2004; Neuman & Celano, 2006). While literacy educators have suggested that reading instruction is enhanced by attention to content (Chall & Snow, 1988), literacy programs have largely emphasized the teaching of process (how) to the exclusion of content (what), distinguishing between learning to read and reading to learn (Palincsar & Duke, 2004). That is, literacy instruction often focuses on teaching students skills and strategies for decoding and comprehending text and pays less attention to the content of the texts. As Palincsar and Duke (2004) point out, one problem with this approach is that it deprives students of the information that they might use to read, write, and think.

Using discipline-based knowledge development as a context for literacy learning provides an opportunity for students to practice and apply their emerging literacy skills in the interest of developing understandings about the world that support their future learning. Knowledge, from this perspective, does not refer to a litany of facts, but rather to the discipline-based conceptual understandings that provide explanatory principles for phenomena in the world (Guthrie & Alao, 1997) and that engage students in becoming experts on the world around them. For example, in the project in which we have been involved over the past 5 years (Cervetti, Pearson, Bravo, & Barber, 2006; Cervetti, Pearson, Barber, Hiebert, & Bravo, 2007), science and literacy instruction are integrated in ways that invite students to become experts on important scientific topics. One unit develops the importance of shorelines as the habitat for innumerable fascinating organisms. Second- and third-grade students develop conceptual understandings that are likely to support their future learning, including the understanding that shoreline organisms have characteristics called adaptations that aid in their survival in a habitat. At the same time, students are learning facts about shoreline organisms such as that seagulls have webbed feet and that pismo clams have hard shells. These facts are grounded in the concept of adaptation, and it is this conceptual grounding that makes this information something more than a mere collection of fascinating facts or seductive details (Garner & Gillingham, 1991). The essential understanding that adaptations help organisms survive guides students in predicting that the webbed feet of gulls aid them in swimming in the shoreline habitat to escape predators and find food, or that clams have hard shells that serve as protection from predators and crashing waves. It is the discipline-based conceptual understanding about adaptation that becomes the readers' newfound "prior" knowledge that will support future learning—and reading—in this subject area.

Supporting Comprehension with Knowledge

There has been a strong emphasis in the research-and-practice literature in reading education on activating prior knowledge for reading (e.g., Harvey & Goudvis, 2007; Pressley et al., 1992; Spires & Donley, 1998) but less emphasis on finding ways to build knowledge to support reading comprehension. The problems with activating prior knowledge without building knowledge is that it privileges the students who have knowledge already and it depends on the knowledge that students bring to school.

Readers who have more knowledge of the topic of a text demonstrate better comprehension and recall (e.g., Tierney & Cunningham, 1984), particularly when reading texts that require more gap-filling inferences—those inferences that require a reader to fill in details that the author omitted (McNamara, Kintsch, Songer, & Kintsch, 1996). In their review of the contribution of factors such as knowledge, strategies, goals, and interest to constructing meaning from text, Jetton and Alexander (2001, ¶19) suggest that nothing exerts a more powerful influence over what students understand and remember from reading a text than their existing knowledge. Prior knowledge has been shown to make a greater contribution to text comprehension than decoding or the reported use of strategies (Samuelstuen & Bråten, 2005) and to make a contribution to comprehension independent of topic interest (Baldwin, Peleg-Bruckner, & McClintock, 1985). Readers with more knowledge of the topic of a text also perform better on comprehension assessments than readers with less knowledge, independent of reading ability (e.g., Recht & Leslie, 1988).

Several decades ago, when schema theory was in the foreground, the research and pedagogical suggestions of researchers and teacher educators emphasized the reciprocal relationship between reading comprehension and knowledge. Schema theory (Anderson & Pearson, 1984) described the relationship of knowledge to comprehension as a cycle wherein knowledge supports comprehension and comprehension in turn builds new knowledge. This understanding of the relationship between comprehension and knowledge suggests that the new knowledge that students develop today, whether from a book or from an experience, is the prior knowledge they will bring tomorrow to another experience or another text. The vestiges of this understanding are still evident in the instructional focus on preparing children to read by activating text-relevant knowledge (Duke & Pearson, 2002).

We suggest, however, that the cognitive revolution's vision of knowledge as the basis of reading comprehension had been only partially realized. Literacy educators attended to activating prior knowledge and teaching students to bring this knowledge to bear on their comprehension of text. At the same time, the other half of the cycle— where comprehension builds new knowledge—was shortchanged as literacy educators moved to literature-based reading programs. While this movement had some positive outcomes (e.g., students got to read real literature), the expanded literacy curriculum has largely squeezed out content-area instruction and, consequently, attention to knowledge-building altogether (Kato & Manning, 2007).

While students acquire pockets of knowledge from wide reading, in-depth knowledge development may provide more benefits. As Jetton and Alexander (2001) point out, substituting superficial coverage of content for in-depth exploration of concepts can form a disjointed and only piecemeal basis for further text-based comprehension and learning. Broader disciplinary knowledge appears to be more powerful in supporting reading comprehension of content-area texts than knowledge of a specific topic. In their study of the role of subject matter knowledge on recall of and interest in science expository text, Alexander, Kulikowich, and Schulze (1994) found that college students who had more content-area knowledge, particularly in the form of domain knowledge, produced higher scores and gave higher interest ratings than those with less content-area knowledge.

Much has been written about the contribution of prior knowledge to comprehension (see, e.g., Stahl, Hare, Sinatra, & Gregory, 1991). A primary way in which prior knowledge supports comprehension is that students with more knowledge can assimilate additional information and distinguish between important and more peripheral information (Alao & Guthrie, 1999). Kintsch and Kintsch (2005) point out that readers must construct a situation model, a mental model of the situation described by the text, requiring an integration of text information with relevant prior knowledge and reader goals. As Garner and Gillingham (1991) point out, "If a topic is entirely unfamiliar, there is no way to relate new information in a text to existing knowledge structures."

In addition, knowledge is needed to understand the relationship between ideas in a text. Stahl et al. (1991) found that readers with low prior knowledge are able to recall as many facts as those with high prior knowledge, but readers with high prior knowledge are better able to infer an organization to those facts and selectively attend to different portions of the text (in particular information that is related to the themes of an article).

In recent years there has been a marked interest in nonfiction and informational text, driven in part by documentation of a genre imbalance in the early grades (Duke, 2000) and by concerns about reading achievement in the upper grades, particularly the drop-off in reading achievement at the fourth-grade level, when students are expected to handle nonfiction texts with increased independence (Gambrell, 2005). Students' struggles with reading and comprehending nonfiction texts have been documented across grade levels (McGee, 1982; Hidi & Hildyard, 1983), and their performances have been found to be poorer with expository than narrative texts (Dreher, 1999). These difficulties, it has been argued, reflect the lack of significant exposure to informational texts in the early grades (Yopp & Yopp. 2000) and little instruction in the structures and functions of informational texts (Duke & Bennet-Armistead, 2003). Students may also lack the knowledge that would make these content-rich texts accessible.

We do not wish to minimize the importance of skills and strategies associated with decoding, fluent oral reading, and reading comprehension. Instead, we want to suggest that knowledge and skills are mutually supportive. Kintsch and Kintsch (2005) suggest that the goal of reading comprehension instruction is to assist students in constructing good situation models from texts in order to understand and retain information. In this view, comprehension requires a combination of knowledge and strategies/skills. In addition, these processes are supported when reading instruction is situated in a meaningful knowledge-building context that fuels literacy development by providing background knowledge for future reading and future learning and that inspires literacy development by engaging students in becoming experts on the world around them. As we describe below, reading about something compelling in the natural world from an increasingly informed knowledge base can provide greater ease of reading as well as a motive for continued reading. In our own work, we connect students' firsthand investigations—of the solar system, energy, and ecosystems—to the texts they read so that they are mutually informing and together build sustained engagement in a set of ideas, yielding opportunities for rich discussions, complex forms of writing, and, indeed, instruction in the skills and strategies of reading.

Building Authenticity with Knowledge

Many arguments for integration of literacy and content instruction stem from notions of increased authenticity and engagement (Guthrie, Wigfield, & Perencevich, 2004a). From this perspective, instruction that situates conceptual understandings or knowledge as the ends of instruction and that positions reading, writing, and discourse as tools to achieve these ends creates the kind of need to know that can motivate engaged reading and propel literacy development ahead.

Reading for Real Reasons

Several studies have offered compelling evidence that growth in reading engagement and reading comprehension is accelerated when students are involved in authentic reading activity (e.g., Knapp. 1995; Purcell-Gates, Duke, & Martineau, 2007). By "authentic," we mean reading real texts for real purposes—that is, where the goal of reading is understanding the material well enough to use it for other purposes, such as making an argument, applying a concept in some way, or engaging in a firsthand investigation. Hiebert (1994) similarly defines authentic tasks as "ones in which reading and writing serve a function for children" and "involve children in the immediate use of literacy for enjoyment and communication" (p. 391). Authentic literacy tasks focus on student choice and ownership, extend beyond the classroom walls, involve a variety of reading and writing opportunities, promote discussion and collaboration, and build upon students' interests, abilities, background, and language development (Hiebert, 1994).

Purcell-Gates et al. (2007) examined student growth in reading-and-writing informational text genres. The project infused second- and third-grade classrooms with the target text genres and monitored, among other things, the degree of authenticity of literacy activities in these classrooms. Authentic literacy activity was defined as (1) the reading and writing of text genres that serve a communicative purpose that can occur *outside of* a learning-to-read-and-write context and purpose (e.g., reading for information that one wants or needs to know, such as reading instructions to complete a task); and (2) the match between the genres that students read in school and the actual tasks that those genres might be used for in the world outside of school. Purcell-Gates and her colleagues reported that student growth in reading and writing the target genres did not relate to the amount of time spent reading and writing the genres alone or even explicit teaching of genre features. The crucial ingredient was the nature of the interaction with the text. Students in classrooms with more authentic reading and writing of science informational and procedural texts (that is tied to authentic communicative purposes and an authentic need to know) grew in reading ability at a faster rate than those using texts with less authenticity.

An Emphasis on Deep Understanding

A number of studies, including the CIERA School Change study (Taylor, Pearson, Peterson, & Rodriguez, 2003), have found that reading achievement is higher the more that teachers emphasize deep understanding of text rather than literal comprehension or recall. Readers who are driven by a learning goal and engaged in deep processing of information are more likely to recall information from text (Graham & Golan, 1991). Participation in knowledge building, or reading with a knowledge goal, demands a level of involvement in text and a level of meaning making that might not be demanded of reading isolated texts. A knowledge goal provides opportunities for deep processing of textual information, for connecting ideas across texts, and for making meaning of information through writing and, in science, through subsequent investigations.

In addition, Guthrie et al. (2004a) suggest that conceptual goals for reading increase interest and enjoyment. They point out that it is motivating to develop expertise—to know about something, to learn more about it, to connect it to other learning, and to be able to explain it. Jetton and Alexander (2001) similarly conclude that, while the skills and strategies of reading are important, readers "also need a commitment or will to explore text in a deep or meaningful way." Ongoing investigations of the natural and social world provide reasons to persist in the reading of challenging texts. Learning what others have discovered about the world and sharing one's own discoveries can be powerful motivators for learning to read, write, and speak effectively.

There is some evidence that students are more strategic when reading and writing are associated with a learning goal that extends beyond the particular text at hand. Examining the role of a learning goal orientation in reading, Alao and Guthrie (1999) found that, after controlling for prior knowledge, a learning goal orientation accounted for 34% of the total variance in students' use of higher-level reading strategies, such as monitoring and elaboration. In fact, in the Alao and Guthrie study, learning goals was a better predictor of strategy use than prior knowledge. A large body of research demonstrates the association between learning goal orientations and learning outcomes.

Both of these principles—reading for real purposes and reading for deep understanding—are supported by knowledge goals. Approaches to reading in contexts where the learning goals emphasize acquiring the knowledge or skills of another discipline may tend toward a more functional view of literacy, that is, one that emphasizes employing reading, writing, and discourse as a set of tools and processes that people use to acquire knowledge in other domains. Not only do content-area disciplines create a setting in which students can "practice" applying their discrete reading and writing strategies, they also foster opportunities for sophisticated and dynamic enactment of these strategies in the service of learning about the world. When a knowledge goal is positioned as the "end" of instruction, even discrete skills can be taught in the context of meaningful reading rather than out-of-context reading. That is, even when one is teaching skills, knowledge goals keep the focus on meaning and render transparent the relationship between the skills and the goal of constructing meaning from text. As Goodlad and Su (1992) point out, an integrated curriculum can build close relationships among concepts, skills, and values so that they are mutually reinforcing.

The Evolving Relationship of Reading and Content

Having put forth three arguments for focusing on knowledge in reading instruction, we shift our attention to the attempts that schools have made to explore and implement this relationship. Over the past hundred years, a number of educational movements have embraced the idea of combining the development of reading, writing, speaking, listening, and viewing processes with content-area learning goals. In essence, we want to distinguish the approach we advocate—an integrated approach to literacy and content-area instruction—from related instructional approaches that have come before, making sure to emphasize both their commonalities and differences.

Origin in the Progressive Movement

The origin of integrated approaches to reading and content-area instruction is often associated with the progressive movement in education that started in the first half of the 20th century. The progressive tradition did not separate reading instruction from subject matter instruction (Zirbes, 1918). Rather than isolating literacy skills instruction, many progressive educators believed that reading was to be "organically bound up" with all of the other content-based learning work of the school (Thorne-Thomsen, 1901). Progressive educators such as Francis Parker and John Dewey argued that all reading should be focused on the study of subject matter. In this way, the learning of reading, writing, speaking, listening, and viewing was necessarily integrated with and *in the service of* content-area learning. Characteristic of this movement was Parker's (1894) declaration that "in the school all the reading should be a direct means of intensifying, enhancing, expanding, and relating the thought evolved by the study of the subjects. ... Reading in botany, in zoology, in history—in fact, all reading—should be concentrated upon the study of the central subjects" (p. 220).

In 1925, the National Committee on Reading stressed the importance of *reading for a reason*, characterizing the relationship between reading and subject matter as follows: "The difficulty which constantly confronts the teacher is to keep the reading skills sufficiently in the foreground that they may be improved and refined, yet at the same time make them subservient to the real interests and larger purposes for which pupils read" (Whipple, 1925, p. 140).

While the initial basis for this integrated approach to reading and content-area instruction was largely theoretical rather than empirical, this element of the progressive movement underpinned the Eight Year Study from the 1930s. The study found that college students who had attended progressive high schools with integrated instruction across disciplines as one of its foundations outperformed students from traditional high schools on standardized tests (Chamberlin, Chamberlin, Drought, & Scott, 1942). Nevertheless, by the middle of the 20th century, many of the principles guiding the progressive movement in education, including those associated with integrated instruction, were subjected to serious criticism. Some held the movement responsible for producing citizens who were underprepared for careers in science and technology, advocating a return to instruction that emphasized more traditional disciplinary lines. As a result, instruction shifted to more a reductionist and behavioristic view of reading (Moore, Readance, & Rickelman, 1983).

Thematic Instruction

In the last part of the 20th century, integrated instruction reemerged in different forms, including thematic instruction. Thematic instruction commonly refers to instruction organized around broad topics in order to facilitate connection making across academic domains (Lederman & Niess, 1997). Some educators distinguish thematic instruction from other forms of integrated instruction that organize different subject areas around narrower real-world problems to form a "seamless whole" wherein distinctions among academic disciplines melt away. We use *thematic instruction* to refer to a broad set of approaches that uses themes as a framework on which to merge language and literacy learning with content-area learning.

While thematic instruction invited subject matter topics back into language arts instruction, its focus was on supporting literacy more than serving knowledge development or content-area learning. In the 1970s and 1980s, the emergence of whole language brought with it a form of instruction designed to make literacy learning more meaningful and authentic by centering reading and writing activities around content-relevant themes (Morrow, 2001). In her review of how thematic instruction found a comfortable home in the whole-language movement, Morrow explains that whole language, with its focus on teaching literacy skills as needed depending on what the children were reading or writing, freed teachers to use different kinds of organizing heuristics for literacy instruction, including themes. With these early forms of whole-language thematic units, literacy instruction remained the primary goal, and eventually thematic language arts basal programs followed suit.

While many basals have been organized thematically since this time, the lack of attention to subject matter-relevant content has long been noted (e.g., Flood & Lapp. 1987; Stotsky, 1997). Even as basals have included more expository text in recent years, attention has not been paid to substantial knowledge development (Walsh, 2003). Possibly in part as a reflection of this, the latest rendering of thematic instruction as it is embodied in basal programs and implemented in language arts instruction often incorporates themes as loose umbrellas for literacy instruction. These themes (e.g., "bears," "water," and "change") allow teachers and publishers to identify materials and activities that are topically related, but the latter probably do not realize the potential of integrated instruction for disciplinary knowledge development.

While contemporary thematic instruction is often a testament to teachers' creativity and ability to build connections across domains, the possibility remains that the connections may be tenuous (Holdren, 1994). Because the focus is squarely on supporting literacy development, activities are typically chosen based on their link to the theme rather than their potential to deepen students' knowledge of the domain. And although classroom experiences centered on a unifying theme may provide students with multiple exposures to related academic vocabulary, such instruction does not guarantee that this is done is any systematic way. Indeed, some research suggests that students engaged in thematic instruction develop less conceptual understanding than they would with more scaffolded approaches (Lederman & Niess, 1997). Although the instructional approach we propose in this chapter centers around topics or themes in particular domains, it considers the goal of instruction to be not only connection making but also building deep conceptual knowledge of the domain.

Reading Instruction in the Content Areas

Reading instruction in the content areas most commonly refers to content-area teachers' providing students with explicit instruction on various "good reader strategies" to facilitate word identification, vocabulary development, and comprehension while reading content-area texts. As early as the 1920s, major figures in education were calling for reading instruction that included specific skills needed for content-area study (Moore et al., 1983). It was Gray (1925) who popularized the slogan "Every teacher a teacher of reading." Recent attention to content-area reading came about in response to research that has documented that students across grades struggle with reading and understanding content-area and other expository texts and the recognition that different reading strategies may be needed, depending on the nature of the reading material and the purpose (Dreher, 1999; Hidi & Hidyard, 1983; McGee, 1982; Moore et al., 1983).

Content-Area Reading Instruction

It is reasonable to expect that strategic reading can enhance content-area learning; however, it is important to bear in mind that text is typically operationalized as traditional textbooks rather than the broad range of nonfiction genres that readers are likely to encounter beyond the classroom. Consequently, it may be the case that the notion of text in content-area reading instruction is not rich enough to help students acquire a wide range of understandings about content and literacy (Beck & McKeown, 1991).

Alternatively, some curricular embodiments of content-area reading programs commonly take the form of more traditional content-area instruction, augmented by the use of nonfiction trade books (Palmer & Stewart, 1997). As Palmer and Stewart point out, "Increasing numbers of teachers are supplementing or supplanting textbooks with nonfiction trade books" (p. 630). Important to take into account, however, is the fact that making effective use of nonfiction trade books may require supplemental support for both teacher and student so that these new texts are not simply treated as another textbook (Palmer & Stewart, 1997). We suggest that true integration of literacy and content-area instruction can provide the opportunity for students to deepen their learning of the content as they broaden their understanding of, and facility with, the skills and strategies of nonfiction reading and writing.

Use of Nonfiction or Informational Texts

As Duke (2000) pointed out nearly a decade ago, students in many classrooms get much smaller doses of informational texts than the narrative fiction texts that often dominate much of their home and early school literacy experiences. This research, in combination with research documented in the report *Reading for Understanding* (RAND Reading Study Group. 2002), calls into question the decades-long assumption that text is text—that students can and will transfer generic reading skills from fictional literature to other genres of text. The research summarized in the Rand report indicates that, for students to use nonfiction text effectively, teachers need to instruct students directly on how to navigate and extract information from text. Such instruction on the part of teachers, Palmer and Stewart (1997) stress, depends on adequate training in using such texts, especially content-area teachers who may have more limited text-based pedagogical knowledge.

In the intervening years there has been a strong resurgence of interest in nonfiction and informational text. Further, evidence has verified that many students are genuinely interested in reading nonfiction texts (Duke & Bennett-Armistead, 2003; Edmunds & Bauserman, 2006; Mohr, 2006). As a result, many teachers have expanded the number of nonfiction texts in their classroom libraries, basal programs have boosted the proportion of nonfiction selections, and publishers have increased their selections of nonfiction trade books. Most educators will agree that it makes sense to provide students with exposure to a broader range of the nonfiction text structures and features that they are likely to encounter outside the classroom. Even so, simply giving students nonfiction texts—especially ones that superficially address various topics—may be an insufficient means of developing bodies of background knowledge and engaged reading. As we discuss further in the next section, evidence is mounting that experiences with nonfiction texts can be most powerful when they are related to and situated within content-area instruction that has the potential to build students' skills with, and extend their conceptual understandings of several *different* genres of text.

Integrated Instruction that Foregrounds Knowledge

The instruction in reading that we envision is more than the opportunity to read—it is the opportunity to learn *something meaningful* through text and related activities around text (i.e., discussion and also hands-on learning experiences). McRae and Guthrie (Chapter 3, this volume) have described this phenomenon as "beyond opportunity to read." Our way of conceptualizing the phenomenon is "opportunity to learn"— something that we believe is best achieved through the integration of content-area learning and literacy learning. The instruction we envision integrates content-area learning with an emphasis on reading and writing in the context of knowledge development and with a related emphasis on the cultivation of shared and reciprocal processes across domains. In our work on science—literacy integration, we have often used the word *synergistic* to describe this relationship (Cervetti et al., 2006).

In many respects, this synergistic approach harkens back to the earlier forms of integrated instruction from the progressive era in education. In this approach, reading skills and strategies are taught and learned in a context that supports the development of disciplinary knowledge and skills with high level of integrity. Scientific inquiry, reading, writing, and discussing are woven together in mutually reinforcing ways and always in the interest of important scientific understandings. In this approach, the concepts and skills of science are in the foreground. The content provides an engaging and enriching context for teaching the skills, strategies, and dispositions of literacy.

To provide a concrete example, consider an astronomy unit for fourth and fifth graders that we developed recently for the Seeds of Science/Roots of Reading program that manifests our approach (Seeds of Science/Roots of Reading, 2009). In this unit, students investigate the ways that scientists and engineers use technology to learn about distant solar system objects (mainly planets and moons). Having studied many of these solar system objects earlier in the unit, students read about space scientists and space missions and engage in the activity of designing a spacecraft that might be successful in landing on and gathering data about a solar system object characterized by specific environmental conditions and surface features. Students write scientific explanations about how their spacecraft design and mission goals are suited to the conditions on the solar system object they intend to study. They learn about the models that scientists use to study their designs in advance of the missions. They learn about the determination and persistence that are necessary to engage in the challenging enterprise of space exploration. They learn a great deal about the solar system in which they live and the conditions, features, and movement of many of its objects. In the meantime, they learn about and engage in reading and writing scientific genres of text, learn the language and structures of scientific argumentation, and engage in rich discussions of the nature of science, scientific design, and our solar system.

Approaches to the integration of literacy and content-area instruction that foreground knowledge development are not simply intuitively appealing; their efficacy is increasingly borne out by rigorous research studies. This research is providing increasingly compelling evidence that these instructional approaches result in greater growth in literacy and disciplinary knowledge development than isolated instruction (Gavelek, Raphael, Biondo, & Wang, 2000). Two programs have particularly impressive records of research: Concept-Oriented Reading Instruction (CORI) and In-Depth Expanded Application of Science (IDEAS). Each program has accumulated a record of learning outcomes across a number of studies using a variety of literacy measures, including standardized measures.

John Guthrie, Alan Wigfield, and their colleagues developed CORI to integrate inquiry-based science and reading strategy instruction in order to enhance elementary students' use of reading strategies, motivation to read, and conceptual knowledge in science and social studies (see Guthrie, Wigfield, & Perencevich, 2004b). The CORI program uses content goals for reading instruction and creates a highly collaborative learning environment that engages students in hands-on activities and the reading of interesting texts related to the content goal.

The IDEAS project (Romance & Vitale, 1992, 2001) is an instructional model that integrates science and literacy instruction by providing students with opportunities to access and build upon their prior knowledge; do hands-on science activities; read, write, and journal about science; and use a variety of instructional tools to build meaningful connections and increase their conceptual science understandings. Romance and Vitale (1992, 2001) have reported that what seemed to make the IDEAS model effective with students was the fact that it provided them with an opportunity to pursue an in-depth understanding of conceptually meaningful structured knowledge, not just simple or superficial connections.

Similarly, while the objective of CORI is to increase the amount of engaged reading students do, CORI situates direct instruction of reading strategies within a context that allows students to develop in-depth knowledge on a science or social studies topic with a high degree of disciplinary integrity. In both programs, students construct meaningful knowledge and then use that knowledge to support future learning. An important characteristic of both programs is what CORI researchers call "coherence," or the linking of activities and content in ways that enable students to make connections between experience and reading, strategies and content, and among different texts.

While other forms of thematic instruction in reading allow for connection making, the repetition of vocabulary, and possibly the development of some background knowledge, both of these programs pursue substantive knowledge goals within the domain of science and use reading, writing, speaking, concept mapping, strategy instruction, and so on to further these goals. CORI and IDEAS not only use the context of science to build on students' curiosity about the world and allow that curiosity to drive reading instruction, but they also establish knowledge goals and a context of developing expertise that drives students' literacy development.

Conclusion

The schism between learning to read and reading to learn has been extensive and long-standing. We suggest that it is time to reconsider this schism. There are many reasons to believe that knowledge development may be the necessary next frontier in reading education. Progress has been made over the past decade in students' fundamental capacity to read, but the gains have not been commensurate in students' ability to comprehend and remember critical information. And the knowledge gap between wealthier students and lower-SES students persists. Knowledge is a necessary and natural outcome of reading, and evidence is beginning to demonstrate that reading instruction is more potent when it builds and then capitalizes upon the development of content knowledge.

Equally important, though, is the potential of knowledge goals to engage students in reading (and writing and speaking). If we want students to persevere through the challenges of learning to read, we need to provide a motive for reading that makes it worth the effort. If we want to inspire students to love reading, we need to give them opportunities to experience firsthand reading's power to expose them to amazing new ideas and communities, to help them explore and explain the world around them, and to answer their questions. Knowledge goals provide motives for reading that go beyond getting the words straight or reading through to the end of the text. Children should be learning real things for real reasons as they read. We should not deliberately delay students' involvement in reading to learn until they necessarily have all of the skills of reading in place. Practicing for years on end without ever getting to play the game is no fun. And there is compelling evidence that those students who view reading as important are also those who like it best (Scholastic, 2008). To ensure that our students develop the skills to participate in the complex literacy experiences of the digital age and to help assure that they become truly engaged as readers, the first priority of literacy educators is to make reading genuinely important to students.

References

Alao, S., & Guthrie, J. T. (1999). Predicting conceptual understanding with cognitive and motivational variables. *Journal of Educational Research, 92*(4), 243–254.

Alexander, P. A., Kulikowich, J. M., & Schulze, S. K. (1994). How subject-matter knowledge affects recall and interest. *American Educational Research Journal, 31*(2), 313–337.

Anderson, R. C., & Pearson, P. D. (1984). *A schema-theoretic view of basic processes in reading comprehension.* In P. D. Pearson, R. Barr, M. L. Kamil, & P. B. Mosenthal (Eds.), *Handbook of reading research* (pp. 255–291). New York: Longman.

Baldwin, R. S., Peleg-Bruckner, Z., & McClintock, A. H. (1985). Effects of topic interest and prior knowledge on reading comprehension. *Reading Research Quarterly, 20*(4), 497–504.

Beck, I. L., & McKeown, M. G. (1991). Social studies texts are hard to understand: Mediating some of the difficulties (Research Directions). *Language Arts, 68*(6), 482–90.

Cervetti, G. N., Pearson, P. D., Barber, J., Hiebert, E., & Bravo, M. (2007). Integrating literacy and science: The research we have, the research we need. In M. Pressley, A. K. Billman, K. Perry, K. E. Refitt, & J. M. Reynolds (Eds.), *Shaping literacy achievement: Research we have, research we need* (pp. 157–174). New York: Guilford Press.

Cervetti, G., Pearson, P. D., Bravo, M. A., & Barber, J. (2006). Reading and writing in the service of inquiry-based science. In R. Douglas, M. Klentschy, & K. Worth (Eds.), *Linking science and literacy in the K–8*. Arlington, VA: NSTA Press.

Chall, J. S., & Snow, C. E. (1988). Influences on reading in low-income students. *Education Digest, 54*, 53–56.

Chamberlin, D., Chamberlin, N., Drought, E., & Scott, W. E. (1942). *Did they succeed in college?* New York: Harper.

Dochy, F., Segers, M., & Buehl, M. M. (1999). The relation between assessment practices and outcomes of studies: The case of research on prior knowledge. *Review of Educational Research, 69*(2), 145–186.

Dorph, R., Goldstein, D., Lee, S., Lepori, K., Schneider, S., & Venkatesan, S. (2007). *The status of science education in the Bay Area*. Berkeley, CA: Lawrence Hall of Science, UC-Berkeley.

Dreher, M. J. (1999) Motivating children to read more nonfiction. *The Reading Teacher, 52*(4), 414–417.

Duke, N. K. (2000). 3.6 minutes per day: The scarcity of informational texts in first grade. *Reading Research Quarterly, 35*, 202–224.

Duke, N. K., & Bennett-Armistead, V. S. (Eds.). (2003). *Reading and writing informational text in the primary grades: Research-based practices*. New York: Scholastic.

Duke, N. K., & Pearson, P. D. (2002). Effective practices for developing reading comprehension. In A. E. Farstrup & S. J. Samuels (Eds.), *What research has to say about reading instruction* (3rd ed., pp. 205–242). Newark, DE: International Reading Association.

Edmunds, K. M., & Bauserman, K. L. (2006). What teachers can learn about reading motivation through conversations with children. *The Reading Teacher, 59*(5), 414–424.

Flood, J., & Lapp, D. (1987). Forms of discourse in basal readers. *The Elementary School Journal, 87*(3), 299–306.

Gambrell, L. (2005). Reading literature, reading text, reading the Internet: The times they are a'changing. *The Reading Teacher, 58*(6), 588–591.

Garner, R., & Gillingham, M. G. (1991). Topic knowledge, cognitive interest, and text recall: A microanalysis. *Journal of Experimental Education, 59*(4), 310–319.

Gavelek, J. R., Raphael, T. E., Biondo, S. M., & Wang, D. (2000). Integrated literacy instruction. In M. L. Kamil, P. B. Mosenthal, P. D. Pearson, & R. Barr (Eds.), *Handbook of reading research* (Vol. III). Mahwah, NJ: Erlbaum.

Goodlad, J. I., & Su, Z. (1992). The organization of the curriculum. In P. W. Jackson (Ed.), *Handbook of research on curriculum* (pp. 327–344). New York: Macmillan.

Graham, S., & Golan, S. (1991). Motivational influences on cognition: Task involvement, ego involvement, and depth of information processing. *Journal of Educational Psychology, 83*, 187–194.

Gray, W. S. (1925). *Summary of investigations relating to reading*. Supplementary Educational Monograph, No. 28. Chicago: University of Chicago Press.

Guthrie, J. T., & Alao, S. (1997). Designing contexts to increase motivations for reading. *Educational Psychologist, 32*(2), 95–105.

Guthrie, J. T., Wigfield, A., & Perencevich, K. C. (Eds.). (2004a). Scaffolding for motivation and engagement in reading. In J. T. Guthrie, A. Wigfield, & K. C. Perencevich (Eds.), *Motivating reading comprehension: Concept-Oriented Reading Instruction* (pp. 55–86). Mahwah, NJ: Erlbaum.

Guthrie, J. T., Wigfield, A., & Perencevich, K. C. (Eds.). (2004b). *Motivating reading comprehension: Concept-Oriented Reading Instruction.* Mahwah, NJ: Erlbaum.

Hailikari, T., Nevgi, A., & Komulainen, E. (2008). Academic self-beliefs and prior knowledge as predictors of student achievement in mathematics: A structural model. *Educational Psychology, 28*(1), 59–71.

Harvey, S., & Goudvis, A. (2007). *Strategies that work: Teaching comprehension for understanding and engagement* (2nd ed.). Portland, ME: Stenhouse.

Hidi, S., & Hildyard, A. (1983). The comparison of oral and written productions of two discourse types. *Discourse Processes, 6,* 91–105.

Hiebert, E. H. (1994). Becoming literate through authentic tasks: Evidence and adaptations. In R. Ruddell & M. R. Ruddell (Eds.), *Theoretical models and processes of reading* (4th ed.). Newark, DE: International Reading Association.

Holdren, J. (1994). Is "interdisciplinary" better?: The limits of thematic instruction. *Common Knowledge, 7*(4). Available at *www.coreknowledge.org/ck/about/print/thematic.htm.*

Jetton, T. L., & Alexander, P. A. (2001, July/August). Learning from text: A multidimensional and developmental perspective. *Reading Online, 5*(1). Available at *www.readingonline.org/articles/art_index.asp?HREF=/articles/handbook/jetton/index.html.*

Kato, T., & Manning, M. (2007). Content knowledge—the real reading crisis. *Childhood Education, 83*(4), 238.

Kintsch W., & Kintsch, E. (2005). Comprehension. In S. G. Paris & S. A. Stahl (Eds.), *Current issues in reading comprehension and assessment* (pp. 71–92). Mahwah, NJ: Erlbaum.

Knapp, M. S. (1995). *Teaching for meaning in high-poverty classrooms.* New York: Teachers College Press.

Lederman, N. G., & Niess, M. L. (1997). Integrated, interdisciplinary, or thematic instruction?: Is this a question or is it questionable semantics? *School Science and Mathematics, 97,* 57–58.

Marzano, R. J. (2004). *Building background knowledge for academic achievement: Research on what works in schools.* Alexandria, VA: Association for Supervision and Curriculum Development.

McGee, L. M. (1982). Awareness of text structure: Effects on children's recall of expository text. *Reading Research Quarterly, 17,* 581–590.

McMurrer, J. (2008). *Instructional time in elementary schools: A closer look at changes for specific subjects.* Washington, DC: Center on Education Policy. Retrieved July 15, 2008, from *www.cep-dc.org.*

McNamara, D. S., Kintsch, E., Songer, N., & Kintsch, W. (1996). Are good texts always better?: Interactions of text coherence, background knowledge, and levels of understanding in learning from text. *Cognition and Instruction, 14,* 1–43.

Mohr, K. A. J. (2006). Children's choices for recreational reading: A three-part investigation of selection preferences, rationales, and processes. *Journal of Literacy Research, 38*(1), 81–104.

Moore, D. W., Readance, J. E., & Rickelman, R. J. (1983). An historical exploration of content area reading instruction. *Reading Research Quarterly, 18,* 419–438.

Morrow, L. M. (2001). *Literacy development in the early years: Helping children read and write.* Boston: Allyn & Bacon.

Neuman, S. B., & Celano, D. (2006). The knowledge gap: Implications of leveling the playing field for low-income and middle-income children. *Reading Research Quarterly, 41*(2), 176–201.

Palincsar, A. S., & Duke, N. K. (2004). The role of text and text-reader interactions in young children's reading development and achievement. *The Elementary School Journal, 105*(2), 183–197.

Palmer, R. G., & Stewart, R. A. (1997). Nonfiction trade books in content area instruction: Realities and potential. *Journal of Adolescent and Adult Literacy, 40*(8), 630–641.

Parker, F. W. (1894). *Talks on pedagogics: An outline of the theory of concentration.* New York: Kellogg.

Pressley, M., El-Dinary, P. B., Gaskins, I., Schuder, T., Bergman, J. L., Almasi, J., et al. (1992). Beyond direct explanation: Transactional instruction of reading comprehension strategies. *The Elementary School Journal, 92*(5), 513–555.

Purcell-Gates, V., Duke, N. K., & Martineau, J. A. (2007). Learning to read and write genre-specific text: Roles of authentic experience and explicit teaching. *Reading Research Quarterly, 42*(1), 8–45.

RAND Reading Study Group. (2002). *Reading for understanding: Towards an R&D program in reading comprehension.* Retrieved November 16, 2007, from *www.rand.org/multi/achievementforall/reading/readreport.html.*

Recht, D. R., & Leslie, L. (1988). Effect of prior knowledge on good and poor readers' memory of text. *Journal of Educational Psychology, 80*(1), 16–20.

Romance, N. R., & Vitale, M. R. (1992). A curriculum strategy that expands time for in-depth elementary science instruction by using science-based reading strategies: Effects of a year-long study in grade four. *Journal of Research in Science Teaching, 29*(6), 545–554.

Romance, N. R., & Vitale, M. R. (2001). Implementing an in-depth expanded science model in elementary schools: Multi-year findings, research issues, and policy implications. *International Journal of Science Education, 23*(4), 272–304.

Samuelstuen, M. S., & Bråten, I. (2005). Decoding, knowledge, and strategies in comprehension of expository text. *Scandinavian Journal of Psychology, 46*(2), 107–117.

Scholastic. (2008). *2008 kids and families reading report.* New York: Author.

Seeds of Science/Roots of Reading. (2009). *Planets and moons.* Nashua, NH: Delta Education.

Spires, H., & Donley, J. (1998). Prior knowledge activation: Inducing engagement with informational texts. *Journal of Educational Psychology, 90*(2), 249–260.

Stahl, S. A., Hare, V. C., Sinatra, R., & Gregory, J. F. (1991). Defining the role of prior knowledge and vocabulary in reading comprehension: The retiring of number 41. *Journal of Reading Behavior, 23*(4), 487–508.

Stanovich, K. E. (1986). Matthew effects in reading: Some consequences of individual differences in the acquisition of literacy. *Reading Research Quarterly, 21,* 360–380.

Stotsky, S. (1997). Why today's multicultural basal readers may retard, not enhance, growth in reading. In L. R. Putnam (Ed.), *Readings on language and literacy; Essays in honor of Jeanne S. Chall.* Cambridge, MA: Brookline Books.

Taylor, B. M., Pearson, P. D., Peterson, D. S., & Rodriguez, M. C. (2003). Reading growth in high-poverty classrooms: The influence of teacher practices that encourage cognitive engagement in literacy learning. *The Elementary School Journal. 104,* 3–28.

Thorne-Thomsen, G. (1901). Reading in the third grade. *The Elementary School Journal and Course of Study, 2,* 227–229.

Tierney, R. J., & Cunningham, J. W. (1984). Research on teaching reading comprehension. In P. D. Pearson, R. Barr, M. L. Kamil, & P. Mosenthal (Eds.), *Handbook of reading research* (pp. 609–655). New York: Longman.

U.S. Department of Education. (2001). *No Child Left Behind.* Retrieved September 16, 2008, from *www.ed.gov/policy/elsec/leg/esea02/index.html.*

Walsh, K. (2003). Basal readers: The lost opportunity to build the knowledge that propels comprehension. *American Educator, 27*(1), 24–27.

Whipple, G. M. (1925). Report of the National Committee on Reading. In *Twenty-fourth yearbook, part 1, National Society for the Study of Education.* Bloomington, IL: Public School Publishing.

Yopp, R. H., & Yopp, H. K. (2000). Sharing informational text with young children, *The Reading Teacher, 53*(5), 410–423.

Zirbes, L. (1918). Diagnostic measurement as a basis for procedure. *Elementary School Journal, 18,* 505–512.

5

SERIES BOOKS, GRAPHIC NOVELS, COMICS, AND MAGAZINES

Unauthorized Texts,
Authorized Literacy Practices

ANNE MCGILL-FRANZEN
STERGIOS BOTZAKIS

Although educators, parents, and psychologists often complain that children's obsession with "pop culture" is at best a dumbing-down phenomenon and, at worst, a manipulation of youth by media moguls, no one disputes the influence of Hannah Montana, Lizzie McGuire, Britney Spears, or, for that matter, Superman on the minds and mores of kids today. Ways of being in the world—one's identity as a first grader, a third grader, or adolescent—may be actualized in the characters seen in movies, cartoons, TV shows, comics, and their cousins—graphic novels and series books. In her ethnography of the literacy practices of young urban "brothers and sisters" in school, Dyson (2003) noted that the children "did not use dress and makeup to create new realities and identities for themselves; they used talk and, more particularly, shared references to popular media" (p. 106). As Dyson pointed out, children's preferences for media stars and media productions (including books) index their membership in particular peer groups and enable them to take on the attributes of different identities—wealthy, glamorous, admired, heroic.

In 2006 *USA Today* (October 17, 2006) published a list of "imaginary luminaries"—famous yet fictional people. Taken from the book *The 101 Most Influential People Who Never Lived: How Characters of Fiction, Myth, Legends, Television, and Movies Have Shaped Our Society, Changed Our Behavior, and Set the Course of History* (Karlan, Lazar, & Salter, 2006), the list was loaded with icons of popular culture, many with particular relevance to students' out-of-school lives. The Marlboro Man, Santa Claus, Mickey Mouse, and Smokey Bear made the top 25; Barbie, GI Joe, Bambi, Superman, and Batman, the top 100. Of special note is that the Lil' Engine That Could and the Ugly Duckling, both imaginary luminaries originating in books rather than the nonprint media, were also deemed influential. Indeed, we would argue that nowhere in this Harry Potter world is the intersection of literacy and popular culture more apparent than in the book selections of children. In this chapter we build a case for acknowledging the importance of popular culture in literacy development; we unpack the reading preferences of children and adolescents and suggest venues for capitalizing on what they want to read, building a bridge to more ownership of "school-authorized" literacy. Thus, in this chapter we explore what motivates children and adolescents to want to read, what kinds of texts they select to read, and why children's preferences matter for educators.

What Motivates Children to Read?

Why should literacy educators care about the influence of popular culture on children? In a word, because we want to motivate children to read—and read more. Providing student choice, interesting texts, the opportunity to collaborate with peers and dig deeper into a topic of importance are classroom practices that enhance motivation and produce powerful effects on reading comprehension and achievement (McRae and Guthrie, Chapter 3, this volume; Guthrie & Humenick, 2004). Student engagement with interesting texts, defined as those relevant to the learner and approached with authentic purpose, is the single most important factor in the motivation to read. Motivated readers read more, and they read more outside of school, thereby increasing reading volume and accruing the benefits of sustained engagement with text (Allington, Chapter 2, this volume; Cunningham & Stanovich, 1998). Most notably, reading volume develops vocabulary and supports knowledge acquisition. In other words, reading more makes children smarter—it bears a reciprocal relationship to cognition, language development, and knowledge of the world. A series of studies (Cunningham & Stanovich, 1998) demonstrated that reading volume, significantly and independent of general intelligence and decoding ability, predicted variance in vocabulary knowledge among upper elementary students and reading comprehension from the third to fifth grade.

Similarly, fourth graders who reported reading almost every day scored significantly higher on the 2002 National Assessment of Educational Progress (Daane et al., 2005) than those who reported reading less frequently ("hardly ever" or "once or twice a week"). Students whose teachers used primarily trade books, or trade books in addition to a textbook, achieved a higher average score on the NAEP than those in classrooms where a single reading textbook formed the core of the curriculum. In other words, experience with a wide range of books— reading volume—supported children's reading development on this challenging national assessment.

What Do Children Want to Read?

A recent experimental longitudinal study of the influence of summer access to books on the achievement of 852 low-income minority youth (McGill-Franzen & Allington, 2008) yielded a serendipitous finding: regardless of whether the children lived in central city or rural farmland communities, or whether they were first graders or fourth graders, they self-selected the 12 same or similar books from among over 400 choices offered to them in a free book fair. Lending a fair amount of credence to the construct of an "everyday culture" (Alvermann & Xu, 2003) that may transcend racial and ethnic divisions, the top choice of the predominately (89%) African American respondents in the first year of this study was the "unauthorized biography" of *Britney Spears* (Talmadge, 2001). Rounding out the top choices were *Hangin' with Lil' Romeo* (Walsh, 2002); *Scooby-Doo and the Haunted Castle* (Gelsey, 1998); *Captain Underpants and the Invasion of the Incredible Naughty Cafeteria Ladies from Outer Space* (Pilkey, 1999); *Junie B. Jones Is A Party Animal* (Park, 1997); the unauthorized biography of the World Wrestling Federation's "The Rock," *Rock Solid* (Preller, 2000); *Scary Creatures: Big Cats* (Clarke, Riley, & Bergen, 2003); *Scary Creatures: Alligators and Crocodiles* (Legg & Hewetson, 2002); *Clifford the Big Red Dog* (Bridwell, 1962/1995); and *Superman's First Flight* (Friedman, 2000).

Although the book access study (McGill-Franzen & Allington, 2008) involved two cohorts of children, one beginning as first graders, the other as second graders, and extended across three summers, the children, as third and fourth graders, did not select substantively different types of books (see Table 5.1). Children maintained their interest in pop culture personalities, making the biography series the most highly sought books, followed by the *Captain Underpants* series. When asked why, this fourth grader's response was typical: "[Hilary Duff] plays on Lizzie McGuire, and that's my favorite show" (Williams, 2005; p. 119). The *Captain Underpants* series books were especially popular among both girls and boys for humor and text features: "The people's names and other stuff [are funny in *Captain Underpants*]. Like this one you get to make your own stories and draw your own people in it. And this one. It's got stickers" (Williams, 2005, p. 78). Of course, students selected new titles in the series, for example, *The Adventures of Super Diaper Baby* (Pilkey, Hutchins, & Beard, 2002); *Captain Underpants and the Big, Bad Battle of the Bionic Booger Boy, Part 1: The Night of the Nasty Nostril Nuggets* (Pilkey, 2003a) and *Part 2: Revenge of the Ridiculous Robo-Boogers* (Pilkey, 2003b); or *Pop People: Destiny's Child* (Glass, 2001). At this same time, the *Harry Potter* series was offered, and, consistent with the popularity of Harry with children from all types of communities, the sample of children selected *Harry Potter and the Goblet of Fire* (number 6 in popularity; Rowling, 2002) even though it was a challenging book for most of them to read.

Consistent with prior research on the effects of reading on achievement, and the contribution of student choice and interesting texts on motivation to read, the high-poverty students in the summer books study scored significantly higher than children without such access to books on the Florida Comprehensive Achievement Test as third- and fourth graders. Those who benefited the most were students whose book choices were somewhat challenging for them to read—not too difficult but not too easy, either—as measured by a match between the average lexile level of selected books and students' reported reading scores (Allington et al., 2007).

Do Children's Preferences and Media Attachments Matter?

What do children learn from popular texts, including those of the media, and how does this learning fit school literacy practices? According to Dyson (2003), very young children initially appropriate content that they can fit into school forms, such as "I like [name of football team]"

TABLE 5.1. Top 10 Books over 3 Years

Year 1	Year 2	Year 3
Superman's First Flight	Britney Spears	Hangin' with Lil' Romeo
Arthur's Underwear	Pokemon Pop Quiz	Pop People: Lil' Romeo
NBA Action from A to Z	Mojo Jojo's Rising	Pop People: Destiny's Child
Chomp!	I Choose You	Hangin' with Hilary Duff
If You Give a Mouse a Cookie	Paste Makes Waste	How to Draw Spiderman
Itchy Itchy Chicken Pox	Attack of the Prehistoric Pokemon	What Did I Do to Deserve a Sister Like You?
The Very Hungry Caterpillar	Scooby-Doo and the Sunken Ship	Meet the Stars of Professional Wrestling
Junie B. Jones and the Mushy Gushy Valentine	Rock Solid	The All New Captain Underpants Extra-Crunchy Book o' Fun #2
The Magic School Bus in the Time of the Dinosaurs	Scooby-Doo and the Snow Monster	The Adventures of Super Diaper Baby
Arthur Goes to Camp	The Island of Giant Pokemon	The Captain Underpants Extra-Chunky Book o' Fun

or "I went to [Disney]" but they also "lift" (p. 107) familiar and important (to them) communicative practices, such as sports announcements or songs. Over time children appropriated not only content (names of characters in books and TV shows) in their written and oral productions but also themes like heroism, good guys with supernatural powers, and the like. They reported on events, often reenacting episodes from TV and movies, "revoicing" dialogue, inserting codas or "summarizing claims" ("He saved the world!"), and using exclamations, stylized print, and drawings. Dyson contends that children's literacy development is a process of text appropriation and recontextualization (p. 179), not simply a reinvention of the orthographic system or apprenticeship into official school practices. As such, different children enter into literate practice at different points, using different textual tools, building on what they know—the "cultural landscape" and personal repertoire of communicative practices from which they draw (p. 170).

An example provided by Dyson (2000) is that of second graders appropriating the identities of Frog and Toad characters in an improvised role-playing activity in which they negotiate dialogue and study the texts for inspiration in what she called the "collective zone" (p. 152) of the classroom community. These second graders were not simply involved in dyadic interactions with the teacher, but they also participated in scaffolding interactions involving one another with familiar texts and literacy activities. By participating in literacy events such as these, Dyson suggested that children gain understandings of literary discourse and genre expectations that eventually transform into disciplinary knowledge.

The School Shift from Pleasure to Academic Texts

In their report *To Read or Not to Read: A Question of National Consequence*, the National Endowment for the Arts (2007) reports that there has been a decline in reading activity in the general U.S. population, especially among high school students. In part, a shift to reading to learn rather than for pleasure is cited for this decline in interest, and this shift in purpose for reading has been identified as a major contributor to the academic downturn known as the "fourth-grade slump" (Chall & Jacobs, 2003). The change in reading purposes is often compounded by the texts used in schools, with the inclusion of more textbooks and more technical readings. The types of texts that students would like to read are typically excluded, and as a partial consequence secondary students' most negative experiences with reading are associated with texts required by the curriculum (Ivey & Broaddus, 2001). Assigned texts, although they are used with good intentions in order to broaden student knowledge, are often hard to connect with, contain difficult language and ideas, and also can be seen as dry or dull. As Worthy, Morman, and Turner (1999) have remarked, what students like to read is "hard to find in school" (p. 12).

Education research has suggested that regular and frequent engagement in reading has positive effects on learning and scholastic performance (Brozo, 2002; Schwanenflugel, Hamilton, Kuhn, & Stahl, 2004). Because secondary students are far less likely to read on their own, it comes within the purview of classroom teachers to promote reading whenever they can. This shortage of reading time is not limited to the United States; a recent comparison of three English-speaking PISA (Program for International Student Assessment) countries (Brozo, Shiel, & Topping, 2008) advanced the suggestion that secondary students generally need to increase the amount of time spent reading, particularly in classrooms, the environment in which teachers can ensure that it happens.

Given the need for all students to read more in classrooms in order to promote reading skills as well as an enthusiasm to read not just for academic reasons, we next examine what motivates adolescents to read, what we know about adolescents' reading choices, and in the last section what uses can be made in school of these unofficial or unauthorized texts for students of all ages.

What Motivates Adolescents to Read?

In Western culture in general and U.S. culture specifically, reading is psychologically tied to the "arts of existence" (Foucault, 1984/1985), where people try to maximize their potential and develop themselves as best they can mentally and physically (i.e., having a sound mind in a sound body). Reading is frequently associated with the art of self-improvement (Long, 2003) through developing one's intellect and engaging in thoughtful reflection. This sentiment has been reflected in research done with adolescents regarding their reading choices and practices. For many adolescents, reading is a means to an end and not something done just for its own sake (Hughes-Hassell & Rodge, 2007; Reeves, 2004), with one of the most common reasons given to read being to learn something. Reading in this case is not something done purely as a pleasurable activity but is bound up in other contexts and activities, such as learning about a topic for school, catching up on their interests such as sports news or celebrity gossip, or sharing a specific book or book series with friends to talk about (Stairs & Stairs, 2007). It is not the act of reading itself that gives students something; rather, it is through reading that they get the chance to interact with a topic or other people. As Reeves (2004) puts it, students may enjoy something such as sports, and "reading is just one way to fill their minds with sports" (p. 236). Most adolescent students read to get something out of the text and mostly not necessarily for some aesthetic experience.

The features about adolescents' engagement with reading were further explored in a study of adolescent males' reading habits done by Smith and Wilhelm (2002). They found that the youths they worked with overwhelmingly engaged in reading that was built into social connections. The males they interviewed stated that they read materials such as magazines and sports pages from newspapers because these tied into their interests and hobbies outside of school. They also described how they engaged in such popular culture reading because then they could keep up with conversations with their peers, and they also described how they read a particular text or book because one of their friends or teachers had recommended it. For many of these young males, reading was most valuable when there was a personal or social connection involved. They valued reading that helped them interact with their friends, that was connected to an activity or hobby in which they were expert or even just interested, or that they could do with a degree of competence. The male readers Smith and Wilhelm talked to especially felt that reading texts that they were comfortable with and capable of understanding led to some of their most successful reading experiences.

Conversely, many of students' most negative experiences with reading involve assigned texts and confusion about the aims of instruction (Ivey & Broaddus, 2001). Even though well intentioned, classroom activities may not connect with students to whom "the purpose of specific drills and lessons seems opaque" (Csikszentmihalyi, 1990, p. 135). Fostering positive and productive reading experiences in classrooms involves paying attention to what motivates students (Guthrie, 2004) and providing meaningful and engaging instruction that relates to students' lives. One pathway to this goal involves using texts that interest students, as those texts are more immediately taken up and read when they have a direct bearing on students' lives and social circles (Alvermann, Moon, & Hagood, 1999; Xu, Perkins, & Zunich, 2005). But before we get to the question of how we can use student interest to foster educational motivation, we turn our attention to the question of what it is that students like to read.

What Do Secondary Students Like to Read and Why?

Before answering this question, we begin with a caveat: secondary students are a hugely diverse bunch, and there is no such thing as a unitary youth culture (Sutherland, Botzakis, Moje, & Alvermann, 2008). What is popular, relevant, or interesting to one student may not be to another. With this caveat in mind, we explore what research tells us about what students prefer to read without reference to specific titles but rather to general trends.

In general, studies with urban adolescents (Hughes-Hassell & Rodge, 2007) and eighth-grade students in Maine (Stairs & Stairs, 2007) have shown that students prefer to read series books, comics, magazines, and the Internet. In a seminal study of the reading preferences of middle school students, Worthy et al. (1999) surveyed and interviewed sixth-grade students from nine middle schools in a diverse area in Texas. They identified that in general students preferred recently published series books, books based on movies and television shows, specialty magazines (i.e., video games), comic and cartoons, and horror stories. Also, although personal tastes resulted in a wide range of authors being described as a student's favorite, two authors were cited as favorites significantly more than the others, horror writers Stephen King and R. L. Stine. Almost half of the students stated that they had no favorite author. As for how they chose which books to read, students described "word-of-mouth" recommendations from their friends or teachers as being a powerful factor in their reading choices. As for how and where students obtained texts to read, a slight majority (56%) stated that they bought them from a store, while others (44%) stated that they borrowed them from the library.

In part, economic constraints limited students' access to the types of texts that they liked to read, with school being one of the few places where students had free access to texts, but in the recent past teenagers have been buying books at the fastest rate in decades (Goodnow, 2007). In part, this recent surge in sales has been attributed to publishers catering more to younger audiences. Although there is a huge range of books aimed at younger readers, from established classics to romance, horror, informational, or humor books, series such as *Harry Potter* books as well as fantasy and graphic novels have been noted as being particularly "hot" among young consumers (p. 12). Graphic novels and *manga* (serialized graphic novels from Japan), in particular, have doubled their sales volume since 2002 (Glazer, 2005). In fact, out of the top twenty best-selling graphic novels in 2006, nineteen were *manga* (with the top 9 being in the *Naruto* series), while the one exception was *V for Vendetta* (Moore & Lloyd, 1995), an original graphic novel that was made into a movie (Hibbs, 2007, p. 56). There is a trend here with books with other media tie-ins, as *Naruto* (Kishimoto, 2003) is also a popular cartoon series on television, and this trend has continued more recently, with a spike in the popularity of the *Watchmen* graphic novel (Moore & Gibbons, 1986), which also has been adapted into a major motion picture.

Other studies concerning adolescents' reading choices have addressed the reasons that students give for their reading choices in addition to recording what they liked to read. In their study of middle school students and their relationships to reading, Ivey and Broaddus (2001) found that students cited magazines and genre fiction, particularly adventure and mysteries, as their overall favorite types of texts. They also found that students, in the course of their school activities, valued time for personal reading the most. The most motivating factors that students cited were their personal connections with a text as well as such emotional sensations as humor and suspense that stimulated their interests and pleasure in the texts. Furthermore, another consistent thread throughout students' responses was that being able to choose which text to read was highly valued.

The link between choice, social practice, and academic value is reinforced by research done with students. Ivey and Broaddus (2001) found that many students linked dissatisfaction with reading directly to instruction and that students' most negative associations with reading were linked to assigned texts. When there was no room for choice or personal connections in the interests of curricular demands, students felt a conflict between their in- and out-of-school reading practices. Standard curricula did not account for their interests or their own inquiries, and this disconnect led to disinterest, confusion, and even rejection of school reading. As can be seen from the studies cited above, in regard to the general types of texts preferred by students, most if not all are typically excluded from standard school curricula.

This disconnection looks like another case of what Ronnie, a participant in an interview study, described, namely, that "popular culture is something that school doesn't know what to do with" (Botzakis, 2006, p. 3). Often popular culture texts, such as series books, graphic novels, or magazines, are left out of school because they are regarded as facile, possibly questionable in content, or too ephemeral in terms of popularity. Popularity is a fleeting concept; general popularity does not guarantee universal acceptance or enthusiasm by all readers, and many educators are loath to buy materials and texts that may not appeal to students after a year or two.

Using texts that students find interesting requires that one adopt different ways of employing such texts in the classroom. Although some extra effort is needed when using such texts mindfully, researchers have been extolling the benefits of such an approach, particularly for struggling readers who might be more motivated to engage with texts that appeal to their expertise, background knowledge, and interest (Alvermann, 2001; Brozo, 2002; O'Brien, 1998; Smith & Wilhelm, 2002). The call for integrating popular culture into schools is not new or original, but it has been gaining momentum in recent times (e.g., Alvermann et al., 1999; Hull & Schultz, 2002; Morrell, 2004; Xu et al., 2005). In what follows, we do not describe specific practices for using the texts that students prefer for scholastic purposes, as it is difficult to determine specific practices for what can quite diverse students in many different contexts. Rather, we describe general features of texts, in particular series books, genre fiction, and graphic novels, that educators can capitalize on in creating activities and contexts for student learning. We provide the case for how using texts that students prefer can benefit teachers and students in an effective and engaging academic environment.

What Uses Can Be Made of These Texts in School?

Series Books

Although "the importance of background knowledge for reading comprehension is widely acknowledged and documented" (Pikulski, 2006, p. 88), we often overlook these advantages when confronted with the conventions of series books. The very features that often are criticized about series books—the repetitive plots, clichéd characters, and simplistic writing (Bucher & Manning, 2006)—can also be among their most useful aspects when working with beginning, struggling, or reluctant readers.

The very redundancy of the language of series books supports inexperienced readers. Many particular words and phrases are constantly repeated, providing the needed practice that leads to automaticity. In the fluency studies conducted by Melanie Kuhn, Paula Schwanenflugel, and their colleagues (see Kuhn and Schwanenflugel, Chapter 7, this volume), wide reading with different texts proved more efficient than repeated readings of the same texts in bringing primary grade children to proficiency. According to the instance theory of automaticity, which the authors invoke to explain the earlier gains associated with wide reading, each time a text is read, an instance at the phrase, lexical (word), or sublexical level (patterns) is encoded in memory. Because wide reading enabled rarely encountered words, word patterns, or phrases to be encoded in memory, it supported the development of early fluent reading.

Series books would appear to be a good match for wide reading that aims to develop automaticity for readers at any grade level. Not only do series books sustain a narrative over many pages of text, they also sustain student involvement over multiple books. Given the pervasive links to popular media and everyday culture, engagement in a book series supports students not only in developing fluent and automatic processing of text but also, perhaps more important, in building their identify through talk, reading, and writing within their peer community. Repeated readings require authentic purposes for reentering the text, such as rehearsing for a reading performance and other purposes described by Worthy and Broaddus (2002), or the earlier example of second graders consulting *Frog and Toad* books for the exact dialogue and voice of the characters (Dyson, 2000). Series books provide many different exposures to the same or similar characters, settings, and episodes, lending extra support to students who may be struggling, reluctant, or uninitiated in particular genres.

Although series books can be seen as formulaic, even hackneyed, many readers warm up to familiar stories and characters. What is more, the familiar characters, settings, and situations provide readers with schemata to hang their comprehension on and also an opportunity to move beyond simple questions of plot to more critical questions about characterizations or a global look at the story across books that can tap higher-level thinking skills.

There are also other outcomes that can accompany reading series books. Students' familiarity and enjoyment of the narratives can lead to rereading opportunities that can help them gain different understandings of the books over time (Faust & Glenzer, 2000) as well as an opportunity to develop their reading fluency. Additionally, social connections made with friends concerning series books, such as the ones between Maine middle school students and the series of *Cirque Du Freak* novels (Stairs & Stairs, 2007), can turn into opportunities for discussion in and outside of classrooms. These discussions can turn into debates over style, content, tastes, and opinions about the relative worth of individual titles within the series (Worthy, 1998), much like ones a classroom teacher would promote in a class setting.

Comics and Graphic Novels

Many of the same benefits that apply to series books can also be applied to the increasingly popular graphic novels, comics, and *manga*, and the sequential art format of comics and graphic novels also affords opportunities for students to make meaning of texts with the contextual support of pictures. This feature can be of great assistance to second-language learners, who might have the background knowledge to understand a narrative or exposition but not the specific vocabulary to deal with a typical text or textbook (Cary, 2004). Many other students can also benefit from the use of images in making inferences (Frey & Fisher, 2004). Students often struggle with the idea of making inferences in texts when they have difficulty with reading comprehension and vocabulary, but they can feel more at ease making predictions and observations from a picture. Students can make quite complex, informed, and insightful comments from a small series of pictures, and this ability can then be extrapolated into the world of more traditional texts. The use of the comics format here provides a more comfortable, nonthreatening entry into more complex thinking and learning.

Furthermore, the comics format can also be a favorable alternative for reluctant writers. Students who create their own comic strip narratives must consider the format, style, and conventions that they will use in their creations (Xu et al., 2005). These choices reflect the choices writers also make when they are composing texts, and teachers can take advantage of this opportunity to do some informal writing instruction. Also, many reluctant writers prove to be more willing artists, and the sequential art format allows them an opportunity to express themselves in a manner in which they feel more expert.

Magazines

Magazines, particularly the ones favored by students—which include those that focus on celebrities, sports, teen issues, and music (Hughes-Hassell & Rodge, 2007)—are typically considered as being inappropriate for school because of their shallow and sometimes crass or questionable content; but there are opportunities for learning even within the pages of those often disparaged texts. Using a media literacy stance (Thoman & Jolls, 2004), teachers and students can approach these texts from a more critical angle, asking questions about the content of these magazines, who put them together, and what messages are being conveyed by them. One way to do this is simply to examine the images within as well as the techniques used to attract the readers' attention (Botzakis, 2007). Looking at these can help students ask questions about why they are looking at these magazines, about whether or not what they are looking at is realistic or desirable, and also about how or how not they are encouraged as consumers.

These texts can also be examined for how certain social, ethnic, or gender groups are depicted (Morrell, 2004) and whether or not those depictions are fair. This last exercise can be especially powerful when students are afforded the opportunity to examine these different depictions across a number of different magazines. This activity can be accompanied by a productive extension where students are asked to design and create their own magazines to show how they would like themselves and their social groups to be portrayed. The relatively short types of writing that are included in magazines, such as the captions, sidebars, and news items, can even put some of the most reluctant writers at ease.

Conclusion

Our students are attracted to texts where they can encounter a wide array of characters, ranging from Hilary Duff to Scooby-Doo, Captain America to Captain Underpants, and the Shinigami death god of the *Deathnote* series (Ohba & Obata, 2003) to the death eaters of the *Harry Potter* series. Connections among their peers, situations that relate to their lives, suggestions from family and teachers, and things that they see on television and movies compel them to explore the worlds around them. Often these texts may seem to be silly, inconsequential, and even commercially predatory, and we are not suggesting that educators should approach them uncritically. But we also believe that "if children are to engage meaningfully with text, they need to have a sense of ownership that pleasure derives" (Norton, 2003, p. 146) and that these books can serve at least dual purposes. They can serve as attractive entry points into learning and literacy, where students are more motivated to take up and engage with texts because they are actually interested in their content. This motivation may work wonders for developing reading fluency as well as general reading skills (Allington, Chapter 2, this volume; Schwanenflugel et al., 2004). Additionally, popular texts can be used as vehicles for teachers to get students to ask more critical questions about their worlds, such as why they like these particular texts and what messages the authors might be attempting to send (Dyson, 2003; Morrell, 2004). By working with our students in places where they are comfortable and familiar, we might be able to encourage them to take more chances, ask more questions, and in the process learn more about the world around them.

References

Allington, R., McGill-Franzen, A., Williams, L., Zmach, C., et al. (2007, April 11). *Ameliorating summer reading loss among economically disadvantaged children.* Paper presented at the American Educational Research Association Conference, Chicago.
Alvermann, D. E., & Xu, S. (2003). Children's everyday literacies: Intersections

of popular culture and language arts instruction. *Language Arts, 81*(2), 145–154.

Alvermann, D. E. (2001). Reading adolescents' reading identities: Looking back to see ahead. *Journal of Adolescent and Adult Literacy, 44*(8), 676–690.

Alvermann, D. E., Moon, J. S., & Hagood, M. C. (1999). *Popular culture in the classroom: Teaching and researching critical media literacy.* Chicago: National Reading Conference.

Botzakis, S. (2006). *Reading when they don't have to: Insights from adult comic book readers.* Unpublished doctoral dissertation, University of Georgia, Athens.

Botzakis, S. (2007). *Pretty in print: Questioning magazines.* Mankato, MN: Capstone Press.

Bridwell, N. (1995). *Clifford the Big Red Dog.* New York: Scholastic. (Original work published 1962)

Brozo, W. G. (2002). *To be a boy, to be a reader.* Newark, DE: International Reading Association.

Brozo, W. G., Shiel, G., & Topping, K. (2008). Engagement in reading: Lessons learned from three PISA countries. *Journal of Adolescent and Adult Literacy, 51*(4), 304–315.

Bucher, K., & Manning, M. L. (2006). *Young adult literature: Exploration, evaluation, and appreciation.* Upper Saddle River, NJ: Pearson.

Cary, S. (2004). *Going graphic: Comics at work in the multi-lingual classroom.* Portsmouth, NH: Heinemann.

Chall, J. S., & Jacobs, V. A. (2003). Poor children's fourth-grade slump. *American Educator, 27*(1), 14–15, 44. Retrieved August 12, 2008, from *www.aft.org/pubs-reports/american_educator/spring2003/chall.html.*

Clarke, P., Riley, T., & Bergen, M. (2003). *Scary creatures: Big cats.* New York: Scholastic.

Csikszentmihalyi, M. (1990). Literacy and intrinsic motivation. *Daedalus, 119,* 115–140.

Cunningham, A. E., & Stanovich, K. E. (1998, Spring/Summer). What reading does for the mind. *American Educator, 22*(1–2), 1–8.

Daane, M. C., Campbell, J. R., Grigg, W. S., Goodman, M. J., Oranje, A., & Goldstein, A. (2005). *The Nation's Report Card: Fourth-grade students reading aloud—NAEP 2002 special study of oral reading.* Washington, DC: U.S. Department of Education, Institute of Education Sciences, National Center for Education Statistics.

Dyson, A. H. (2000). Writing and the sea of voices: Oral language in, around and about writing. In R. Indrisano & J. R. Squire (Eds.), *Perspectives on writing: Research, theory, and practice* (pp. 45–65). Newark, DE: International Reading Association.

Dyson, A. H. (2003). *The brothers and sisters learn to write: Popular literacies in childhood and school cultures.* New York: Teachers College Press.

Faust, M. A., & Glenzer, N. (2000). "I could read those parts over and over": Eighth graders rereading to enhance enjoyment and learning with literature. *Journal of Adolescent and Adult Literacy, 44*(3), 234–239.

Foucault, M. (1985). *The use of pleasure: Volume 2 of the history of sexuality* (R. Hurley, Trans.). New York: Vintage Books. (Original work published 1984)

Frey, N., & Fisher, D. (2004). Using graphic novels, anime, and the Internet in an urban high school. *English Journal, 93*(3), 19–25.

Friedman, M. (2000). *Superman's first flight.* New York: Scholastic.

Gelsey, J. (1998). *Scooby-Doo and the Haunted Castle.* New York: Scholastic.

Glass, E. (2001). *Pop people: Destiny's child.* New York: Scholastic.

Glazer, S. (2005, September 18). Manga for girls. *The New York Times Book Review,* 16–17.

Goodnow, C. (2007, March 7). Teens buying books at fastest rate in decades. Retrieved September 21, 2008, from *seattlepi.nwsource.com/books/306531_teenlit08.html?source=mypi.*

Guthrie, J. T., & Humenick, N. M. (2004). Motivating students to read. In P. McCardle & V. Chhabra (Eds.), *The voice of evidence in reading research* (pp. 329–354). Baltimore: Brookes.

Hibbs, B. (2007). Tilting@windmills #37: Bookscan 2006. Retrieved February 21, 2007, from *www.newsarama.com/Tilting2_0/Tilting37.html.*

Hughes-Hassell, S., & Rodge, P. (2007). The leisure reading habits of urban adolescents. *Journal of Adolescent and Adult Literacy, 51*(1), 22–33.

Hull, G., & Schultz, K. (2002). *School's out! Bridging out-of-school literacies with classroom practice.* New York: Teachers College Press.

Ivey, G., & Broaddus, K. (2001). "Just plain reading": A survey of what makes students want to read in middle school classrooms. *Reading Research Quarterly, 36*(4), 350–377.

Karlan, D., Lazar, A., & Salter, J. (2006). *The 101 most influential people who never lived: How characters of fiction, myth, legends, television, and movies have shaped our society, changed our behavior, and set the course of history.* New York: HarperCollins.

Kishimoto, M. (2003). *Naruto, volume 1.* San Francisco: VIZ Media.

Legg, G., & Hewetson, N. (2002). *Scary creatures: Alligators and crocodiles.* New York: Scholastic.

Long, E. (2003). *Book clubs: Women and the uses of reading in everyday life.* Chicago: University of Chicago Press.

McGill-Franzen, A., & Allington, R. (2008). Got books? *Educational Leadership, 65*(7), 20–23.

Moore, A., & Gibbons, D. (1986). *Watchmen.* New York: DC Comics.

Moore, A., & Lloyd, D. (1995). *V for vendetta.* New York: Vertigo Comics.

Morrell, E. (2004). *Linking literacy and popular culture: Finding connections for lifelong learning.* Norwood, MA: Christopher—Gordon Publishers.

National Endowment for the Arts. (2007). *To read or not to read: A question of national consequence.* Washington, DC: Author.

Norton, B. (2003). The motivating power of comic books: Insights from Archie comic readers. *Reading Teacher, 57,* 140–147.

O'Brien, D. G. (1998). Multiple literacies in a high school program for "at-risk" adolescents. In D. E. Alvermann, K. A. Hinchman, D. W. Moore, S. Phelps, & D. Waff (Eds.), *Reconceptualizing the literacies in adolescents' lives* (pp. 27–49). Mahwah, NJ: Erlbaum.

Ohba, T., & Obata, T. (2003). *Deathnote, volume 1.* San Francisco: VIZ Media.

Park, B. (1997). *Junie B. Jones Is a Party Animal.* New York: Scholastic.

Pikulski, J. J. (2006). Fluency: A developmental and language perspective. In S. J. Samuels & A. E. Farstrup (Eds.), *What research has to say about fluency research* (pp. 70–93). Newark, DE: International Reading Association.

Pilkey, D. (1999). *Captain Underpants and the invasion of the incredible naughty cafeteria ladies from outer space.* New York: Scholastic.

Pilkey, D. (2003a). *Captain Underpants and the big, bad battle of the Bionic Booger Boy, part 1: The night of the nasty nostril nuggets.* New York: Scholastic.

Pilkey, D. (2003b). *Captain Underpants and the big, bad battle of the Bionic Booger Boy, part 2: Revenge of the ridiculous robo-boogers.* New York: Scholastic.

Pilkey, D., Hutchins, H., & Beard, G. (2002). *The adventures of Super Diaper Baby.* New York: Scholastic.

Preller, J. (2000). *Rock solid! The slammin' unauthorized biography of The Rock.* New York: Scholastic.

Reeves, A. R. (2004). *Adolescents talk about reading: Exploring resistance to and engagement with text.* Newark, DE: International Reading Association.

Rowling, J. K. (2002). *Harry Potter and the goblet of fire.* New York: Scholastic.

Schwanenflugel, P. J., Hamilton, A. M., Kuhn, M. R., & Stahl, S. A. (2004). Becoming a fluent reader: Skill and prosodic features in the oral reading of young children. *Journal of Educational Psychology, 96*(1), 119–129.

Smith, M. W., & Wilhelm, J. D. (2002). *"Reading don't fix no Chevys": Literacy in the lives of young men.* Portsmouth, NH: Heinemann.

Stairs, A. J., & Stairs, S. A. (2007). Recommended reading for young adults from young adults. *SIGNAL Journal, 30*(2), 17–22.

Sutherland, L. A., Botzakis, S., Moje, E. B., & Alvermann, D. E. (2008). Drawing on youth cultures in content learning and literacy. In D. Lapp, J. Flood, & N. Farnan (Eds.), *Content area reading and learning: Instructional strategies* (2nd ed., pp. 133–156). Englewood Cliffs, NJ: Prentice-Hall.

Talmadge, M. (2001). *Britney Spears* (Celebrity Bios). New York: Scholastic.

Thoman, E., & Jolls, T. (2004). Media literacy—a national priority for a changing world. *American Behavioral Scientist, 48*(1), 18–29.

USA Today. (2006, October 17). Influential people list. Retrieved September 10, 2008, from *www.usatoday.com/life/people/2006-10-16-influential-people-list_x. htm.*

Walsh, K. (2002). *Hangin' with Lil' Romeo: Backstage pass.* New York: Scholastic.

Williams, L. (2005). *Book selections of economically disadvantaged Black students.* Unpublished doctoral dissertation, University of Florida, Gainesville.

Worthy, J. (1998). "On every page someone gets killed!": Book conversations you don't hear in school. *Journal of Adolescent and Adult Literacy, 41*(7), 508–517.

Worthy, J., & Broaddus, K. (2002). Fluency beyond the primary grades: From group performance to silent, independent reading. *The Reading Teacher, 55*(4), 334–343.

Worthy, J., Morman, M., & Turner, M. (1999). What Johnny likes to read is hard to find in school. *Reading Research Quarterly, 34*(1), 12–27.

Xu, S. H., Perkins, R. S., & Zunich, L. O. (2005). *Trading cards to comic strips: Popular culture texts and literacy learning in grades K–8.* Newark, DE: International Reading Association.

6

HOW MUCH AND WHAT ARE THIRD GRADERS READING?

Reading in Core Programs

DEVON BRENNER
ELFRIEDA H. HIEBERT
RENARTA TOMPKINS

On a typical Tuesday in October, Jamal—a third grader—starts reading instruction by responding to the teacher as she asks questions about the vocabulary words introduced the preceding day. He spends the next 35 minutes turn-taking, or round-robin, reading a story about a trip to the North Pole from the anthology of the core reading program. While his classmates read aloud, Jamal looks around. When Jamal's turn comes, his teacher has to tell him where to begin reading. His teacher stops periodically to ask students to define words or to answer comprehension questions. After the selection has been read and the vocabulary words discussed again, the class constructs a summary of the text. Students dictate sentences that the teacher writes in a graphic organizer on the overhead projector. The teacher leads the whole class in choral reading the summary a few times, then leads a discussion on making words past tense by adding -d and -ed to the ends of words. After this exercise, the class is divided into three achievement-based groups that rotate through small-group learning centers, each of them lasting 15 minutes.

At the first center, Jamal and his group match the vocabulary words from the anthology selection with their definitions. When they finish early, each listens to a different story read aloud on the computer. Jamal listens along as paragraphs from a passage about a ladybug light up in red. Some of the time, Jamal appears to be following along as the voice on the computer reads the story. Other times, he seems to be waiting to click at the end of each paragraph but not reading along. At the next center, Jamal and his partner complete a worksheet on synonyms and antonyms, filling in the blanks with synonyms and antonyms of words from the week's text. When they finish, they talk for a few minutes (not about the text). At the third center, Jamal and his group work with the teacher. Yesterday the teacher led each small group in turn-taking reading of a leveled text that accompanies the week's story and a discussion of using context clues and the *ou* vowel pattern. Today the students reread the last few pages silently, and then the teacher asks the students to select one picture from the text, name all the nouns they see in the illustration, and then sort those into common versus proper nouns.

Jamal is well behaved and participates in the assigned tasks of the reading block, all of which are suggested in the teacher's edition of the reading core program and many of which have been recommended as exemplifying scientifically based reading research (SBRR; National Research Council, 2002). But, in spite of all of his teacher's efforts to follow the guidelines in the reading core program, Jamal may not be getting enough reading practice to become a proficient reader. On this typical school day with about 90 minutes of reading instruction, Jamal spent only 9 minutes independently reading connected text and just another 9 minutes engaged in assisted reading.

Jamal is a hypothetical child, a composite of the students we observed in a study that was conducted in the fall of 2006 in 32 Mississippi schools participating in Reading First, a federally funded reform effort aimed at increasing reading achievement in grades K–3. As a requirement of Reading First funding in the state of Mississippi, reading instruction must be based on an approved scientifically based reading program. The study that is the centerpiece of this chapter describes the amount of time and the types of texts students spent reading in classrooms required to use a core reading program. Our interest in documenting the reading in which students engaged emanates from the consistent conclusion in past reform efforts that time in itself is not the distinguishing feature of increased performance (Jackson, 1968). What matters in becoming a proficient reader is *how* students spend their time in schools and, in particular, the amount of time spent reading in which students are actively engaged. Since the contexts that we were studying have been influenced strongly by Reading First mandates, we consider first the role of core reading programs and Reading First.

Reading First and Core Reading Programs

Current core reading programs—also called basal reading programs—revolve around anthologies of narrative and expository texts that are organized loosely into themes such as survival, adventures, or friendship. The student anthologies are accompanied by teacher's editions, which provide resources and directions for teaching the passage and related reading and language arts skills and strategies, including comprehension, fluency, writing, grammar, phonics, and cross-curricular connections. Additional resources accompanying the text can include sets of trade books, small, single-text books described as little books, guided or leveled readers, phonics readers, practice books or workbooks, CD-ROMs, recordings of the anthology texts being read aloud, transparencies, posters, and more.

The core reading program is not a new phenomenon in elementary classrooms. In the 1800s, most teachers used *McGuffey's Reader* (Matthews, 1966) as a source of progressively more difficult reading texts and lists of words for reading instruction. From the early 1930s through the late 1980s, basal reading programs were central to American reading instruction (Austin & Morrison, 1963; Dole & Osborn, 1991). Through that period, readability formulas were influential in determining the vocabulary load. A consequence of this influence was that texts were often bland in vocabulary and had, at least at the primary levels, simplistic syntactic structures that could impede comprehension (Anderson, Hiebert, Scott, & Wilkinson, 1985). As a result of criticisms of the typical fare of basal reading programs (see, e.g., Anderson et al., 1985), trade book selections became central to basal reading programs during the 1990s. Further, many schools and districts began to replace basal reading programs with trade books or leveled books. Baumann, Hoffman, Duffy-Hester, and Ro's (2000) analyses of teacher use of basal reading programs in the late 1990s indicated that the percentage of teachers reporting that they relied primarily on basal reading programs was approximately 58%, and another 27% used a basal at least some of the time, down from 97% of schools using basals alone or in conjunction with phonics or experience charts in 1961 (Austin & Morrison, 1963).

Since 2000 and the advent of the No Child Left Behind Act (NCLB), the influence of core reading programs has grown substantially, particularly in primary grade classrooms (Simmons & Kame'enui, 2003). A main focus of NCLB has been reforming reading through an emphasis on "selecting and implementing a learning system or program of reading instruction based on scientifically based reading research that ... includes the essential components of reading instruction" (NCLB, Part B, Section 1202, item 7). Reading First, the largest reading reform effort in the United States, aimed to improve the reading achievement of students in kindergarten through third grade by applying teaching practices based on SBRR (U.S. Department of Education, 2003). Reading First requires schools to implement "a program of reading instruction that is based on scientifically based reading research and that includes the essential components of reading instruction and provides such instruction to children in kindergarten through grade 3" (U.S. Government Accountability Office, 2007). Typically, state departments of education that submit applications and are awarded Reading First contracts have interpreted reading instructional programs to be one of the mainstream core reading programs.

According to the NCLB and Reading First legislation, reading programs should be built on the five components of reading outlined in the report of the National Reading Panel (NRP; National Institute of Child Health and Human Development [NICHD], 2000), specifically, phonemic awareness, phonics, fluency, vocabulary, and comprehension. While these components are key elements of effective reading instruction, the foreword of the NRP contains this caveat: "The Panel's silence on other topics should not be interpreted as indicating that other topics have no importance or that improvement in those areas would not lead to greater reading achievement" (NRP report, pp. 1–3). Even so, the guidelines of the Reading First program focus almost exclusively on these five components designated by the NRP.

Reading First has encouraged the use of core reading programs under the rubric of SBRR, and publishers advertise their programs as complying with SBRR. Houghton Mifflin Reading, for example, lists "Evidence of Efficacy" and "Scientific Research Base" as features on its front cover (Cooper et al., 2004). Except for phonemic awareness, which is no longer taught by third grade, the five components of reading outlined in the NRP are featured prominently in the teacher's editions and resources provided by reading core programs. A typical week of instruction will provide one or two comprehension strategies such as summarizing, predicting, or making connections, a list of vocabulary words to be learned with the passage, and resources for teaching components of vocabulary such as affixes or synonyms, phonics activities, and suggestions to reread the entire text or a few pages of the text to build fluency.

Simmons and Kame'enui (2003) described the need for core reading programs as follows:

> The requirements of curriculum construction and instructional design that effectively move children through the "learning to read" stage to the "reading to learn" stage are simply too important to leave to the judgment of individuals. The better the core addresses instructional priorities, the less teachers will need to supplement and modify instruction for the majority of learners. (p. 2)

While individual components of core reading programs may have research validation, there is little research to indicate that the careful design that Simmons and Kame'enui described as the benefit of the core reading programs has, indeed, been effectively implemented.

To date, evidence on the efficacy of core reading programs has been less than convincing. Several studies call the efficacy of various core reading programs into question (Block, Cleveland, & Reed, 2006; Kuhn et al., 2006; McGill-Franzen, Zmach, Solic, & Zeig, 2006). McGill-Franzen et al. (2006) studied the impact of two core reading programs on the achievement of students in Florida, particularly low-income students, and found that neither core program sufficiently supported the learning of those students most dependent on school to learn to read. They concluded, in fact, that standardization of the reading program may actually exacerbate disadvantages for low-income students. Block et al. (2006) compared achievement in courses allocating additional time to the core reading program to classrooms that added 20 minutes of additional reading and found that simply adding more reading, including reading of related leveled texts and expository texts, supported achievement more than additional time with the basal. Another group of researchers (Kuhn et al., 2006; Kuhn and Schwanenflugel, Chapter 7, this volume) found that increasing time reading through an emphasis on either repeated reading or wide reading of related grade-level texts boosted second graders' achievement more than the control condition, spending a similar amount of time on core program reading instruction.

These studies suggest that reforms based on mandating core programs as a palliative against reading failure may not achieve desired results. Teachers in Mississippi's Reading First schools have been required to use a core program. At least a 90-minute daily period is devoted to the core program. Teachers also regularly participate in ongoing training on components of reading instruction from the NRP (NICHD, 2000) and/or on the content of their reading programs.

While, for many schools, these practices represented substantial changes, Mississippi experienced only minimal gains in reading achievement during the first 3 years of Reading First. In the spring of 2006, 58% of third graders in Reading First schools remained below the benchmark level on oral reading fluency on the Dynamic Indicators of Basic Early Literacy Skills (DIBELS; Good & Kaminski, 2002); only an additional 4% of third graders had moved from below-average to at least the benchmark level (MGT of America, 2006). One concern might be that core reading programs, as currently designed, do not offer sufficient opportunities to read to build the fluency, comprehension, and vocabulary needed for high levels of reading achievement.

The Eyes on Text Project

Two authors of this chapter, Brenner and Tompkins, were involved in the professional development of the Reading First effort in Mississippi, and Hiebert served as a consultant for the effort. As we observed the state's teachers and administrators working assiduously to comply with the Reading First guidelines, we wondered whether it might be the case that students were receiving consistent and intensive instruction in the five domains of the NRP and Reading First but not having the opportunities to integrate the domains as they read connected text. However, before we could advise teachers to increase the amount of reading of connected text, we needed to know how much students were typically reading. The first aim of a project that we came to call "Eyes on Text" was to establish the level of reading of connected text then occurring in classrooms and to determine how that level related to recommendations in the literature. The remainder of the chapter presents the rationale, procedures, and results of this first phase of the Eyes on Text project.

Rationale for the Eyes on Text Project

As was evident in the framework of opportunity to read presented in the opening chapter of this volume (Hiebert and Martin, Chapter 1, this volume), opportunities for students to read connected text have been shown to be positively associated with students' fluency, vocabulary, and comprehension proficiency. In particular, time spent reading appears to affect two components of reading that are, in turn, related to comprehension—fluency and vocabulary.

The relationship between fluency and comprehension has been explained by theory on automaticity (LaBerge & Samuels, 1974). When students are not fluent with a critical number of words in a text, their attention is diverted to word recognition rather than to the message of the text. The kinds of reading in which such automaticity develops can include, as Stahl (2004) has argued, both the repeated reading of the same text and reading new texts. Without sufficient experience in reading, automatic word recognition in the act of reading texts does not occur.

A link has also been shown between students' reading of connected texts and their vocabularies. Since the vocabulary of written texts is more sophisticated than that of oral language (Hayes, Wolfer, & Wolfe, 1996), those who read more are exposed to more words (Critchley, 1998). Poor readers who read fewer texts (both as a result of reading less and reading more slowly) encounter and learn fewer new words, impeding comprehension of future texts, while good readers who read more texts (both because they read more quickly and are given more opportunity to read) encounter and learn more words, fostering comprehension (and enjoyment) of future texts (Cunningham & Stanovich, 1998). Since vocabulary and comprehension increase as students read more, struggling readers need to spend more time reading. As Baker, Simmons, and Kame'enui (n.d.) note, "The only realistic chance students with poor vocabularies have to catch up to their peers with rich vocabularies requires that they engage in extraordinary amounts of independent reading" (p. 22).

Despite these links between the amount that students read and comprehension, research has been less forthcoming about what constitutes an "extraordinary" amount of independent reading. Several scholars have proposed guidelines. Based on Krashen's (1993) meta-analyses, Allington (2001) proposed that 90 minutes of time be spent engaged in reading during a school day. Fisher and Ivey (2006) have recommended that time spent in engaged reading and writing should be greater than the amount of time spent in instruction and practice of skills and strategies related to literacy. They propose a ratio of approximately two-thirds of a reading period spent on engaged reading and writing and the remaining portion of time devoted to skills and strategy instruction and practice. Fisher and Ivey found that achievement increased when students, including special education students, participated in this volume of engaged reading and writing.

When data have been gathered in classrooms, the amount that students are reading is typically far from these recommended levels. In the 1980s, Gambrell (1984) found that, on average, students individually read approximately only 14 minutes daily. A decade later, Foertsch (1992) documented similar amounts of reading. Most recently, a survey by Donahue, Finnegan, Lutkus, Allen, and Campbell (2001) showed that fourth graders reported, on average, reading 10 or fewer pages per day in school and for homework. Ten pages of text equates with approximately 8–12 minutes of daily reading. The volume of reading in which students engage at school has remained at a relatively low constant over the past 30 years.

Foci of the Eyes on Text Project

By eyes on text, we are referring to the amount of time that students spend holding texts and looking at them. We chose the construct of eyes on text, recognizing the importance of engaged reading, defined by Guthrie, Schafer, and Huang (2001) as the "joint functioning of motivation, strategy use, and conceptual knowledge during reading" (p. 3). Engaged reading is the sort of reading associated with comprehension, fluency, and vocabulary achievement but is an inherently invisible process of constructing meaning. By observing students closely as they engaged in reading instruction, we were able to determine whether they appeared to engage with the texts. We believe this approach provides a more accurate picture of the volume of reading than measuring the amount of time the teacher provides for students to engage in reading practice, as has been the practice in the past (Adler & Fisher, 2001; Fisher et al., 1980). It is possible for the teacher to provide opportunity to read in small groups, for example but for the students to choose not to take advantage of that opportunity. This study focuses on individual students as they engage in reading behaviors with the texts available in their classrooms. In addition to the time students spent with their eyes focused on the text, we examined four aspects of that reading, including whether the reading was assisted or unassisted, the genre of the text, the source of the text and differences in the volume of reading based on reading achievement, that is, proficiency.

Assisted and Unassisted Reading

Unassisted reading occurs when students independently read text, whether this reading is silently or reading aloud with a partner. Assisted

reading occurs when students read chorally or follow along as someone reads aloud, either on a tape or in person. Theoretical and empirical substantiation exists for both assisted and unassisted reading. The
report of the National Reading Panel (NICHD, 2000) brought the role of
assisted reading to the fore, citing a slate of studies on repeated reading,
in particular, that showed an impact on reading fluency. Stahl and Kuhn
(2002) propose that assisted reading gives students access to more challenging text; provides models of fluent reading; and allows struggling
students, in particular, multiple exposures to difficult words that they
would not successfully deal with when reading alone. While assisted
reading may show some value, particularly for beginning readers in
primary grades, third graders should be afforded considerable opportunity to engage in unassisted reading. Unassisted reading is important for applying strategies and developing the habit of reading (Fisher,
2004). Students who are reading without assistance are responsible
for using all of the domains of reading to comprehend, while students
who are following along or repeating text may not be applying complex reading strategies such as making connections or reading ahead to
figure out unknown words. The time spent in both assisted and unassisted reading and the relative distribution of the two within an entire
reading period was of interest.

Genre of the Texts

A second interest of the project was the genre of the text being read.
Many have noted the prevalence of narrative text, particularly in the
primary grade classroom (Duke, 2000; Symons, MacLatchy-Gaudet,
Stone, & Reynolds, 2001). Duke and Bennett-Armistead (2003) argue
that students benefit from the inclusion of informational text in the
classroom because such texts pervade daily life (in newspapers, the
Internet, instructions, workplace reading, etc.), allow exploration of
interests, answer questions, increase knowledge of the world, and build
vocabulary. Cervetti, Hiebert, and Jaynes (Chapter 4, this volume) and
McRae and Guthrie (Chapter 3, this volume) argue for the motivational
and learning benefits that derive from frequent opportunities to read
science texts. Bernhardt (Chapter 9, this volume) makes a compelling argument for the importance of informational texts in the reading
opportunities of English-language learners who gain both vocabulary
and content-area knowledge that supports further reading as they read
informational text. For this study, we wanted to determine the degree

to which implementation of a core reading program curriculum gave students opportunities to read both narrative and informational texts.

Source of the Text

Whether a given text is from a basal anthology, a set of leveled texts, trade books, or digital sources was also of interest. Our interest in the source of the text lay primarily in documenting whether core reading programs provided the primary context of opportunities to read in Reading First classrooms. We divided the core program texts into the anthology and the accompanying leveled readers. The anthologies provide texts, generally reprints of children's literature, primarily intended for whole-class instruction. All of the series except *Reading Mastery* and *Success for All* used in classrooms also provide leveled readers, reprints of trade books, or specially written books intended to supplement the week's passage by providing below-grade-level, on-grade-level, and sometimes above-grade-level texts for additional reading practice and small-group instruction through differentiated instruction.

Except for *Reading Mastery*, the texts in the anthologies of the core programs consist largely of reprints of children's literature. Most units also include literature connections and lists of award-winning and other trade books. Teachers also frequently supplement the core program with additional trade book literature. Trade books are another source of texts that have been shown to improve achievement and motivation when part of classroom instruction by providing meaningful and engaging texts (Morrow, 1992). Gunning (2008) describes the need to supplement the core program with additional trade book literature in this way: "No matter how well the basal program has been put together, students need to read a broader range of fiction and nonfiction materials" (p. 394).

Another possible source of texts documented in this study is technology-based or multimedia texts, sometimes referred to as new literacies (Leu, 2006). Many core programs make at least some technology-based texts available such as CD-ROMs, and some recommend Internet research or other technology connections. However, multimedia texts are not yet a large component of core reading programs. In the 21st century, new literacies are an increasingly important source of texts for reading instruction, in part because of their rapidly increasing presence in our lives both at home and at work and in part because the comprehension and critical thinking strategies that these texts require are different from those of traditional print literacies (Leu, 2006). Street (2006) argues that a changing world calls for schools to respond with changes in literacy instruction that incorporate new literacies and that "these approaches to literacy and learning look somewhat different from those privileged in at least some policy circles, such as the 'No Child Left Behind' framework in the USA" (p. 36).

Reading Proficiency

Examining whether students with different reading proficiency levels are less or more engaged was also of interest. Grouping students by performance levels, while having the goal of focused instruction and texts of appropriate difficulty, can have the unintended effects on low-performing students of lower expectations, fewer opportunities to read, and a less engaging curriculum (Collins, 1986; Pallas, Entwisle, Alexander, & Stluka, 1994). Among the recommended practices implemented in Reading First has been greater differentiation in grouping during core program instruction. Most core programs make at least a few leveled texts available for small-group instruction based on performance. For this study, we examined whether there were differences in the volume of reading engaged in by students of different proficiency levels.

Procedures and Methods of the Project

Participants

In Mississippi, 65 schools from 32 districts (22% of all districts in the state) participated in Reading First. Approximately half (33 schools) made up Cohort 1, which began in Reading First in 2003 (i.e., the fourth year of implementation at the time of the study in 2007). The remaining schools (Cohort 2) joined Reading First in 2005 (i.e., the second year of implementation at the time of the study). Across the schools, 84% of the students were African Americans and 87% received free or reduced-price lunches.

For our sample, schools were randomly selected from each of the state's 32 Reading First districts. Within these 32 schools, the amount of time spent reading was examined in two third-grade classrooms. The sample was representative of the entire population of Reading First schools in terms of the core program implemented, the length of participation in Reading First, geographic location, and the length of the instructional time period. The number of students in the two groups was equivalent: 155 Cohort 1 students and 160 Cohort 2 students.

Observation Procedures

Literacy coaches in each school selected six students for observation, one male and one female from each of three achievement levels—at-risk, at-some-risk, and low-risk—that were established from the Oral Reading Fluency measure of the DIBELS (Good & Kaminski, 2002). When classrooms had fewer than 15 students or did not have students at the high end of the achievement spectrum, as was common in some of the most rural schools, literacy coaches identified students at any achievement level while also maintaining a balance between boys and girls. When students were absent or fewer than six students had been identified for observation in a classroom, the observer collected data on an additional student; however, due to confidentiality issues observers were not able to obtain achievement information for some students used as last-minute substitutions. Each student was observed twice, on two different days of the week. The final sample consisted of 751 cases (each case represents one day's observation), distributed in the following manner: low-risk, 208 cases; at-some-risk, 246 cases; and at-risk, 247 cases.

The observational measure was adapted from prior studies of reading instruction (Adler & Fisher, 2001) and recorded students' "Eyes on Text Events" (ETEs). ETEs are defined as occasions when students have their eyes on text. We recognize, however, that engaged reading-for-meaning is an inherently invisible process. Therefore, we specified ETEs to be those occasions when students had their eyes on connected text for more than 10 seconds out of a 20-second observation period.

A student was observed for the first 20 seconds of a 30-second block of time every 3 minutes, and the student's activities were coded, indicating whether a student was engaged in an ETE or another activity (e.g., writing, listening to the teacher giving directions, transitions). If the student was engaged in an ETE, the event was coded as assisted or unassisted. Unassisted reading was defined as any reading done without the extended assistance of another. Unassisted ETEs included reading aloud in pairs, small groups, or before the whole classroom as well as silent independent reading. Assisted ETEs included repeated reading and any time a child was following along as another (e.g., teacher, peer, voice on CD) was reading aloud.

For all ETEs, the genre and source of the reading material were coded. Sources of text included the basal, leveled texts, trade books, computer-based texts, and other sources. The genre of text could include narrative, expository, or other. Observers also wrote brief qualitative field notes on the teaching practices and the student activities they observed. These field notes were used to verify patterns in the quantitative data.

Members of the research team and literacy coordinators from the Mississippi Department of Education (MDE) who were responsible for technical assistance and professional development for the schools conducted the observations. Two training sessions were conducted with observers to ensure consistency in coding. Literacy coordinators observed in schools other than those for which they were responsible. In order to observe "typical" curriculum, observers gave schools a 2-week range of dates for observations but did not specify particular days they would observe. Each classroom was observed on two occasions, each time on a different day of the week. The classroom that was observed for the first half of the instructional period on the first day of observations was observed for the second half of the instructional period on the second observation, and vice versa. While most schools had chosen to allocate the minimum period of 90 minutes for their reading block, a few taught reading for 100, 105, and even 120 minutes per day.

Findings of the Project

Frequency measures were used to describe the number of ETEs and the types of text read. Because the data are nonparametric, the Kruskal–Wallis test was used to determine whether significant differences in the opportunity to read existed between students at different achievement levels. Quantitative data were substantiated with excerpts from the observers' field notes describing the instructional practices that were observed.

Time Spent Reading

The standard deviations in Table 6.1 give an indication of the range of time allocated to reading in different classrooms. While the average amount of time spent in ETEs (across both the first and second halves of instructional periods in classrooms with different-length reading blocks) was 9.18 minutes, the range was considerable: 0–42 minutes. Nearly one-fourth of the students observed (23.4% of cases) did not read at all during our observations.

On average, students spent 8.71 minutes in ETEs during the first half of instruction and 9.69 minutes during the second half of instruction. This difference was not significant $(z = -.726, p = .468)$. This finding

TABLE 6.1. Means (and Standard Deviations) for Minutes Spent with Eyes on Text

Length of instructional block	Classes (%)	Time with eyes on text	First half of instructional block	Second half of instructional block
90 minutes	81%	9.19 (8.49)	8.54 (7.80)	9.89 (9.14)
100 minutes	3%	8.13 (4.72)	7.50 (3.50)	8.75 (5.79)
105 minutes	10%	9.24 (9.97)	9.43 (8.19)	9.06 (11.55)
120 minutes	6%	9.63 (6.78)	10.50 (6.32)	8.75 (7.24)
All schools	100%	9.18 (8.44)	8.71 (7.65)	9.69 (9.18)

leads to the extrapolation that students spent, on average, 18.40 minutes with eyes on text during the 90- to 120-minute reading instructional period in third-grade Reading First classrooms.

We also considered whether the ETEs were extended events or occurred at discrete points in the reading block. In most classrooms, students changed activities frequently. They engaged in brief ETEs with different, often unrelated, texts for short periods of time across the instructional block. Only in the 2% of classrooms with more than 33 minutes of reading did students read the same text for a sustained period of time, typically partner reading a longer passage from the anthology. A typical instructional block is evident in a literacy coordinator's field notes describing a 2-day period in a classroom.

> First 45 minutes, Tuesday: Teacher-directed lesson to whole class begins with discussion of previous day's text. Teacher reads text selection aloud, pausing with questions about vocabulary words and introduction of new vocabulary. Students move to centers.

> Second 45 minutes, Wednesday: Students moved through centers: (a) vocabulary, which involved completing sentences with vocabulary; (b) spelling, which involved writing words on cards; (c) listening to leveled book on tape; (d) writing about insects and illustrating composition; and (e) teacher-led group where a short expository selection was read and important and unimportant details were identified. Last 10 minutes were spent as a whole class discussing vocabulary.

Assisted and Unassisted Reading

Half of ETEs were spent in assisted reading ($X = 4.59$ minutes, $SD = 6.47$) and the other half in unassisted reading ($X = 4.68$ minutes, $SD = $

6.37). On some days, students engaged primarily in assisted reading; on other days, students primarily read without assistance. On most days, however, students read both with and without assistance. The following field notes illustrate the teaching practices that led to approximately equivalent amounts of assisted and unassisted reading:

> Students were seated on the carpet, holding their basal readers. Teacher started the tape and students tracked print as they listened to the selection. Students then moved to five small groups. Groups rotated when the timer rang. Group 1 students completed comprehension questions about the story, read a short story, and answered questions on worksheets. Group 2 students wrote sentences using the vocabulary listed on the board. Group 3 students made charts that compared and contrasted spiders and tarantulas. Group 4 students took turns reading *Listen for the Rattle* (a leveled text). Group 5 students listened to *Tales of Oliver Pig* (an Easy Reader) on tape. Teacher circulated, checking students' work.

Genres of Texts

Narratives were the most common genre of text during ETEs, accounting for, on average, 70.9% of the time spent reading ($X = 6.51$, $SD = 7.47$). Expository text accounted for 24.0% of the ETEs ($X = 2.20$, $SD = 4.90$). During the other 5% of the time ETEs included poetry and other nonspecified genres of texts.

Sources of Texts

The most common source of texts was the core reading program, accounting for 53.1% of the ETEs ($X = 4.87$ minutes, $SD = 6.40$), followed by leveled texts (21.2%, $X = 1.95$, $SD = 4.61$) and trade books (9.6%, $X = .88$, $SD = 2.94$). Students rarely read texts presented in multimedia or computer formats ($X = .25$ minutes, $SD = 2.07$). The remaining ETEs (9.3%) were coded as "other texts," including teacher-made texts, peers' compositions, and texts on the overhead projector ($X = 0.85$ minutes, $SD = 2.71$).

Amount of Time Reading and Reading Achievement

Data in Table 6.2 indicate the amounts of ETEs for students of different achievement levels. The 0.61-minute difference in overall ETEs between high and low achievers was not statistically significant (chi-square = 3.30, $df = 2$, $p = .19$). Middle achievers read less than either of the other

TABLE 6.2. Means (and Standard Deviations) for Minutes in ETEs for High, Middle, and Low Achievers

Variables	High achievers	Middle achievers	Low achievers
Total ETEs	9.65 (8.036)	8.48 (7.95)	9.04 (8.73)
Assisted reading	4.55 (6.47)	4.45 (6.09)	5.36 (7.32)
Unassisted reading	5.10 (6.41)	4.15 (5.62)	3.83 (5.80)

two groups but not significantly so. Similarly, there were not significant differences in the amount of assisted or unassisted reading engaged in by high-, middle-, and low-achieving students (chi-square = 2.13, df = 2, p = .345). However, low-achieving students spent only 42.4% of time in ETEs engaging in unassisted reading, a statistically significant difference compared to the 52.8% of time that high-achieving students spent in unassisted reading (chi-square = 7.70, df = 2, p = .02).

Summary

Students in Reading First classrooms spent about 18 minutes of the 90–120 minutes of reading instruction with their eyes on texts. Students spent half of this time in assisted reading, typically following along as the text was read aloud, and the other half reading without assistance. Most of the reading was from narrative texts, with informational texts accounting for 25% of the ETEs. Students also primarily read from core program materials, including the basal and its accompanying leveled readers. Students read trade book texts less than 10% of the time and almost never read multimedia texts during reading instruction. There were not significant differences in the volume of reading engaged in by high-, medium-, and low-achieving students, though low-achieving students did spend about 10% more time in assisted reading than their higher-achieving classmates.

Conclusions and Implications

Third-grade students in a sample of classrooms participating in Mississippi's Reading First and where teachers used a core reading program spent an average of 18 minutes a day with their eyes on a text. While this volume of reading practice is less than the amounts found by Allington (2001) and Fisher and Ivey (2006), this amount was greater than the national average of 12 minutes a day reported by Donahue et al. (2001). Even so, nearly one-quarter of students did not read at all during the observed reading periods. Since our observations were confined to the reading/language arts blocks, it may well be that students spent additional time reading at other times during the school day such as during science or social studies instruction. However, students were actively engaged in reading less than 20% of the time designated specifically for increasing capacity in reading.

When they did read text, the third graders in this study read either the week's anthology selection or leveled readers from the core reading program. Core programs provide day-by-day routines for the weeklong treatment of a single text and a limited number of supplemental texts. The typical weekly pattern includes oral language activities and an introduction to the text on Monday, reading and rereading the weekly text on Tuesday through Thursday with related vocabulary and other activities, and assessing comprehension and skills on Friday. When this major pattern for instruction is used, it may not be surprising that students spend minimal time engaged in independent or unassisted reading. One text per week, even when accompanied by leveled readers, does not provide a substantial amount of text for students to read.

Less than 10% of total reading instructional time was allocated to unassisted reading. While the guides for the core reading programs included in-school independent reading, the Reading First teachers in this study had been advised that this activity was not supported in the NRP report and, consequently, should not take place during the reading/language arts block. The NRP's report (NICHD, 2000) concluded that the studies in their review did not show that independent silent reading with minimal guidance and feedback led to gains in reading achievement. While the NRP report did not support unstructured independent reading such as Drop Everything and Read Time, all unassisted reading is not unstructured reading. Unassisted reading can have substantially more scaffolds than typical sustained silent reading practices (Reutzel, Fawson, & Smith, 2005), including feedback and monitoring and text that is matched to students' reading proficiency. Within models of reading development such as Chall's (1983) stages, third graders should be spending increasing amounts of time in contexts that require them to apply decoding, vocabulary, and comprehension knowledge.

The reliance on assisted reading can, at least in part, be attributed to the practice of utilizing a common text for reading instruction. Since students must be familiar with the text to carry out the subsequent skill instruction and complete the workbook pages in the core reading program, the teacher may find that the most expedient method is whole-class assisted reading either through teacher read-aloud, a taped version of the text, or round-robin reading of the text. In such instances, unassisted reading loses out to the most convenient method.

Students primarily read narrative texts. Although the ratio of informational texts in reading programs is reportedly on the rise, narratives still make up the vast majority of texts available for reading instruction in most core programs (Yopp & Yopp. 2006). While some multimedia texts were made available or suggested in the materials for each program, teachers did not select these resources. Basals have been criticized for not doing enough to build content-area domain knowledge, knowledge of informational text structures, and content-area vocabulary (Walsh, 2003). Our data suggest that concerns about exposure to and time spent reading informational and digital texts have not been alleviated by the implementation of the Reading First initiative or by spending extended time on core reading program instruction.

Observations indicated that low-performing students spent about the same amount of time with their eyes on the page as their high- and middle-performing classmates. Low performers did not have fewer opportunities to read, as has previously been reported (Pallas et al., 1994). While this pattern was noteworthy, students of all proficiency levels read the same texts even when they were divided into performance-based groups. Although Reading First professional development encourages teachers to differentiate instruction by providing targeted instruction with accessible texts, typically the same test preparation materials or leveled readers were used for all three groups even during small-group instruction. Because all of the students in the classroom spent the bulk of their reading time reading the same passage, usually the anthology selection for the week, it is possible that many students were reading texts that did not match up with their reading abilities.

Hiebert and Martin (Chapter 1, this volume) describe the need for attending to text difficulty and students' proficiencies as part of an elaborate and thoughtful framework for enhanced opportunities to read. While texts may be appropriate in current core reading programs for students who are at proficient and advanced reading levels, a mismatch exists between texts in core reading programs and the capabilities of students who are at basic and below-basic reading levels (Hiebert, 2009). Hiebert and Martin identify the "one-size-fits-all" perspective within core reading programs as a particular obstacle for providing beginning and struggling readers with the appropriate texts and tasks that increase their reading proficiency. Within current core reading programs, the assumption is that, if fourth graders benefit from extended discussions, so will first graders. If first graders benefit from significant amounts of assisted reading, so will third graders, and so on. The lesson plans in teachers' guides have not been refined to accommodate differences in students' proficiencies. In this study, low-performing students did spend 10% more time in assisted reading than their higher-performing classmates, which provided them a scaffold for reading the challenging text of the anthology. However, these lower-performing students did not have comparable opportunities with text that allowed them to apply strategies and skills with accessible text in unassisted settings.

Most teachers' guides offer additional activities that involve reading on the Internet or using reference tools, and often they recommend related trade book texts to supplement the weekly anthology text. With the extended reading period mandated by Reading First, it would be hoped that sufficient time would be available for teachers to assign at least some of these activities and thereby boost opportunities to read. Many of these potentially reading-rich activities are offered as learning-center or small-group activities. Since the learning-center or small-group activities are not described in the two-page grid that summarizes the weekly instructional plan, these activities are lost among the numerous pages of the teachers' guide.

Teachers are typically not given guidelines for evaluating whether activities in core reading programs involve their students in high-quality reading. The contexts of a top-down mandate such as Reading First can make such adaptations difficult (MacGillivray, Ardell, Curwen, & Palma, 2004). Teachers may be hesitant to select from the more amorphous activities such as Internet research and related reading of a suggested novel or trade book when these activities do not "look like" core program instruction. A small number of teachers in the study adapted the teacher's manual in ways that supported increased opportunities to read. We currently are investigating criteria for differentiating between reading-rich and reading-poor activities within the core reading programs (Brenner, Hiebert, Tompkins, & Riley, 2007).

Reading First has worked to increase instruction based on SBRR in K–3 classrooms largely through an emphasis on core reading program instruction. This study shows that reforms predicated on the belief that the performance of struggling readers will be improved by fuller implementation of a core reading program may be overly optimistic. The literature promoting core reading programs touts their effectiveness and fundamental importance to scientifically based reading research. Reading researchers should address the research underlying recommendations in core reading programs and substantiate whether students can attain the levels of reading proficiency promised by core program publishers if their programs are implemented as designed, and they should provide objective evaluations of the relative merits of core programs. Teachers should be helped by researchers in whatever ways are possible to better implement the many resources the core program provides.

References

Allington, R. (2001). *What really matters for struggling readers*. New York: Addison-Wesley.

Anderson, R. C., Hiebert, E. H., Scott, J. A., & Wilkinson, I. A. G. (1985). *Becoming a nation of readers: The report of the Commission on Reading*. Washington, DC: National Institute of Education/National Academy of Education.

Austin, M., & Morrison, C. (1963). *The first R: The Harvard report on reading in elementary schools*. New York: Macmillan.

Baker, S. K., Simmons, D. C., & Kame'enui, E. J. (n.d.). *Vocabulary acquisition: Synthesis of the research*. Document prepared by the National Center to Improve the Tools of Educators. Retrieved on February 3, 2006, from *idea. uoregon.edu/~ncite/documents/teechrep*.

Baumann, J. F., Hoffman, J. V., Duffy-Hester, A. M., & Ro, J. M. (2000). *The First R* yesterday and today: U.S. elementary reading instruction practices reported by teachers and administrators. *Reading Research Quarterly, 35*(3), 338–377.

Block, C. C., Cleveland, M. D., & Reed, K. M. (2006). Using books to raise student achievement: 2nd, 3rd, 4th, and 6th grade study 2003–2004. In *Scholastic classroom: Books compendium of research* (pp. 18–36). New York: Scholastic.

Brenner, D., Hiebert, E. H., Tompkins, R., & Riley, M. (2007, November). *If I follow the teacher's manual, isn't that enough?: Analyzing opportunity to read afforded by three core programs*. Paper presented at the annual meeting of the National Reading Conference, Austin, TX.

Chall, J. S. (1983). *Stages of reading development*. New York: McGraw-Hill.

Collins, J. (1986). Differential instruction in reading groups. In J. Cook-Gumperz (Ed.), *The social construction of literacy* (pp. 117–137). New York: Cambridge University Press.

Cooper, J. D., Pikulski, J. J., Ackerman, P. A., Au, K. H., Chard, D. J., Garcia, G. G., et al. (2004). *Houghton Mifflin reading: Mississippi teacher's edition: Grade 3, theme 3* (pp. 290A–315R). Boston: Houghton Mifflin.

Critchley, M. P. (1998). Reading to learn: Pedagogical implications of vocabulary research. *The Language Teacher, 22*(9), 10–13.

Cunningham, A. E., & Stanovich, K. E. (1998). What reading does for the mind. *American Educator, 22*(1–2), 1–8.

Dole, J. A., & Osborn, J. (1991). The selection and use of language arts textbooks.

In J. Flood, J. M. Jensen, D. Lapp, & J. R. Squire (Eds.), *Handbook of research on teaching the English/language arts* (pp. 521–528). New York: Macmillan.

Donahue, P., Finnegan, R. J., Lutkus, A. D., Allen, N. L., & Campbell, J. R. (2001). *The nation's report card: Fourth-grade reading 2000.* Washington, DC: U.S. Department of Education, Institute of Education Sciences.

Duke, N. K. (2000). 3.6 minutes per day: The scarcity of informational texts in first grade. *Reading Research Quarterly, 35,* 202–224.

Duke, N. K., & Bennett-Armistead, S. (2003). *Reading and writing informational texts in the primary grades.* New York: Scholastic.

Fisher, C. W., Berliner, D. C., Filby, N. N., Marliave, R., Cahen, L. S., & Dishaw, M. M. (1980). Teaching behaviors, academic learning time, and student achievement: An overview. In C. Denham & A. Lieberman (Eds.), *Time to learn* (pp. 7–32). Washington, DC: U.S. Department of Education.

Fisher, D. (2004). Setting the "opportunity to read" standard: Resuscitating the SSR program in an urban high school. *Journal of Adolescent and Adult Literacy, 48,* 138–151.

Fisher, D., & Ivey, G. (2006). Evaluating the interventions for struggling adolescent readers. *Journal of Adolescent and Adult Literacy, 50(3),* 180–189.

Foertsch, M. A. (1992). *Reading in and out of school: Achievement of American students in grades 4, 8, and 12 in 1989–1990.* Washington, DC: National Center for Educational Statistics: U.S. Government Printing Office.

Gambrell, L. (1984). How much time do children spend reading during teacher-directed reading instruction? In J. A. Niles & L. A. Harris (Eds.), *Changing perspectives on research in reading/language processing and instruction.* Third yearbook of the National Reading Conference (pp. 193–198). Rochester, NY: National Reading Conference.

Good, R. H., & Kaminski, R. A. (Eds.). (2002). *Dynamic indicators of basic early literacy skills* (6th ed.). Eugene, OR: Institute for the Development of Educational Achievement.

Gunning, T. G. (2008). *Creating literacy instruction for all students in grades 4–8* (2nd ed.). Boston: Pearson Education.

Guthrie, J. T., Schafer, W. D., & Huang, C. (2001). Benefits of opportunity to read and balanced instruction on the NAEP. *Journal of Educational Research, 94,* 145–162.

Hayes, D. P., Wolfer, L. T., & Wolfe, M. F. (1996). Schoolbook simplification and its relation to the decline in SAT-verbal scores. *American Educational Research Journal, 33,* 489–508.

Hiebert, E. H. (2009). The (mis)match between texts and students who depend on schools to become literate. In E. H. Hiebert & M. Sailors (Eds.), *Finding the right texts: What works for beginning and struggling readers: Research-based solutions* (pp. 1–20). New York: Guilford Press.

Jackson, P. W. (1968). *Life in classrooms.* New York: Holt, Rinehart & Winston.

Krashen, S. (1993). *The power of reading: Insights from the research.* Englewood, CO: Libraries Unlimited.

Kuhn, M. R., Schwanenflugel, P. J., Morris, R. D., Morrow, L. M., Woo, D., Meisinger, B., et al. (in memoriam). (2006). Teaching children to become fluent and automatic readers. *Journal of Literacy Research, 38,* 357–387.

LaBerge, D., & Samuels, S. J. (1974). Toward a theory of automatic information processing in reading. *Cognitive Psychology, 6*, 293–323.

Leu, D. J. (2006). New literacies, reading research, and the challenge of change: A deictic perspective. In J. V. Hoffman, D. L. Schallert, C. M. Fairbanks, J. Worthy, & B. Maloch (Eds.), *55th yearbook of the National Reading Conference* (pp. 1–20). Oak Creek, WI: National Reading Conference.

MacGillivray, L., Ardell, A. L., Curwen, M. S., & Palma, J. (2004). Colonized teachers: Examining the implementation of a scripted reading program. *Teaching Education, 15*(2), 131–144.

Matthews, M. M. (1966). *Teaching to read, historically considered.* Chicago: University of Chicago Press.

McGill-Franzen, A., Zmach, C., Solic, K., & Zeig, J. L. (2006). The confluence of two policy mandates: Core reading programs and third-grade retention in Florida. *Elementary School Journal, 107*, 67–92.

MGT of America, Inc. (2006). *Evaluation of the Mississippi Reading First Program: Year three evaluation report 2005–2006.* Tallahassee, FL: Author.

Morrow, L. M. (1992). The impact of a literature-based program on literacy achievement, use of literature, and attitudes of children from minority backgrounds. *Reading Research Quarterly, 27*(3), 251–275.

National Institute of Child Health and Human Development. (2000). *Report of the National Reading Panel. Teaching children to read: An evidence-based assessment of the scientific research literature on reading and its implications for reading instruction* (NIH Publication No. 00-4769). Washington, DC: U.S. Government Printing Office.

National Research Council. (2002). *Scientific research in education.* Washington, DC: National Academy Press.

Pallas, A. M., Entwisle, D. R., Alexander, K. L., & Stluka, M. F. (1994). Ability-group effects: Instructional, social, or institutional? *Sociology of Education, 67*, 27–46.

Reutzel, D. R., Fawson, P.C., & Smith, J. A. (2005, May 1). *Reconsidering silent sustained reading (SSR): An exploratory study of scaffolded silent reading.* Paper presented at the annual meeting of the International Reading Association, San Antonio, TX.

Simmons, D. C., & Kame'enui, E. J. (2003, March). *A consumer's guide to evaluating a core reading program grades K–3: A critical elements analysis.* Eugene, OR: Institute for the Development of Educational Achievement, University of Oregon.

Stahl, S. A. (2004). What do we know about fluency?: Findings of the National Reading Panel. In P. McCardle & V. Chabra (Eds.), *The voice of evidence in reading research* (pp. 187–211). Baltimore: Brookes.

Stahl, S. A., & Kuhn, M. R. (2002). Making it sound like language: Developing fluency. *The Reading Teacher, 55*, 582–584.

Street, B. (2006). New literacies, new times: How do we describe and teach the forms of literacy knowledge, skills, and values people need for new times? In J. V. Hoffman, D. L. Schallert, C. M. Fairbanks, J. Worthy, & B. Maloch (Eds.), *55th yearbook of the National Reading Conference* (pp. 1–20). Oak Creek, WI: National Reading Conference.

Symons, S., MacLatchy-Gaudet, H., Stone, T. D., & Reynolds, P. I. (2001). Strategy instruction for elementary students searching informational text. *Scientific Studies of Reading, 5*(1), 1–33.

U.S. Department of Education. (2003). *Reading First.* Retrieved April 13, 2007, from *www.ed.gov/programs/readingfirst/index.html.*

U.S. Government Accountability Office. (2007). *Reading first: States report improvements in reading instruction, but additional procedures would clarify education's role in ensuring proper implementation by states* (U.S. Government Accounting Office Report GAO-07-161). Washington, DC: Author.

Walsh, K. (2003). Basal readers: The lost opportunity to build the knowledge that propels comprehension. *American Educator, 27*(1), 24–25.

Yopp, R. H., & Yopp, H. K. (2006). Informational texts as read-alouds at school and home. *Journal of Literacy Research, 38*(1), 37–51.

7

TIME, ENGAGEMENT, AND SUPPORT

Lessons from a 4-Year Fluency Intervention

MELANIE R. KUHN
PAULA J. SCHWANENFLUGEL

Fluency is often seen as a bridge between decoding and comprehension (Pikulski & Chard, 2005), one that enables students to become accurate, automatic, and expressive readers. However, this transition is a complex one and involves a range of developmental processes (Kuhn et al., 2006). Our chapter discusses these complexities through the lens of our multiyear, Interagency Education Research Initiative/ National Institute of Child Health and Human Development (IERI/ NICHD) intervention on fluency development, focusing on three components that we feel are critical to student growth: the amount of time students spent reading, their level of engagement with challenging material, and the support these students received in reading such texts. We consider each of these to be essential to fluency development, in particular, and skilled reading, in general, and believe that the structure of our lesson plans provide students with access to all three of these factors.

Fluency Defined and Described

There is a growing consensus that fluent reading is made up of three primary components: accuracy, automaticity, and appropriate prosody (e.g., National Institute of Child Health and Human Development [NICHD], 2000). In other words, fluent readers are able to identify the vast majority of the words they encounter both quickly and correctly and are able to read aloud using appropriate pacing, phrasing, and expression. We feel it is important to stress all three components for two reasons. First, there appears to be an overemphasis on fast, accurate reading in some classrooms at present, perhaps driven by the use of correct words per minute as the primary or only measure of fluent reading (e.g., Mathson, Allington, & Solic, 2006; Walker, Mokhtari, & Sargent, 2006). To prevent students from developing the mistaken notion that reading is a race, it is critical that their understanding of reading fluency incorporate prosody so that, when they read aloud, their reading sounds like oral language.

Our second reason for emphasizing accuracy, automaticity, and prosody has to do with their relationship to comprehension (Samuels, 2006). When students are beginning to develop their word recognition, they need to spend significant amounts of time—and attention—identifying each word they encounter in a text. Because these learners are expending so much attention on their decoding, they have little left over to focus on the text's meaning. However, as they develop their familiarity with words, both through decoding instruction in isolation and through extensive practice in reading connected text, their word recognition becomes automatic. As a result, the attention that they previously expended on word recognition is now available for the construction of meaning (Schwanenflugel et al., 2006). Since fluent readers are, by definition, not only accurate but also automatic readers, they are better able to comprehend text than are disfluent readers.

Next, fluent readers are also prosodic readers. Students who are just learning to read are monotonous in their oral reading and tend to group words in ways that diverge from oral language, often in word-by-word or two-word phrases. However, as their reading develops, they learn to read aloud with appropriate phrasing and expression, an indication that they are able to transfer elements present in oral language to print (Dowhower, 1991; Schreiber, 1991). Further, this denotes a level of comprehension regarding their reading, since the use of stress, pitch, and other prosodic elements helps to indicate nuances in the text (Miller & Schwanenflugel, 2006). Although there is a distinct relationship between prosody and comprehension, exactly how the two are related to each other is still unclear—that is, does prosody contribute to comprehension, does comprehension need to occur before prosodic elements can be applied, or is the relationship between the two reciprocal (Erekson, 2003; Miller, 2007; Schwanenflugel, Hamilton, Kuhn, Wisenbaker, & Stahl, 2004)? Despite the need for further research in this area, what is clear is that prosody is an important element in text enjoyment and an essential part of fluency development.

Fluency Involves Practice

When discussing fluency, one element that is considered critical to its development, both in terms of theory (e.g., LaBerge & Samuels, 1974) and in terms of instruction (e.g., Rasinski, 2003), is that of practice. However, the type of practice that learners participate in determines to a large extent whether or not they become fluent readers. First, while word work (decoding, high frequency word instruction) is a necessary component in your students' fluency development, it is not sufficient (e.g., Allington, 1983; Chomsky, 1976; Levy, Abello, & Lysynchuk, 1997). In fact, learners who spend the bulk of their time practicing word identification in isolation without simultaneously practicing their reading of connected text become very skilled at word recognition in isolation; however, this does not necessarily transfer to their reading of connected text. To be skilled at both word and text reading, students must have opportunities to apply what they are learning about words to the reading of connected text. This allows developing readers access to the kinds of material, such as novels, magazines, newspapers, textbooks, and electronic text, that they will eventually want or need to read.

Next, simply asking students who are not yet fluent to read, for example, during independent reading time, often fails to provide them with sufficient support to make this practice effective. Beginning readers tend to select books that are too difficult for them (Donovan, Smolkin, & Lomax, 2000), and struggling readers try to avoid the task altogether (e.g., Hasbrouck, 2006). Although students who are experiencing success with their reading development usually enjoy the opportunity to read for extended periods of time, students who are experiencing difficulties with their reading, including disfluent readers, do not. This can also result in behavioral issues that, in turn, prevent these learners from making the best use of their independent reading time (Bryan, Fawson, & Reutzel, 2003; Lee-Daniels & Murray, 2000). Being unable to engage effectively during independent reading simply makes it too boring and frustrating to take part in day after day. We suggest that, instead of simply asking your students to read on their own for 10- to 20-minute periods and expecting all of them to be engaged, it may be more effective to provide them with options such as partner reading, reading-while-listening, or mumble reading—all of which include greater support—as a means of increasing their ability to make their practice successful. And, by providing all your students rather than just the disfluent ones with these options, you will be increasing the likelihood that your learners will find these alternatives enjoyable rather than embarrassing.

Instructional Features That Foster Fluency

A recent review of the research on fluency instruction (Kuhn & Stahl, 2003) indicated that when sufficient support, or scaffolding, is provided, learners can benefit from reading texts that are far more challenging than their instructional level might indicate. As the result of these findings, challenging material has served as the basis for both our interventions. In fact, one of our research questions was designed to determine whether children who were reading below grade level—sometimes significantly below grade level—could become fluent readers using grade-level material if they were provided with sufficient support. This same review of research also indicated that, given sufficient scaffolding, learners might benefit from the reading of a number of different texts as much as if they were to read a single text repeatedly. Therefore, a second research question for our study involved looking at the relative effectiveness of the repeated reading of a given text and the reading of a greater number of texts for equivalent amounts of time; specifically, we wanted to know whether there was something unique in the repetition of text, a key component in most fluency instruction, that led to the development of automaticity or whether the provision of opportunities to read multiple scaffolded texts led to similar gains in reading development. Before presenting the results achieved over the course of the 4-year intervention, we want to discuss each of the approaches individually.

Fluency-Oriented Reading Instruction

The first instructional approach, Fluency-Oriented Reading Instruction (FORI; Stahl & Heubach, 2005), was designed in response to a district mandate that required students to work exclusively with grade-level text. Since the district in question had high rates of poverty, many of the students within its jurisdiction were reading below grade level. As a result, both the teachers in the district and the authors of the program were concerned about the discrepancy between students' reading ability and the required texts. In order to alleviate some of the difficulties that might arise from the use of these texts and provide the students with means of accessing them, the authors worked with the teachers to design an approach that integrates scaffolding, repetition, and the gradual release of responsibility as part of a 5-day lesson plan (see Figure 7.1). Since the district used a basal reader/literature anthology, the teachers in the initial study built their lessons around these selections; however, any grade-level text could be used.

On the first day, the teacher introduces the text using typical pre-teaching activities (e.g., vocabulary development, building background knowledge, etc.). This is followed by his or her reading of the week's selection to the class while the students follow along in their own copy

Fluency approach	Monday	Tuesday	Wednesday	Thursday	Friday
Fluency-Oriented Reading Instruction Basal lesson	**Teacher introduces story.** Teacher reads story to class; class discusses story. *Option*: Teacher develops graphic organizers. *Option*: Class does activities from basal story.	**Students practice story.** Teacher and students echo read story.	**Students practice story.** Teacher and students choral read story.	**Students practice story.** Students partner read story.	**Students do extension activities.** These may include writing in response to story, etc. *Option*: Teacher does running records of students' reading.
Home reading	Students read 15–30 minutes in a book of their choosing.	Students take story home and practice reading basal story aloud to someone.	Students who need more practice take home the basal story—others take book of their choosing.	Students who need more practice take home the basal story—others take book of their choosing.	Students read 15–30 minutes in a book of their choosing.

FIGURE 7.1. Weekly lesson plan for the FORI approach.

of the material. Upon completion of the first reading, the teacher and students take part in a discussion of the material; the discussion is designed to take place early in the lesson to reinforce the understanding that comprehension rather than word recognition per se is the primary goal of reading (Hoffman & Crone, 1985). On day 2, the teacher and students echo read the passage, with the teacher interspersing questions throughout the selection to refine the students' comprehension (e.g., Stahl, 2007).

The third day involves the final teacher-led rendition of the text and takes the form of a choral reading. While it is reasonable to incorporate additional discussion at this point, the lesson plans do not call for it. Day 4 requires the students to take primary responsibility for the text by partner reading the week's selection. Should time permit, the students can complete a second reading of the text, with the students reading the pages opposite to those they read originally. On the final day, the teacher and students participate in their traditional extension activities (e.g., writing in response to the reading, imagining an alternative ending, etc.). From day 2 onward, students are also asked to read the week's selection at home. As individual students become comfortable with the material, they can choose to read a different text as an alternative; however, students who are still not fluent with the week's selection should continue to read it on Wednesday and Thursday nights as well. During the original 2 years of the intervention, the students participating in the FORI classroom demonstrated 1.8 and 1.7 years' growth, respectively, on an Informal Reading Inventory (IRI). Given these results and the relative simplicity of the approach, we concluded that this would be a useful approach to integrate into our study.

Wide Reading

The original wide reading study was designed to look at the relative effectiveness of repeated reading and wide reading over the same period of time (Kuhn, 2005, 2009). Four groups took part in this intervention: a repeated readings group Fluency-Oriented Oral Reading (FOOR), that read a single text three times over the course of a week; the Wide Fluency-Oriented Oral Reading (Wide FOOR) that read three different texts over the course of a week; a listening-only group whose members listened to three different texts over the course of a week; and a control group that received no additional literacy instruction beyond that which was occurring in the classroom. Each of the first three groups worked with the study's author for 15–20 minutes per session. On Monday, the repeated readings group echo read a text; on Wednesday they partner read the story; and on Friday they choral read the story and, if they chose to, read a portion of the practiced text out loud. The wide reading group, on the other hand, echo or choral read a new text on all 3 days, while the listening-only group listened to the same selections that their peers in the wide reading group read for themselves.

While both of the groups who read the texts as part of the intervention demonstrated better growth in their reading proficiency than either the listening-only or the control groups, the results were not identical. On the measures of word recognition in isolation, prosody, and correct words per minute, both the FOOR and the Wide FOOR groups made similar gains; however, the Wide FOOR group showed greater growth in comprehension than any of the other groups, indicating that the Wide FOOR approach may be the more beneficial of the two. Since there were indications that wide reading might assist learners' reading development as much as (Kuhn & Stahl, 2003), if not more than (Kuhn, 2005), repeated reading, we wanted to use a wide reading approach as part of the intervention as well; but we needed to rework this intervention into a lesson plan that could be implemented on a weekly basis (see Figure 7.2). The modified FORI approach incorporated three grade-level texts, including the class's primary shared text—whether this was a selection from the basal anthology, the literature anthology, or a trade book— over the course of each week. The two additional texts were class sets of grade-level trade books provided by the researchers.

The first 2 days of the Wide FORI approach were designed to parallel the FORI lesson plan. On Monday, the teacher would conduct his or her usual introductory activities as a way of familiarizing students with the material; the teacher would then read the selection to the students while they followed along. This was followed by a discussion of what had been read. On Tuesday, the teacher and students would echo read the text, with the teacher interspersing comprehension questions throughout the material. On Wednesday, the two lessons diverged. Rather than continuing to reread the selection, the students in the Wide FORI approach instead worked on the extension activities for their primary text (paralleling day 5 of the FORI lesson). Finally, on Thursday and Friday, days 4 and 5 of the Wide FORI approach, the teacher would echo read a second and a third text with the students. The teacher was also encouraged to briefly introduce the text, intersperse questions during the echo reading, and hold a discussion with students after the reading of the selection was completed. All of the texts were also sent home for additional reading practice; the primary selection was sent

Fluency approach	Monday	Tuesday	Wednesday	Thursday	Friday
Wide FORI	**Teacher introduces story.** Teacher reads story to class; class discusses story. *Option*: Teacher develops graphic organizers. *Option*: Class does activities from basal (story 1).	**Students practice story.** Teacher and student echo read story 1. *Option*: Students do partner reading.	**Students do extension activities.** These may include writing in response to story, etc. *Option*: Teacher does running records of students' reading.	**Teacher and students echo or choral read trade book (story 2).** *Option*: Students partner read story 2. *Option*: Students do extension activities (writing, etc.).	**Teacher and students echo or choral read trade book (story 3).** *Option*: Students partner read story 3. *Option*: Students do extension activities (writing, etc.).
Home reading	Students read 15–30 minutes per day in a book of their choosing.	Students take story home and practice reading basal story aloud to someone.	Students read 15–30 minutes per day in a book of their choosing.	Students read 15–30 minutes per day in a book of their choosing.	Students read 15–30 minutes per day in a book of their choosing.

FIGURE 7.2. Weekly lesson plan for Wide FORI approach.

home on Tuesday and, possibly, Wednesday for those students who were still not fluent with the piece; the second and third texts, on the other hand, were sent home with the students only on the days they were read (Thursday and Friday, respectively). These modifications allow any teacher using this approach to cover the material required by a district while simultaneously extending students' opportunities to read two additional texts each week.

Nonintervention Classrooms

Before moving on to our results, we briefly outline the range of reading and language arts instruction that the teachers were using in the nonintervention classrooms. There were a number of different literacy activities going on in all of the classrooms, none of which dominated in any single class, including reading workshop, guided reading, writing workshop, round-robin reading, shared reading, and a variety of literacy centers. While some of these approaches are considered to be more effective instructionally than others (e.g., Ash & Kuhn, 2006), we found these activities to be typical of the range of approaches used in the literacy curricula we have encountered over each of our 20-plus years of teaching and conducting research.

What Happened over the Course of the Intervention?

There were several important findings from this study, some of which we determined through assessment measures and others that we ascertained through the use of a version of the CIERA school change classroom observation scheme (Taylor & Pearson, 2000) that was modified to include the fluency practices we presented as part of our intervention's professional development. However, because of the variations that occurred over the course of the intervention, we believe that these results need to be presented on a year-by-year basis.

Years 1 and 2

Our initial data, based on our classroom observations, determined that there was an increase in what we consider to be our core fluency activities in the FORI and Wide FORI classrooms during the first 2 years of the intervention. That is, there was greater emphasis on teacher read-alouds, repeated readings, echo reading, choral reading, and partner reading in the intervention classrooms than in the nonintervention classrooms. In terms of other forms of reading instruction, we found that the teachers in the nonintervention classrooms spent more time on word work and round-robin reading than did their peers in the intervention classrooms. Finally, there was greater emphasis on reading, particularly oral reading, and less emphasis on language arts activities in the intervention classrooms than in the nonintervention classrooms.

The year 1 findings (see Kuhn et al., 2006) indicated that the intervention teachers willingly shifted to more fluency-oriented instructional practices as compared with control teachers and engaged in fewer of the less effective practices such as round-robin reading. As a result, students in both types of intervention classrooms enjoyed better word reading efficiency and comprehension skills than their counterparts in the nonintervention classrooms. However, students in the Wide FORI intervention also demonstrated greater text reading fluency than those in control classrooms (see Table 7.1).

TABLE 7.1. Results for Year 1 Students (2001–2002), Using Test Standard Scores

Assessment point	Condition	TOWRE	GORT-3	WIAT
End of year	Control	98	8.8	99
	FORI	102[a]	9.1	101[a]
	Wide FORI	101[a]	9.3[a]	102

Note. TOWRE, Test of Word Reading Efficiency; GORT-3, Gray Oral Reading Test—Third Edition; WIAT, Wechsler Individual Achievement Test, Reading Comprehension Subtest.

[a]Indicates significant controls at time point, adjusting for preintervention pretest scores, using HLM.

In the second year, we replicated this study but broadened our focus somewhat. We were concerned about long-term consequences and possible "unintended effects" of the interventions. An honest evaluation of any program or, in our case, set of programs should take into account all types of changes that the programs might bring—the good, the bad, and the ugly.

We looked for effects on reading *soft skills*, such as changes in reading motivation and children's general attentiveness during reading lessons. We had been told in informal conversations with our first-year intervention teachers that their students were more motivated to read as compared with approaches these teachers had used previously. If their perceptions were accurate, this endorsement would be an excellent unintended consequence! Thus, in this second year, we evaluated this possibility by expanding our assessments to include the Motivation to Read profile (Gambrell, Palmer, Codling, & Mazzoni, 1996). This scale has two subscales, Value of Reading and Self-Concept as a Reader. Value of Reading assesses how important the respondent believes reading is, how frequently he or she likes to engage in reading-related activity, and generally how useful the respondent believes reading will be in his or her life. Self-Concept as a Reader, on the other hand, measures the respondent's personal assessment of his or her competence in performing reading tasks and his or her view of reading as either easy or difficult.

We also evaluated the student's time on task more closely. Teachers at some of the sites expressed the concern that there was a bit of "social loafing" going on during some of these reading lessons—that is, slacking off during choral reading and echo reading or perhaps kidding around during partner reading. If true, this would be a negative unintended consequence.

Finally, we worried that the emphasis on fluency might detract from other important types of instruction, particularly comprehension instruction. After all, there are only so many minutes in the reading day! We worried that the increase in fluency-oriented instruction came at the expense of this important type of instruction. Consequently, we evaluated whether there was less comprehension instruction happening in our intervention classrooms.

The good news was that, like the first year, teachers were willing to include more fluency-oriented practices in their classrooms, *but their emphasis on comprehension was similar* to that experienced in control classrooms. Fluency practice was not added at the expense of an emphasis on comprehension. On the downside, our classroom observations indicated that some students were, indeed, more likely to be off-task during the reading lessons in the second year. However, in all fairness, some of the classrooms in which these interventions took place did not have the best classroom management techniques to begin with.

Further, by the end of the year, reading fluency had increased over controls, but only for the students in Wide FORI classrooms, despite early gains by the FORI group. There were no other detectable differences between controls and intervention students on reading skills per se. Moreover, students in Wide FORI classrooms rated themselves as having a more positive self-concept as a reader as compared to students in control classrooms, although both groups valued reading similarly (which is close to ceiling at this age).

One year later, fluency was similar for all three groups, but students in both the FORI and Wide FORI groups demonstrated better reading comprehension skills (see Table 7.2). Thus, whatever resource benefits that early fluency had provided intervention children resulted in improved comprehension a year later.

Year 3 (Scaling Up)

Our final year of interventions brought major changes to the implementation of the fluency intervention. Our mandate was to scale up one of these approaches to a large number of classrooms—in our case, it was nearly 60 classrooms. We decided to focus exclusively on the FORI approach because, since it required fewer resources, it was the more practicable alternative; we considered this to be a reasonable decision, given the lack of resources faced by many schools. After 2 years of assisting teachers in providing materials for both approaches, we were well aware that the Wide FORI approach was expensive, perhaps too expensive for resource-strapped low-income schools. A quick calcula-

TABLE 7.2. Results for Year 2 Students (2002–2003), Using Test Standard Scores

Assessment point	Condition	TOWRE	GORT-3	WIAT
End of intervention year	Control	199	8.7	101
	FORI	200	9.0	101
	Wide FORI	203	9.3[a]	103
1 year later	Control	100	8.8	96
	FORI	102	9.2	98[a]
	Wide FORI	102	9.4	99[a]

Note. TOWRE, Test of Word Reading Efficiency; GORT-3, Gray Oral Reading Test—Third Edition; WIAT, Wechsler Individual Achievement Test, Reading Comprehension Subtest.

[a]Indicates significant increase over controls at time point, adjusting for pretest scores, using one-tailed HLM test.

tion, for example, suggests that, for the typical 35-week school year, 105 separate class sets of grade-level texts would have to be bought or found to carry out Wide FORI effectively. Although we do not think this is an insurmountable number, even for low-income schools, we do think that it requires considerable imagination for large-scale implementation (although we present some possibilities later in this chapter).

It also appeared that the Wide FORI approach requires greater professional development and support with regard to finding grade-level texts than the FORI approach. Thus, while the FORI approach could be carried out with the basal materials provided by one's school system and with virtually no time spent in identifying appropriate texts, the Wide FORI approach would require time, energy, and expertise for finding enough grade-level classroom sets to provide wide reading practice for the whole year. Up to this point, significant amounts of professional development support had been provided by us through trained assistants who visited the schools often *and* through meetings that were scheduled between the researchers, faculty, and students' families. In the final year, however, we included only a standard professional development training session and one follow-up meeting with each teacher after we carried out a formative classroom observation. This was more typical of, or even better than, the professional development teachers often receive, but it was certainly well below what might be considered ideal.

The results were incredibly disappointing. After 24 weeks, students in FORI classrooms experienced no benefits over those in control classrooms in word reading efficiency or reading comprehension. Even more surprising, students in FORI classes performed even *worse* than control students in terms of the number of words correct per minute (wcpm)! What happened?

To better understand the statistical results, we reverse engineered the issue by turning to our observations for answers. What we found was an inconsistency in the implementation of FORI over the course of the year. In terms of basic fidelity to the research plan, we found that 49% of the intervention teachers followed the basic format, but 22% used it only part of the time and 29% did not use it at all. This level of fidelity was well below what we had calculated during our first intervention year. Further, the core activities were seen in only 23% of the 5-minute segments we observed in the FORI classrooms, not all that different from the 15% of the segments observed in the nonintervention classrooms. This finding also implies that even the teachers who were following the basic format were not implementing it for the significant lengths of time that we recommended.

In addition to looking at the observations directly, we also tried to reason backward by comparing the seven most successful classes in terms of improved fluency (measured by the increase in wcpm over the course of the year) to the seven least successful classes regardless of condition. What exactly were the effective teachers doing that the ineffective teachers were not? When comparing the classes that made the most improvement with those that made the least, we found that the difference could be captured largely by one simple fact—namely, there was a noticeable difference in the amount of reading that was occurring during the students' shared reading instruction. Specifically, the students in the classes that showed the greatest growth in reading proficiency read approximately 7 minutes more per day on days we observed than did their peers in the least successful classes; if extrapolated over the full 24-week period, this totals 840 additional minutes of reading over the course of the intervention for successful classes. Moreover, the teachers in the classes with the greatest growth demonstrated better classroom management, and, not surprisingly, their students exhibited more on-task behavior than was the case in the least successful classes.

Thoughts, Theory, and Some Questions

Thoughts

Given the findings from our multiyear intervention, we have several insights regarding the relative effectiveness of the two approaches.

First, we feel fairly confident that the Wide FORI approach—that is, the use of multiple challenging texts with significant support—is more consistently effective in assisting students in their reading development. This finding has begun to be confirmed in other studies as well (e.g., Mostow & Beck, 2005; Schwebel, 2007). Although we initially had reservations regarding recommending this approach over the FORI approach because of the difficulty some schools may have in finding sufficient materials, we think our evidence for Wide FORI is strong enough to recommend it. We believe the materials issue can be solved through some creative "scavenging." For example, it is quite likely that most schools have retained earlier versions of basal readers or literature anthologies; these can serve as the basis of some additional selections. Similarly, many schools receive weekly magazines designed for young readers, and these can serve as another source for selected texts. Also, many schools have enough copies of a given title available to make up a class set of a text. For example, one school we worked with had six copies of *Frog and Toad Are Friends* (Lobel, 1970) in each of the three second-grade classrooms, and there were several other copies in the school and various classroom libraries; taken all together, there were enough to make a class set. Finally, we have found numerous grade-level texts available on the Internet that can be downloaded. Allowing for the use of these various options, we believe it is reasonable to recommend the Wide FORI approach as the basis of a fluency curriculum.

Second, we believe the FORI approach might be deceptively simple—so simple, in fact, that teachers may think that they do not need to attend to the implementation of the instruction as carefully as they might for other, more complex, literacy programs. This lack of attention may, in turn, have led to insufficient amounts of time being spent reading the actual texts, creating what amounts to a haphazard implementation of the approach. In fact, because of repeated readings, children do quickly become fluent on the weekly selection. As a result, we saw teachers in less successful classrooms moving on from FORI practice after a single quickly executed reading on a given day. This leads to insufficient reading practice on the children's part. We consider 20–40 minutes, depending upon the daily activity, to be a reasonable amount of time to spend on the FORI selections. Although the approach is very straightforward, teachers still need to ensure that the selections are sufficiently challenging and of sufficient length to warrant being read between four and seven times weekly. Teachers also need to continue preparing appropriate introductory and conclusion activities for the material, along with comprehension questions to be used after the first reading and during the echo reading of the selection, rather than assuming that the repetition of the material is, in and of itself, sufficient for dealing with a complex shared text.

Third, the final year left us wondering (we do not yet have a clear answer) as to how important the integration of consistent feedback and monitoring is to the implementation and maintenance of a new curricular element. Professional development, whether teacher-driven (as in study groups) or district-driven (as in professional workshops), is central to change in our schools. However, exactly how this development is structured may make a significant difference in the effectiveness of a new approach. While we believe there is great value in 1-day presentations, if the notes that teachers take are just put into a drawer, they will do little to bring about improved instruction. Instead, if the research is to be applied in practice, it seems likely that the creation of a support group is needed to share positive ideas, questions that may arise, and frustrations encountered in implementation of the new approach. Given the relative ease of implementing the FORI procedure, the importance of continuing professional development becomes even more critical in our minds.

The second piece of the professional development puzzle has to do with the length of time such support needs to be available for the implementation of an approach to become a permanent part of the curriculum. Is 1 year sufficient, or does this need to be a multiyear process? In our own experience, we have found that old habits die hard; given this reality, how long does it take for an ineffective instructional approach, such as round-robin reading, to be replaced with a more effective approach, such as Wide FORI, in such a way that the new method is truly integrated into a teacher's core instruction? We would argue that, as a profession, we need to rethink instructional change in a systematic way if teachers are going to embrace new approaches. At present, many teachers have seen so many trends in the teaching of reading—both good and bad—come and go that they have developed a healthy distrust of the newest instructional method, whether research-based or not.

Theory

In our research we have been struck by the effectiveness of the Wide FORI approach for enhancing fluency. In each year that we tried it, students who received the Wide FORI program displayed better fluency than control students. We think the explanation for its success can be traced to the way that automaticity develops in a wide reading environment as compared to a repeated-reading one.

To some extent the ideas expressed in the FORI approach emerge from an earlier view of automaticity (LaBerge & Samuels, 1974). In these earlier views, the emphasis was on repetition as the key to automaticity. However, recent versions of automaticity theory, in particular, the instance theory of automaticity proposed by Logan (1997), imply that there may be benefits from a more distributed approach to practice over a purely repetitive one. It is important for reading theory to consider these changes and integrate them into thinking about the development of automaticity. The implications for reading instruction from these newer views are intriguing.

From an instance theory point of view, each time a child attends to text, an instance, or trace, of that text is automatically encoded in memory at the sublexical, lexical, phrase, and text levels. As these multileveled instances build up and their learning levels off, within a relatively few repetitions (three to five, according to many authors; e.g., O'Shea, Sindelar, & O'Shea, 1985, 1987; Reutzel, 2003) they become reasonably easy to retrieve.

In the FORI approach, a relatively small set of phrase, word, and sublexical instances are encoded and reactivated on each reading, allowing these and only these particular traces to be easily retrieved. In the Wide FORI approach, many instances at the phrase, word, and sublexical level are encoded through exposure to a variety of texts. In the Wide FORI approach described here, there is some repetition also, albeit less than in the FORI approach. There is probably enough repetition that the text instances are relatively easily retrieved. Children are likely to be able to read a number of text segments several times during the course of the week, but each one only two or three times. As a result, in the Wide FORI condition, children may have a great range of higher-level traces (i.e., a greater diversity of phrases and words) encoded well enough to become activated automatically during reading. Thus, because of wide reading, students are more likely to have similar traces available in memory to become activated, which would lead to overall improvement in their oral reading fluency. By contrast, reading approaches that emphasize constant repetition of only sublexical information (i.e., strict phonics and rime approaches), isolated sight-word repetition, or text repetition (such as FORI) might not create a diverse enough set of high-level traces to enable students to benefit from the activation of these traces in the way that wide reading does.

Consequently, we find more consistent theoretical and empirical support for Wide FORI approaches.

Questions

Although we have referred to some of our questions in the previous sections, we want to end this chapter with issues we feel are specific to the title of our chapter and are worthy of further research. First, we believe it is important to determine the extent to which common words appear specifically in the texts that we used in our two approaches, a question that is currently being pursued by Hiebert (2007) and, more broadly, in second grade leveled material (or texts that range from the late first grade through the early third grade since that was the range used in the study). This information will better allow us to determine the degree to which the diversity of traces at the lexical and sublexical level may influence the development of fluency. We think it is important to determine how much the recurrence of words affects students' retention of those words; in other words, how does seeing the same words or phrases in multiple texts help develop learners' word recognition? We also wonder what happens as the texts become increasingly challenging and the number of shared words decreases? That is, are there optimal levels of shared words, new vocabulary, and unknown concepts for developing learners' word recognition and fluency? And are these levels the same for developing students' knowledge of a construct as well? While we feel this study has increased our knowledge of the importance of time, engagement, and support in the development of reading fluency and has begun to clarify the role text plays in this process, there are still important research questions remaining. As such, we hope our work can serve as a stepping stone to the further clarification of these issues in future research.

References

Allington, R. L. (1983). The reading instruction provided readers of differing abilities. *Elementary School Journal, 83,* 95–107.

Ash, G. E., & Kuhn, M. R. (2006). Meaningful oral and silent reading in the elementary and middle school classroom: Breaking the Round Robin Reading addiction. In T. Rasinski, C. Blachowicz, & K. Lems (Eds.), *Fluency instruction: Research-based best practices* (pp. 155–172). New York: Guilford Press.

Bryan, G., Fawson, P. C., & Reutzel, D. R. (2003). Sustained silent reading:

Exploring the value of literature discussion with three non-engaged readers. *Reading Research and Instruction, 43,* 47–73.

Chomsky, C. (1976). After decoding: What? *Language Arts, 53,* 288–296.

Donovan, C. A., Smolkin, L. B., & Lomax, R. G. (2000). Beyond the independent-level text: Considering the reader–text match in first graders' self-selections during recreational reading. *Reading Psychology, 21,* 309–333.

Dowhower, S. L. (1991). Speaking of prosody: Fluency's unattended bedfellow. *Theory into Practice, 30*(3), 158–164.

Erekson, J. (2003, May). *Prosody: The problem of expression in fluency.* Paper presented at Preconference Institute 15 of the International Reading Association, Orlando, FL.

Gambrell, L. B., Palmer, B. M., Codling, R. M., & Mazzoni, S. A. (1996). Assessing motivation to read. *The Reading Teacher, 49,* 518–533.

Hasbrouck, J. (2006, Summer). Drop everything and read—but how?: For students who are not yet fluent, silent reading is not the best use of classroom time. *American Educator, 30*(2). Retrieved September 11, 2008, from *www. aft.org/pubsreports/american_educator/issues/summer06/fluency.htm.*

Hiebert, E. H. (2007). The word zone fluency curriculum: An alternative approach. In P. Schwanenflugel & M. Kuhn (Eds.), *Fluency in the classroom* (pp. 154–170). New York: Guilford Press.

Hoffman, J. V., & Crone, S. (1985). The oral recitation lesson: A research-derived strategy for reading basal texts. In J. A. Niles & R. V. Lalik (Eds.), *Issues in literacy: A research perspective, 34th yearbook of the National Reading Conference* (pp. 76–83). Rochester, NY: National Reading Conference.

Kuhn, M. R. (2005). A comparative study of small group fluency instruction. *Reading Psychology, 26,* 127–146.

Kuhn, M. R. (2009). *The hows and whys of fluency instruction.* Boston: Allyn & Bacon.

Kuhn, M. R., Schwanenflugel, P. J., Morris, R. D., Morrow, L. M., Woo, D., Meisinger, B., et al. (2006). Teaching children to become fluent and automatic readers. *Journal of Literacy Research, 38,* 357–387.

Kuhn, M. R., & Stahl, S. (2003). Fluency: A review of developmental and remedial practices. *Journal of Educational Psychology, 95,* 1–19.

LaBerge, D., & Samuels, S. A. (1974). Toward a theory of automatic information processing in reading. *Cognitive Psychology, 6,* 293–323.

Lee-Daniels, S. L., & Murray, B. A. (2000). DEAR me: What does it take to get children reading? *Reading Teacher, 54,* 154–155.

Levy, B. A., Abello, B., & Lysynchuk, L. (1997). Transfer from word training to reading in context: Gains in fluency and comprehension. *Learning Disability Quarterly, 20,* 173–188.

Lobel, A. (1970). *Frog and Toad are friends.* New York: HarperCollins.

Logan, G. D. (1997). Automaticity and reading: Perspectives from the instance theory of automaticity. *Reading and Writing Quarterly: Overcoming Learning Difficulties, 13,* 123–146.

Mathson, D. V., Allington, R. L., & Solic, K. L. (2006). Hijacking fluency and instructionally informative assessments. In T. Rasinski, C. Blachowicz, &

K. Lems (Eds.), *Fluency instruction: Research-based best practices.* New York: Guilford Press.

Miller, J. (2007). *The development of prosodic text reading as a dimension of oral reading fluency in early elementary school children.* Unpublished dissertation, University of Georgia.

Miller, J., & Schwanenflugel, P. J. (2006). Prosody of syntactically complex sentences in the oral reading of young children. *Journal of Educational Psychology, 98*, 839–853.

Mostow, J., & Beck, J. (2005, June). *Micro-analysis of fluency gains in a reading tutor that listens.* Paper presented at the Society for the Scientific Study of Reading annual meeting, Toronto, Ontario.

National Institute of Child Health and Human Development. (2000). *Report of the National Reading Panel. Teaching children to read: An evidence-based assessment of the scientific research literature on reading and its implications for reading instruction* (NIH Publication No. 00-4769). Washington, DC: U.S. Government Printing Office.

O'Shea, L. J., Sindelar, P. T., & O'Shea, D. J. (1985). The effects of repeated readings and attentional cues on reading fluency and comprehension. *Journal of Reading Behavior, 17*, 129–142.

O'Shea, L. J., Sindelar, P. T., & O'Shea, D. J. (1987). The effects of repeated readings and attentional cues on the reading fluency and comprehension of learning disabled readers. *Learning Disabilities Research, 2*, 103–109.

Pikulski, J. J., & Chard, D. J. (2005). Fluency: The bridge between decoding and reading comprehension. *The Reading Teacher, 58*, 510–519.

Rasinski, T. V. (2003). *The fluent reader: Oral reading strategies for building word recognition, fluency, and comprehension.* New York: Scholastic.

Reutzel, D. R. (2003, May). *Fluency: What is it? How to assess it? How to develop it!* Paper presented at Preconference Institute 15 of the International Reading Association, Orlando, FL.

Samuels, S. J. (2006). Reading fluency: Its past, present, and future. In T. Rasinski, C. Balachowicz, & K. Lems (Eds.), *Fluency instruction: Research-based best practices* (pp. 7–20). New York: Guilford Press.

Schreiber, P. A. (1991). Understanding prosody's role in reading acquisition. *Theory into Practice, 30*, 158–164.

Schwanenflugel, P. J., Hamilton, A. M., Kuhn, M. R., Wisenbaker, J., & Stahl, S. A. (2004). Becoming a fluent reader: Reading skill and prosodic features in the oral reading of young readers. *Journal of Educational Psychology, 96*, 119–129.

Schwanenflugel, P. J., Meisinger, E., Wisenbaker, J. M., Kuhn, M. R., Strauss, G. P., & Morris, R. D. (2006). Becoming a *fluent* and automatic reader in the early elementary school years. *Reading Research Quarterly, 41*, 496–522.

Schwebel, E. A. (2007). *A comparative study of small group fluency instruction—a replication and extension of Kuhn's (2005) study.* Unpublished master's thesis, Kean University, Union, NJ.

Stahl, K. A. D. (2007). Creating opportunities for comprehension instruction within fluency-oriented reading. In M. R. Kuhn & P. J. Schwanenflugel (Eds.), *Fluency in the classroom* (pp. 55–74). New York: Guilford Press.

Stahl, S. A., & Heubach, K. (2005). Fluency-oriented reading instruction. *Journal of Literacy Research, 37,* 25–60.

Taylor, B. M., & Pearson, P. D. (2000). *The CIERA school change classroom observation scheme.* Minneapolis: University of Minnesota.

Walker, B. J., Mokhtari, K., & Sargent, S. (2006). Reading fluency: More than fast and accurate reading. In T. Rasinski, C. Blachowicz, & K. Lems (Eds.), *Fluency instruction: Research-based best practices.* New York: Guilford Press.

PART III

*

CRITICAL FACTORS IN SUPPORTING MORE AND BETTER READING

8

THE CHALLENGE
OF ADVANCED TEXTS

*The Interdependence
of Reading and Learning*

Marilyn Jager Adams

As I write this chapter, it has been 25 years since the release of *A Nation at Risk* by the National Commission on Excellence in Education (NCEE; 1983). The NCEE was specifically authorized by the U.S. Congress and created by then Secretary of Education Terrence Bell to examine the quality of teaching and learning in our nation's schools, with special attention to the experience of teenaged youths.

The principal motivation for the report was a growing concern that the United States's "once unchallenged preeminence in commerce, industry, science, and technological innovation is being overtaken by competitors throughout the world" (National Commission on Excellence in Education [NCEE], 1983, p. 1). This, the NCEE warned, was the wave of the future: we were to expect an ever increasing redistribution of competitive capability throughout the globe. "Knowledge, learning, information and skilled intelligence are the new raw materials of international commerce. ... If only to keep and improve on the slim competitive edge we still retain in the world markets, we must dedicate ourselves the reform of our educational system" (NCEE, 1983, p. 2).

The NCEE also concluded that such educational reform was long overdue and direly needed:

> Our Nation is at risk. Our once unchallenged preeminence in commerce, industry, science, and technological innovation is being overtaken by competitors throughout the world. ... We report to the American people that the educational foundations of our society are presently being eroded by a rising tide of mediocrity that threatens our very future as a Nation and a people.
>
> If an unfriendly foreign power had attempted to impose on America the mediocre educational performance that exists today we might well have viewed it as an act of war. ... As it stands, we have allowed this to happen to ourselves. ... We have, in effect, been committing an act of unthinking, unilateral educational disarmament. (NCEE, 1983, p. 1)

Particularly worrisome at the time was a prolonged downward trend in the scores of U.S. high school students on the Scholastic Aptitude Test (SAT), as shown in Figure 8.1. From 1963 to 1980, the average score on the math section of the SAT had fallen by 36 points; on the verbal section, it had fallen by 54 points, an equivalent of 0.49 standard deviations (Price & Carpenter, 1978).

When the SAT score decline stretched into the 1970s, the College Board engaged a panel to try to identify the underlying causes (College Entrance Examination Board, 1977). A first hypothesis to be checked, of course, was that the difficulty of the test had somehow shifted to students' disadvantage. But, no, to the contrary, indications were that scoring had become more lenient (Beaton, Hilton, & Schrader, 1977) and that the verbal passages had become slightly easier (Chall, Conard, & Harris, 1977). A second prominent hypothesis was that the decline was due to changes in the demographics of the test takers. In this case, the answer was positive, but only in part. Statistics showed that, over the 1960s, changes in the composition of the tested population accounted for as much as three-quarters of the test score decline—and, no wonder, for during this period the number of students taking the SAT tripled. However, when the test-taking population stabilized over the 1970s, the scores did not. Instead, the decline continued, even steeper than before, while the extent to which it could be ascribed to demographic shifts shrank to 30%, at best (Stedman, 1993). Furthermore, it was the scores of the strongest students, those in the top 10% of their class, that dropped the most; the scores of students toward the bottom of the distribution were holding steady or even gaining (Turnbull, 1985).

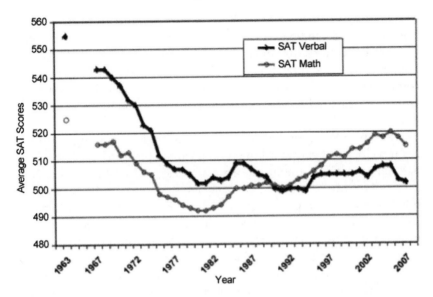

FIGURE 8.1. Average SAT scores in 1962–1963 and from 1966–1967 to 2006–2007. Data from Turnbull (1985) and National Center for Education Statistics (2007, Table 132).

By the early 1990s, SAT scores appeared to have plateaued. The College Board decided to "recenter" the scale, basically adding about 25 points to the math scores and about 80 to the verbal scores so as to return the mean of each test to a value close to 500 points. (The scores in Figure 8.1 have been adjusted so that all are on the current "recentered" scale.) Beleaguered, the College Board also changed the name of the test from the Scholastic Aptitude Test to simply the SAT, with the letters standing for nothing.

Unfortunately, if the downward trend of the SAT scores had slowed, their levels have even today not recovered (see Figure 8.1.). "SAT Records Biggest Score Dip in 31 Years," headlined the *Washington Post* in 2006 (Matthews, 2006). "SAT Scores Drop for Second Year in a Row," headlined *U.S. News and World Reports* in 2007 (Kingsbury, 2007).

Not Just the SAT Scores

To be sure, whether scores on the SAT exams truly reflect relevant or important intellectual or academic proficiencies remains a topic of discussion (e.g., College Entrance Examination Board, 1977; Lewin, 2006; Rothstein, 2004; Stedman, 1996). On the other hand, there are a number of other indications that the development of more advanced levels of literacy is a special problem in the United States, and this is so whether compared with the literacy proficiency of other countries around the world or measured against our country's own standards and expectations.

Recent international studies of fourth graders' reading and literacy development show children in the United States to be above average, ranking ninth among the 35 countries participating in the 2001 assessment (Mullis, Martin, Gonzalez, & Kennedy, 2003). By contrast, relative to the 30 OECD (Organization for Economic Cooperation and Development, a.k.a. "developed") countries, U.S. high school students performed below average, ranking 17th of 30 and significantly outperforming only 5 of the others. The top 10% of U.S. high school students scored comparably to the top 10% of students in the other countries. However, when the scores are broken into reading levels, the United States showed a significantly smaller proportion of high school students at intermediate levels of proficiency and a significantly greater proportion at the lowest levels. Thus, while it seems the best of our students are world-class, our educational system is somehow failing the majority. With time, as so strongly voiced in *A Nation at Risk*, this will matter increasingly, both personally and nationally.

Based on data from the International Adult Literacy Survey (IALS), the average literacy of U.S. adults ranked 12th among 20 countries of comparably high income (Sum, Kirsch, & Taggart, 2002). Moreover, within the five performance categories defined by the assessment framework, 45% of U.S. adults fell within the lowest two, placing them 16th among the 20 countries in the study. This relative underperformance occurred despite the fact that U.S. adults ranked first in the number of years of schooling and in academic degree completion. A particularly troubling aspect of Sum et al.'s (2002) analysis was the precipitous rate at which the relative literacy levels of U.S. adults seemed to be falling. As compared with their peers in other countries, the literacy levels of older U.S. adults (ages 36–45, 46–55, and 56 and older) ranked in the top 5. In contrast, the average literacy performance of U.S. adults younger than 35 years old ranked in the bottom half of the distribution by every measure. Closer analyses of these younger adults showed that, among participants with just a high school diploma or less, those from the United States fell at the bottom of the pile, ranking 19th out of 20. Although scores were far higher for young U.S. adults who had completed 4 or more years of postsecondary education, they were still below the average of their same-aged and like-educated peers in the other countries.

Results of domestic assessments are not inconsistent with the international results. The 2003 National Assessment of Adult Literacy (Kutner et al., 2007) found more than 40% of U.S. adults unable to comprehend texts of moderate everyday difficulty. Only 13% of U.S. adults could read and understand the longer and more complex documents included in the assessment—and these documents were neither very long nor very complex.

Returning to school students, the National Assessment of Educational Progress (NAEP) documents slight but significant improvement in the average reading scores of fourth graders (4 points) and eighth graders (3 points) between 1992 and 2007. Similarly, the percentage of fourth- and eighth-grade students performing at grade level ("proficient") or above has increased over that period from 29% to 33% and from 29% to 31%, respectively (Lee, Grigg, & Donahue, 2007).

For 12th graders, by contrast, the average reading score on the NAEP *fell* by 6 points between 1992 and the most recent assessment in 2005. Between 1992 and 2005, the percentage of 12th graders performing at or above grade level ("proficient") fell from 40% to 35%; at the other end of the spectrum, those who scored *below* the basic level rose from 20% to 27% (Grigg, Donahue, & Dion, 2007).

The NAEP scores of the 12th graders are jarring not just because they are so low but also because they are low compared to the 4th and 8th graders and even, working backwards in time, within same cohorts when in the 4th and 8th grades. Bear in mind, too, that 25% of 8th graders, nationwide drop out of school before completing high school (Seastrom, Hoffman, Chapman, & Stillwell, 2005); presumably, then, those who stay in school, and therefore participate in the NAEP in the 12th grade, disproportionately include the more successful and motivated students. In short, one can't help but wonder whether the 12th graders were trying. After all, 12th graders are an ultraworldly group, and there is little personal consequence for doing well or poorly on the NAEP.

Yet, college entrance examinations are voluntary, and performing well on them is the very point of taking them. In analyzing scores from its own college admissions exam, ACT, Inc. (known until 1996 as the American College Testing Program) compared them within-cohort to scores on its tests for 8th and 10th graders. For each of the cohorts examined and regardless of gender, race/ethnicity, or household income, the students were collectively on track in the 8th and 10th grades for better scores than they ultimately obtained in the 12th grade. The report (ACT, 2006) concludes that there is a specific problem at the high school level. The same conclusion was drawn by the College Entrance Examination Board (1977) in the mid-1970s and again in the mid-1980s (Turnbull, 1985).

What Could Be the Problem?

The College Board's 1977 panel examined a number of factors that might have contributed to the SAT score decline. One of these, proposed by Jeanne Chall, was that the reading selections on the tests had somehow become too hard for the students. To test this hypothesis, Chall and her colleagues (1977) sampled passages from SAT tests administered between 1947 and 1975, using readability analyses to compare their difficulty. Yet, the data indicated that the SAT passages had become easier, not harder. Between 1963 and 1975, during the years of the score decline, the average difficulty of the test passages lay at the 11th-grade level, which should have been solidly in range for 12th-grade college-bound students. However, Chall et al. also evaluated popular 11th-grade textbooks in history, literature, grammar, and composition. The average difficulty of the textbooks lay between the 9th- to 10th-grade levels. Could the SAT score decline have been due to this difference in the relative difficulty of the test and the school books? If students had neither practiced nor been instructed with reading materials as hard as the SAT passages, then one could hardly expect them to read the latter with competence and confidence.

Following on Chall et al.'s (1977) hypothesis, Hayes, Wolfer, and Wolfe (1996) undertook a complementary study in which they analyzed the difficulty of popular reading textbook series over time. Their results indicated that the difficulty of the text in these books, especially in grades 4 and up, had been reduced and, further, that this reduction was temporally aligned with the SAT score decline. As one indication, the average length of sentences in books published between 1963 and 1991 was shorter than that in books published between 1946 and 1962. In seventh- and eighth-grade textbooks, for example, the mean length of sentences decreased from 20 to 14 words—"the equivalent of dropping one or two clauses from every sentence," observed Hayes et al. (1996, p. 497). Meanwhile, the sophistication of the books' wording also declined. Hayes et al.'s analysis concluded that the wording of school books published from 1963 onward for 8th graders was as simple as that in books used by 5th graders before 1963, while the wording of 12th-grade literature texts published after 1963 was simpler than 7th-grade texts published prior to 1963.

Such a disparity between the students' school books and the passages on the tests might well explain students' poor performance on their college entrance exams. More significantly, however, failing to provide instruction or experience with "grown-up" text levels seems a risky course toward preparing students for the reading demands of college and of life in general.

This concern was recently raised again by ACT, Inc. (2006) in reviewing the poor performance of students on its college entrance exam. The maximum score on the reading component of the ACT college entrance exam is 36. ACT has found that scores of less than 21 predict reading difficulties in college coursework and also in the workplace. Among students who took the ACT exam in 2005, the scores of 51%—more than half—fell below the 21-point cutoff for college readiness in reading ability. Through analyses of student performance, ACT determined that the major stumbling block for the students was complex texts. More specifically, the ACT reading assessment is designed around three levels of textual complexity. For students whose overall performance fell below the 21-point benchmark, average response accuracy on the complex texts was at chance levels. As students scored beyond the 21-point benchmark, their performance on the complex texts steadily increased but reached levels comparable to performance on texts classified as moderate and simple only among those students who scored at least 35 of the 36 points possible.

The Wording of Natural Language

Hayes et al.'s (1996) analysis of shifts in the difficulty levels of school books was based on a clever and conceptually straightforward approach. As a reference against which to gauge usage of words in everyday "grown-up" text, they sampled words from a large number of English-language newspapers. To represent the wording of the textbooks, they sampled approximately 1,000 words from each of more than 800 different school books, divided into sets corresponding to the particular era (prior to 1962 and subsequent to 1962) and the grade level (each of grades 1–12). They then developed separate word-frequency corpora for each of the sets of school book samples and for the reference sample in the standard way, by counting the number of times each different word occurred and then ordering the words in each set of texts from most to least frequent (see, e.g., Carroll, Davies, & Richman, 1971, for a fuller explanation of the process of generating word frequency counts). Eliminated from the corpora were all proper nouns and also, so as to focus on meaning-bearing words, all closed-class words (i.e., grammatical words such as prepositions, determiners [e.g., *the, this, some*], conjunctions, and pronouns). In addition, all but the 10,000 most frequent words were eliminated from the reference sample (because word counts of low-frequency words are more sensitive to sample size and more susceptible to sampling error). After converting frequencies of the remaining words in each of the corpora to proportions (so that all were on the same scale regardless of the size of the sample), the researchers basically computed the extent to which words in the textbook samples were overused or underused relative to the reference sample taken from the newspapers and, by the same metric, relative to each other. Hayes et al.'s (1996) conclusion that the vocabulary of school books had been simplified was based on their finding that the wording of post-1962 school books had shifted toward more common words, as gauged by word frequencies in the reference sample.

Hayes et al. (1996) found that it was especially school books for students in grades 4 and up that were simplified in the years after 1962. They also found that, although the wording of school books for children generally increased with the grade-level from grades 1 through 8, the same was not true of high school books. Instead, across grades 9 through 12 (including texts for Advanced Placement courses), the difficulty levels of the literature books were shown to differ little from one another or from the grade 7 and grade 8 offerings. High school students' science texts were significantly more difficult than their English books. However, even among science texts, only those designated for Advanced Placement coursework evidenced difficulty levels comparable to the newspaper sample used as the benchmark reference. Because Hayes et al.'s high school text sample was relatively sparse, it is possible that it is not wholly representative. On the other hand, the measured simplicity of the high school books is consistent with the conclusions and speculations of others (e.g., ACT, 2006; Chall et al., 1977).

Over the years, following basically the same approach, Hayes and his colleagues quantified the relative lexical demands of a number of language domains. Many of his analyses affirmed that the lexical difficulty of texts varied predictably with the maturity or sophistication of the audience for which each was written. As examples, his analyses showed that the wording of scientific publications aimed at scientists, such as *Cell*, *Nature*, and *Science*, is more sophisticated than the wording of those written for lay persons, such as *Scientific American* (Hayes, 1992); that the wording of scientific publications, including college textbooks, is more difficult than that of newspapers (Hayes, 1992); that the wording of newspapers is significantly more difficult than the wording of popular adult novels (Hayes & Ahrens, 1988); that the wording of adult novels is generally more difficult than that found in novels written for grade-school children (Hayes & Ahrens, 1988); and that the wording of school children's books, with the exception of preprimers, is more difficult than that of books written for preschoolers (Hayes & Ahrens, 1988).

On the other hand, the results of some of Hayes's analyses are quite provocative with respect to the nature of literacy challenge. For example, while his analyses showed that textbooks had become progressively easier over this century (Hayes et al., 1996), they also indicated that the lexical difficulty of English-language newspapers had remained nearly constant (Hayes et al., 1996). Could this disparity be a factor in the declining circulation of newspapers?

In contrast, analyzing the wording of scientific magazines and journals published between 1930 to 1990, he found that the sophistication of every single one that he evaluated, whether professional or lay, had increased dramatically over the decades (Hayes, 1992). If it is a national goal to inspire more students to become engineers and scientists, then shouldn't the difficulty of our school books have increased as well? If a goal is to ensure that our students will be able to stay sufficiently informed about scientific progress to conduct business, reflect on policy, and manage their family's health and education, then at a minimum shouldn't the difficulty of our school books keep pace with the difficulty of scientific publications aimed at the general public?

Even so, it was Hayes's comparisons of spoken and written language sources that seemed most telling. For these analyses, Hayes and Ahrens (1988) compiled and analyzed a variety of oral language samples, including language from prime-time adult television shows, children's television shows, mothers' speech to children ranging in age from infancy to adolescence, conversations among college-educated adults (including from the Oval Office), and adults providing expert witness testimony for legal cases. Regardless of the source or situation and without exception, the lexical richness of the oral language samples paled in comparison with the written texts. Indeed, of all the oral language samples evaluated, the only one that exceeded even preschool books in lexical range was expert witness testimony.

This difference between the wording of oral and written language must lie at the crux of the literacy challenge, as it points up a profound dilemma. On the one hand, the extent of this disparity implies that the great majority of words needed for understanding written language are likely to be encountered, and thus can only be learned, through experience with written text. On the other hand, research has taught us that written text is accessible, and thus permits learning, only if the reader or listener already knows the vast majority of words from which it is constructed. Indeed, research indicates that reading with comprehension depends on understanding at least 95% of the words of a text (Betts, 1946; Carver, 1994; Hu & Nation, 2000; Laufer, 1988).

The Word Frequency Spectrum

As it happens, the distribution of words in natural language conforms closely to certain mathematical functions. This fact has been very useful for computational linguists. It enables them, for example, to detect bias in their sampling and to determine the costs versus benefits of increasing their sample sizes. It has also been highly useful for corpus researchers. As a case in point, it enabled Hayes to derive quantitative indices of lexical richness. Representing the distribution of the words in each corpus mathematically, he needed only to take the integral of the function describing each curve to find the area beneath and then to subtract the area beneath the first curve from the area beneath the second to compare the lexical density of the two distributions.

As another example, in building the corpus for the *American Heritage Word Frequency Book*, Carroll et al. (1971) took 10,000 samples of 500 words from texts written for children in grades 3 through 8. Across those 5 million words, the total number of different words found was 86,741. Using the mathematics of word frequency distributions, Carroll et al. estimated that the actual number of different words in such materials—that is, the number that they would have found had they counted such texts exhaustively rather than sampling just 5 million words of excerpts—would have totaled more than 609,606.

Again, all of the materials from which Carroll et al. sampled were indeed specifically written for and meant to be understood by school children in grades 3 through 8. But how can grade school children possibly be expected to know more than 600,000 different words? Can Carroll et al.'s estimate possibly be correct?

Of the 5 million words of text from which Carroll et al. built their corpus, 50% of the sample was represented by just 109 very frequent words and 90% of the sample by just 5,000 frequent words. At the other extreme, 35,079 of the 86,741 distinct words in the corpus—more than 50%—turned up only once in the entire sample. Further, the 86,741 distinct words that showed up at all in the sample represent only 15% of the total number of different words estimated to arise in texts for children in grades 3 through 8. The problem, explain Carroll et al., is that a sample of 5 million words is just plain too small to capture but a fraction of the total distribution.

In recent years, the proliferation of electronic texts has made it possible to compile much larger word frequency corpora. The British National Corpus was built from 100 million words taken from 4,124 different sources. Approximately 10% of the corpus was sampled from spoken language sources and 90% from written texts. Because the goal was to create a profile of present-day English, all of the sources were published after 1985, and the distribution of topics and text was guided by the pattern of print publishing in the United Kingdom. Ten percent of the corpus was drawn from imaginative texts and 90 percent from informative texts (Leech, Rayson, & Wilson, 2001).

As described on the British National Corpus's website, this is a very large corpus: "To put these numbers into perspective, the average paperback book has about 250 pages per centimeter of thickness; assuming 400 words a page, we calculate that the whole corpus printed in small type on thin paper would take up about ten metres of shelf space. Reading the whole corpus aloud at a fairly rapid 150 words a minute, 8 hours a day, 365 days a year, would take just over four years" (British National Corpus, 2008).

Another drawback to Carroll et al.'s (1971) estimate of the total vocabulary in school children's texts is that words in the American Heritage corpus are distinguished solely by their spellings. Conflicting with this practice, research suggests that nouns and their regular plurals, such as *cat* and *cats*, share a common mental representation (Sereno & Jongman, 1997), as do the basic conjugations of the verbs, such as *walk, walks walked*, and *walking* (Stanners, Neiser, Hernon, & Hall, 1979). As Carroll et al. point out, had each noun and verb been counted only once rather than separately for each of its inflected forms, their estimate of the total number of words in schoolchildren's texts would have been considerably smaller. Thus, a further advantage of the British National

Corpus for purposes of investigating the lexical demands of texts is that, within it, each word is tagged with its part of speech.

In a challenge to develop a vocabulary assessment for the National Assessment of Adult Literacy (Adams & Spoehr, in press), Kathryn Spoehr and I turned to the British National Corpus in quest of a means of examining the feasibility of selecting a spectrum of test items as a function of their frequencies. Because we were interested only in words that occurred sufficiently often that their relative frequency estimates might be reliable, we restricted attention to those that appeared at least 10 times in the full corpus or, equivalently, with a minimum probability of about once per 10 million words. Because our interest was in vocabulary, we focused exclusively on adjectives, adverbs, common nouns, and verbs. So as to afford a cleaner view of the number of different words available at each frequency, we included only the base forms of the nouns and verbs. The resulting distribution is shown in Figure 8.2.

In Figure 8.2, a separate line is accorded to each of the four major parts of speech. The x axis represents the frequency of the words, ranging from 100 or more per million to 1 per million. The y axis indicates the number of words found at each frequency. As can be seen from the small spike on the far left of each curve, there are a few dozen words for each part of speech with frequencies of 100 per million or greater. Excepting those words, however, the graph shows that the frequency of occurrence of the vast majority of the words is extremely low. Fully 60% of the words that we counted had frequencies of less than one per million. Had we included proper nouns in our count, the number of infrequent words would have swelled still further and, in the present context, it is important to recognize that gaining familiarity with a great abundance of proper nouns is a key and core component of becoming literate. Further, though the total number of different words in the British National Corpus is 757,087, nearly 10 times more than captured in the American Heritage sample (Carroll et al., 1971), the percentage of different words that turned up only once was nearly identical in the two corpora (52% and 54%, respectively).

The formal explanation of this distribution of words is known as Zipf's law, named for the linguist who discovered it (Zipf, 1935). According to Zipf's law, the distribution of words in natural language discourse conforms to an inverse power function, and research confirms this to be true regardless of the topic, genre, language, level, or modality of the source of the word count.

In a nutshell, Zipf's law states is that every natural language sample is made up of relatively few words that recur over and over again

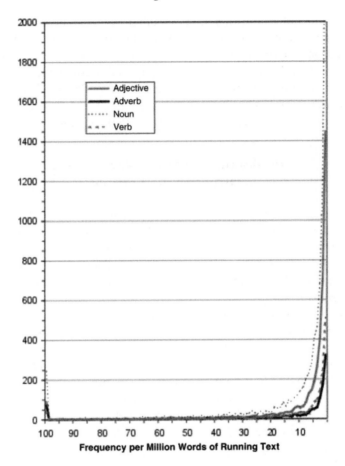

FIGURE 8.2. Frequency counts from the British National Corpus (2001) for adjectives, adverbs, verbs, and common nouns. For common nouns and verbs, counts are for base (uninflected) forms.

and many, many words that arise very infrequently—just as seen in the American Heritage and British National corpora. In turn, the J-shaped nature of such word frequency distributions developmentally divides their utility for guiding educational practice. Because large-scale corpora quite reliably index the relative frequency of the most common words (the initial "curl" on the J), they can be fruitfully used to design or evaluate texts and tests for primary grade students (see, e.g., Hiebert, 2005). In contrast, word frequency statistics from such corpora can offer little if any useful guidance where interest is shifted to the middle and upper grades, and this holds whether the focus is on vocabulary instruction, on methods or formulas for evaluating the readability or difficulty of text, or on assessments of vocabulary breadth. The impasse is that even in the largest corpora, the counted frequencies of the vast majority of words—nearly all beyond those few thousand most common words—are too low to be statistically meaningful or trustworthy and are tied with thousands of other words, in any case.

Developing Students' Vocabulary: Examining the Options

Having a better sense of the magnitude of the challenge, let us turn to the question of how best to help students master enough words to understand advanced texts. In broad terms, there appear to be only two options: (1) to endeavor to teach students the words they will need to know and (2) to expect students to learn new words on their own through reading.

Is direct vocabulary instruction worthwhile? Based on a meta-analysis by Stahl and Fairbanks (1986), the answer seems to be a resounding "yes." Across studies involving a variety of students, instructional specifics, and outcome measures, Stahl and Fairbanks found that direct vocabulary instruction significantly increases knowledge of words that are taught. Just as important, students who received vocabulary instruction were found to perform significantly better on global nonspecific vocabulary measures such as standardized tests, indicating that such instruction promotes learning of words beyond those that have been explicitly taught.

In the present context, however, we must also bear in mind that, by its very nature, direct vocabulary instruction admits coverage of precious few words relative to the magnitude of the challenge. Even if, beginning in grade 1 and continuing through grade 12, teachers consistently taught—and students perfectly retained—20 vocabulary words each and every week, the gain in vocabulary would total only 8,640 words in all (20 words × 36 weeks of school × 12 years), many times fewer than what is required.

Such considerations have led some scholars to conclude that the only feasible means by which students might acquire an adequate reading vocabulary is through the process of inferring the meanings of new words from their contexts during the course of reading (see Nagy, Herman, & Anderson, 1985). Upon scrutiny, however, this explanation is also inadequate.

Let us suppose that, as Anderson, Wilson, and Fielding (1988) have estimated, median fifth-grade students read approximately 700,000 words of text per year. If these students were to read the 5 million words of text from which the American Heritage corpus was compiled, it would take them about 7 years—through the 12th grade. If we suppose that these students already know 12,000 of these words, then—again based on the American Heritage corpus—we can expect them to encounter about 75,000 new words in the course of this reading. Using Nagy, Anderson, and Herman's (1987) estimate of 0.05 as the probability that students retain the meaning of any given new word they encounter during reading, the upshot is that such students will have learned only 3,750 new words by the time they graduate, equaling about 550 words per year. Counting time with informal text (e.g., mail) as reading and generously assuming that an estimated 15 minutes per day of in-school reading time is spent, without pause, reading at 200 words per minute, Nagy et al. (1987) boost the estimated amount read per year to 1 million words, yielding a total of nearly 4,700 new words in just 5 years, or about 840 per year. No matter; recalling that even texts written for students in grades 1 through 8 presume knowledge of more than 600,000 different words, it is clear that both estimates fall way short of the challenge. At the same time, however, both seem at odds with the intuitive sense that a high school student need be neither a genius nor a tireless scholar to read and understand most materials written for grade school children.

Insights from Computational Models of Vocabulary Acquisition

Working from corpus statistics, the prospect of raising students' vocabulary to the demands of advanced texts seems a nearly impossible task. Yet, recent computation models such as the latent semantic analysis (LSA) model developed by Tom Landauer and his colleagues (e.g., Landauer, 1998; Landauer & Dumais, 1997; see also Griffiths, Steyvers, & Tenenbaum, 2007) offer a different way of viewing the challenge.

The core mechanism underlying the LSA model is associative learning. The first step in training the model consists in inputting large quantities of text, where the computer is programmed to remember each word and the context in which it occurred. The second step in training the model consists in creating associations or connections between the words and contexts and then mathematically collapsing or bundling them according to their commonalities and distinctions. The connections between words and their contexts are bidirectional and are weighted positively by the number of times the word occurs in the context and inversely by the number of different contexts in which the word occurs. By interconnecting all of the words and contexts in this way, a rich matrix of associations arises between the words, between the contexts, and between the words and the contexts in both directions.

As a concrete example, Landauer and Dumais (1997) trained the computer by having it "read" each of 30,473 articles (or, for long articles, the first 2,000 words) from the *Grolier Encyclopedia*. The sample totaled 4.6 million words of text in all, which the researchers estimated to be comparable in magnitude to the lifelong learning of a seventh grader. From these readings, the researchers created a matrix in which the 30,473 articles (the "contexts") stood as the columns and the rows were populated by each of the 60,768 words that had arisen in at least two of the encyclopedia articles. The researchers then used a mathematical procedure (singular value decomposition) to condense the separate connections between each word and context to a smaller set that optimally captured their overlap and separation. Again, the connections are bidirectional in the LSA model. As they extend both from words to contexts and from contexts to words, they also extend, by derivation, from words to other words, contexts to other contexts, and between words and contexts that did not co-occur in training.

To evaluate what the model had "learned," Landauer and Dumais (1997) then tested it with 80 retired items from the synonym subtest of the Test of English as a Foreign Language (TOEFL). Each of these items presents an isolated test word for which the test taker is to select the best synonym from four alternative words. The model's performance, as based on the knowledge it gained from "reading" the encyclopedia articles, was then compared to performance of a large sample of applicants to U.S. colleges from non-English-speaking countries. The model's score was 64.4%; the people's score averaged 64.5%. Similarly, after the LSA model "read" an introductory psychology text, it performed nearly as well as college students on a multiple-choice exam (Landauer, 1998).

The LSA model has also been used with impressive success to gauge the quality and content of student essays and the coherence and conceptual density of reading materials. In one study, for example, students were first asked to write essays about the heart and circulatory system, and LSA was used to benchmark their prior knowledge based on what they wrote (Wolfe et al., 1998). Each student was then asked to read one of four passages on the topic, where the four passages ranged in sophistication from elementary level to medical school level. The results showed that students learned most when given a passage that was just a little—but not too much—more sophisticated than the knowledge shown in their essays.

To investigate LSA's vocabulary more closely, Landauer and Dumais (1997) compared the word learning of the model to that of school children. In simulating school children, results showed that the probability that the model learned any given new word in any given new text was approximately 0.05, just like the students in Nagy et al.'s (1987) study.

Within the LSA model, any new input is represented in terms of the overall structure of the network or, equivalently, in relation to the representations of other words within it. It is for this reason that, like people, the amount that the LSA model learns from any set of readings depends on how much it already knows; for any given text, the larger its starting vocabulary, the more it learns.

But there is something else, too. Because the meaning is represented relationally, the connections that effectively define the meanings of words grow, shrink, and shift continuously, continually, and always in relation to one another. Thus, the addition or modification of any one connection impacts many others, pulling some closer together, pushing some farther apart, and otherwise altering the strengths and patterns of connections among words and contexts. Due to this dynamic, Landauer and Dumais (1997) found that with each reading the model effectively increased its understanding not just of words that were in the passage but also of words that were *not* in the passage. Measured in terms of total vocabulary gain, the amount the model learned about words that did *not* appear in a given reading was three times as much as what it learned about words that were in the reading.

"What?" we cry, "How can that be? How can reading a text produce increases in knowledge of words that it does not even contain! That is not credible! It makes no sense!" But wait. If we were talking about knowledge rather than words, then it would make lots of sense. Every concept—simple or complex, concrete or abstract—is learned in terms of its similarities, differences, and relationships with other concepts with which we are familiar. As a simplistic example, when we read about tigers, then by dint of both similarities and contrasts, we learn more about all sorts of cats and, further, about every subtopic mentioned along the way. The more deeply we read about tigers, the more nuanced and complex these concepts and their interrelations become.

Words are not just words. They are the nexus—the interface—between communication and thought. When we read, it is through words that we build, refine, and modify our knowledge. What makes vocabulary valuable and important is not the words themselves so much as the understandings they afford. The reason we need to know the meanings of words is that they point to the knowledge from which we are to construct, interpret, and reflect on the meaning of the text.

What is unique about the LSA model is not its implications about the essential structure of semantic memory. Cognitive psychologists broadly agree that the meaning of any word consists of bundles of features and associations that are the cumulative product of the reader's experience with both the word in context and the concepts to which it refers. In any given instance, only that subset of a word's meanings, usages, or features that are contextually relevant is activated (see, e.g., Gorfein, 2001). As examples, the activated meaning of the word *fan* differs, depending on whether the text is about a *soccer fan*, a *ceiling fan*, or a *peacock's fan*. What is unique about the LSA model is its demonstration that this structure and this dynamic can so richly and powerfully evolve through accrued experience with the various contexts in which words do and do not occur—that is, through reading.

There are potential extensions of the LSA model that also beg attention. For example, the concepts and relations that emerge and are strengthened through reading may belong to words that the student does not already know. That is exactly the point. As they grow in richness and complexity, the relationships that evolve within the network will increasingly support many new words and many new spheres of knowledge, whether in abstract or tied to related concepts or situations. Perhaps this is why people's vocabulary correlates so strongly with the amount and kinds of reading in which they have engaged (Gradman & Hanania, 1991; Stanovich & Cunningham, 1992, 1993).

Another thought that comes to mind is that, if reading results in so rich a network of knowledge through nothing more than overlaps and contrasts in association, then shouldn't students learn far more efficiently, given active, incisive comprehension strategies? Research indicates that comprehension strategies can be taught and suggests that doing so may improve comprehension (National Institute of Child Health and Human Development [NICHD], 2000). However, comprehension strategies seem to do little to compensate for poor reading ability or weak domain knowledge (O'Reilly & McNamara, 2007). Instead, research repeatedly shows prior domain knowledge to be a prepotent predictor of students' ability to comprehend or to learn from advanced texts (Dochy, Segers, & Buehl, 1999; Shapiro, 2004). In themselves, strong reading skills are also important, but they, too, seem to be of greatest advantage to students with strong domain knowledge (O'Reilly & McNamara, 2007).

Perhaps such findings should not be surprising. As broadly accepted by cognitive psychologists, there are two modes of reasoning (see Sloman, 1996, 2005). The first, most common, mode is knowledge-based. This sort of reasoning is rapid, extensive, and automatic; it is the sort of reasoning that LSA and neural networks statistically emulate. The second mode of reasoning is conscious and rule-based. Such logical analytic thought also warrants instructional attention in our schools, as it is our means of monitoring internal consistency and vetting our thoughts for bias and happenstance. However, no reasoning strategy, however well-structured, can rival the speed, power, or clarity of knowledge-driven understanding (Ericsson, Charness, Feltovich, & Hoffman, 2006); nor can it compensate for an absence of sufficient information.

Still another idea that raises itself is that the pathway to advanced texts might be well paved through other media such as educational videos. That is, if domain knowledge is the ticket to understanding advanced texts, then might the entry of students with less relevant knowledge or weaker reading skills be accelerated through well-designed videos? Unfortunately, evidence so far indicates that even while such educational media can be valuable for developing students' interest in a topic, their impact on the knowledge structures underlying language development and reading comprehension is minimal (Bus, de Jong, Verhallen, & van der Kooy-Hofland, 2008; Echols, West, Stanovich, & Zehr, 1996; West & Stanovich, 1991).

In keeping with this, the J-shaped curve that characterizes the word frequency distributions of large-scale corpora can be seen to represent two different categories of words. The high frequency words—those clustering at the curl of the J—are the nuclear or matrix words of the language. Writers depend on these words to carry the structure and flow of the language regardless of topic or genre. The low frequency words—those clustering at the staff of the J—are the information-bearing words. As such, the usage of these low-frequency words is tied to specific topics and genre. Conversely, mastery of their meanings depends on learning about the specific topics and genre to which they pertain—

and, in turn, such learning is strongly dependent on reading within those domains.

There may one day be modes and methods of information delivery that are as efficient and powerful as text, but for now there is no contest. To grow, our students must read lots, and, more specifically, they must read lots of "complex" texts—texts that offer them new language, new knowledge, and new modes of thought. Beyond the basics, as Hirsch (2006) has so forcefully argued, the reading deficit is integrally tied to a knowledge deficit.

Back to the Classroom:
A Strategy for Developing Advanced Reading

The capacity to understand and learn from any text depends on approaching it with the language, knowledge, ideas, and reading skill that it presumes. It follows that, when assigning materials from which students are to learn, there are basically but two choices. Either the materials must be sufficiently accessible in language and concept for the students to read and understand on their own, or the students must be given help as they read. Some students receive such help in their homes, but many do not and, as I have argued elsewhere, this may be the major factor underlying the achievement gap (Adams, 2006, 2008). In any case, opportunity for one-on-one reading assistance in the typical school setting is limited, leaving for educators only the alternative of restricting assignments to materials that are within their students' independent reach. For weaker students, there follows the popularity of so-called high–low texts, intended to offer high interest or information along low demands on vocabulary and reading skill.

Although the relaxation of school book complexity may be the consequence of our earnest efforts to ensure full curricular access to all, it is a solution with serious problems of its own. In terms of literacy growth, it is a solution that is vortically self-propagating and self-defeating, for it is a solution that denies students the very language, information, and modes of thought that they need most in order to move up and on.

Many have suggested using word-frequency information from large corpora to sequence vocabulary instruction or to evaluate readability, but this will not work. The five most frequent common nouns in the British National Corpus are *time, year, people, way,* and *man*. In the American Heritage corpus, they are *time, people, way, words,* and *things*. These are not the sorts of words that distinguish advanced literacy status. Yet, as described earlier, the reader would need to cover massive amounts of text to encounter the sorts of words that do. Indeed, Carroll et al. (1971, p. xxii) estimate that the likelihood of encountering a word of just average frequency within the domain of grade school texts is about 1 in 13 billion. The problem with using these corpora for instructional guidance or readability estimates relates to the fact that in creating them, the goal was to capture as broad and representative a range as possible of their target domains, thus sampling reading materials so as to minimize redundancy and bias. In effect, then, both of these corpora are topic-neutral. If people were similarly to read a little of this and a little of that, and to retain the words they encounter independently of their contexts, then the likelihood of their knowing any given word might well resemble the probabilities reflected in these corpora.

An alternate and far more promising strategy follows directly from Zipf's law. Again, according to Zipf's law, every natural language discourse comprises a few words that recur again and again and many words that occur just once or only a few times. And, again, Zipf's law is shown to hold for virtually every natural language domain, regardless of its size, topic, modality, or sophistication. But do not be confused here: it is the shape of the distribution that does not change—the words underlying the curve vary from source to source.

In particular, the most frequent words in any language domain relate directly to its topic. Indeed, it is this fact that enables automatic topic spotting by computers. For example, a quick sampling of informational texts on Mars that I picked off the Internet affirms that, without exception and whether the intended audience was young children or scientists, the nouns *Mars* and *planet* are among the five most frequent in each. The balance of the dominant nouns in each text depend on the subtopic in focus—variously, its moons, its geography, our efforts at its exploration, etc.

In other words, combined with what else we know about literacy growth, Zipf's law prescribes a self-supporting strategy for developing the sorts of knowledge structures that complex texts require. We know that, even for young (Cunningham, 2006) and delayed (Share & Shalev, 2004) readers, any new word encountered (and attended) in print becomes a sight word through little more than a single encounter, provided its meaning is known (see Adams, 2008). We know that the more that students already know about the topic of a text, the greater their understanding and learning from its reading (O'Reilly & McNamara, 2007; Shapiro, 2004). We know that prior vocabulary strength predicts the speed and security with which students learn the meanings of unfamiliar words through direct instruction or study (Biemiller & Boote, 2006; Jenkins, Stein, & Wysocki, 1984; Perfetti, Wlotko, & Hart, 2005; Robbins & Ehri, 1994). Prior knowledge also predicts the likelihood that students will learn the meanings of new words through context during reading (Daneman & Green, 1986; Herman, Anderson, Pearson, & Nagy, 1987; Shefelbine, 1990; Sternberg & Powell, 1983). It predicts the probability with which readers correctly infer a new word's meaning from context (Morrison, 1996; Nassaji, 2004), and it predicts both the amount and the nature of the reasoning that is evidenced when they are asked to try to do so (Calvo, Estevez, & Dowens, 2003; Nassaji, 2004).

The challenge, then, lies in organizing our reading regimen such that each text bootstraps the language and knowledge that will be needed for the next. Zipf's law tells us that this can be done by scaffolding students' reading materials within topic.

Pick any topic about which you would like your students to learn—once started, there will be plenty of time for others. If the students are below-level, begin with shorter, simpler texts. Teach the key words and concepts directly, engaging students in using and discussing them so as to be sure they are well anchored. As the students learn the core vocabulary, basic concepts, and overarching schemata of the domain, they will become ready to explore its subtopics, reading as many texts as needed or appropriate on each subtopic in turn. Gradually and seamlessly, they will find themselves ready for texts of increasingly greater depth and complexity. Better yet, as their expertise on, say, Mars, expands, they will find themselves in far better stead to read about Venus, Jupiter, earth sciences, and so on.

Even while making incremental progress in this way, some may question whether offering advanced texts to reluctant readers is a realistic plan. Consider, however, that while no text on dinosaurs would pass a readability criterion for second graders, many second graders nonetheless read about dinosaurs with great satisfaction. Similarly, I have rarely met a Boston cabbie—no matter how much he might decry his ability or interest in reading—who wasn't quick to pick up and read a news article about the Red Sox.

Knowledge is the prepotent determinant of reading comprehension. In theory—and as these two examples perhaps attest—the greatest cognitive and literacy benefits of text-based expertise depend on reading deeply in multiple domains and about multiple topics. We can and must do a better job of leading—and enabling—our students to do so. If education is the key to opportunity, then their options, in school and beyond, depend on it.

References

ACT, Inc. (2006). *Reading between the lines: What the ACT reveals about college readiness in reading.* Iowa City, IA: Author.

Adams, M. J. (2006). The promise of automatic speech recognition for fostering literacy growth in children and adults. In M. McKenna, L. Labbo, R. Kieffer, & D. Reinking (Eds.), *Handbook of literacy and technology* (Vol. 2, pp. 109–128). Hillsdale, NJ: Erlbaum.

Adams, M. J. (2008). The limits of the self-teaching hypotheses (and how technology might help). In S. B. Neuman (Ed.), *Literacy achievement for young children from poverty.* Baltimore: Brookes.

Adams, M. J., & Spoehr, K. T. (in press). *Framework for the vocabulary assessment for the National Assessment of Adult Literacy (NAAL).* Washington, DC: National Center for Education Statistics, Institute of Education Sciences, U.S. Department of Education.

Anderson, R., Wilson, P., & Fielding, L. (1988). Growth in reading and how children spend their time outside of school. *Reading Research Quarterly, 23,* 285–303.

Beaton, A. E., Hilton, T. L., & Schrader, W. B. (1977). *Changes in the verbal abilities of high school seniors, college entrants, and SAT candidates between 1960 and 1972.* New York: College Entrance Examination Board.

Betts, E. A. (1946). *Foundations of reading instruction.* New York: American Book Company.

Biemiller, A., & Boote, C. (2006). An effective method for building meaning vocabulary in primary grades. *Journal of Educational Psychology, 98*(1), 44–62.

British National Corpus, version 2 (BNC World). (2001). Distributed by Oxford University Computing Services on behalf of the BNC Consortium. Available at *www.natcorp.ox.ac.uk/.*

British National Corpus. (2008). The BNC in numbers. Retrieved June 15, 2008, from *www.natcorp.ox.ac.uk/corpus.*

Bus, A. G., de Jong, M. T., Verhallen, M. J. A. J., & van der Kooy-Hofland, V. A. C. (2008). Design features in living books and their effects on young children's vocabulary. In S. Neuman (Ed.), *Educating the other America.* Baltimore: Brookes.

Calvo, M. G., Estevez, A., & Dowens, M. G. (2003). Time course of elaborative inferences as a function of prior vocabulary knowledge. *Learning and Instruction, 13*(6), 611–631.

Carroll, J. B., Davies, P., & Richman, B. (1971). *The American Heritage word frequency book.* Boston: Houghton Mifflin.

Carver, R. P. (1994). Percentage of unknown vocabulary words in text as a function of the relative difficulty of the text: Implications for instruction. *Journal of Reading Behavior, 26,* 413–437.

Chall, J. S., Conard, S. S., & Harris, S. H. (1977). *An analysis of textbooks in relation to declining SAT scores.* New York: College Entrance Examination Board.

College Entrance Examination Board. (1977). *On further examination: Report of the Advisory Panel on the Scholastic Aptitude Test Score Decline.* New York: Author.

Cunningham, A. E. (2006). Accounting for children's orthographic learning while reading text: Do children self-teach? *Journal of Experimental Child Psychology, 95,* 56–77.

Daneman, M., & Green, I. (1986). Individual differences in comprehending and producing words in context. *Journal of Memory and Language, 25,* 1–18.

Dochy, F., Segers, M., & Buehl, M. (1999). The relation between assessment practices and outcomes of studies: The case of research on prior knowledge. *Review of Educational Research, 69(1),* 145–186.

Echols, L. D., West, R. G., Stanovich, K. W., & Zehr, K. S., (1996). Using children's literacy activities to predict growth in verbal cognitive skills: A longitudinal investigation. *Journal of Educational Psychology, 88,* 296–304.

Ericsson, K. A., Charness, N., Feltovich, P. J., & Hoffman, R. R. (2006). *The Cambridge Handbook of expertise and expert performance.* Cambridge, UK: Cambridge University Press.

Gorfein, D. (2001). *On the consequences of meaning selection: Perspectives on resolving lexical ambiguity.* Washington, DC: American Psychological Association.

Gradman, H., & Hanania, E. (1991). Language learning background factors and ESL proficiency. *Modern Language Journal, 75,* 39–51.

Griffiths, T. L., Steyvers, M., & Tenenbaum, J. B. (2007). Topics in semantic representation. *Psychological Review, 114(2),* 211–244.

Grigg, W., Donahue, P., & Dion, G. (2007). *The nation's report card: 12th-grade reading and mathematics 2005* (NCES 2007-468). Washington, DC: National Center for Education Statistics, Institute of Education Sciences, U.S. Department of Education.

Hayes, D. P. (1988). Speaking and writing: Distinct patterns of word choice. *Journal of Memory and Language, 27,* 572–585.

Hayes, D. P. (1992). The growing inaccessibility of science. *Nature, 356,* 739–740.

Hayes, D. P., & Ahrens, M. G. (1988). Vocabulary simplification for children: A special case of "motherese"? *Journal of Child Language, 15,* 395–410.

Hayes, D. P., Wolfer, L. T., & Wolfe, M. F. (1996). Schoolbook simplification and its relation to the decline in SAT-verbal scores. *American Educational Research Journal, 33(2),* 489–508.

Herman, P. A., Anderson, R. C., Pearson, P. D., & Nagy, W. E. (1987). Incidental acquisition of word meaning from expositions with varied text features. *Reading Research Quarterly, 22,* 263–264.

Hiebert, E. H. (2005). In pursuit of an effective, efficient vocabulary curriculum for the elementary grades. In E. H. Hiebert & M. Kamil (Eds.), *The teaching and learning of vocabulary: Bringing scientific research to practice* (pp. 243–263). Mahwah, NJ: Erlbaum.

Hirsch, E. D. (2006). *The knowledge deficit: Closing the shocking education gap for American children.* Boston: Houghton Mifflin.

Hu, M., & Nation, P. (2000). Unknown vocabulary density and reading comprehension. *Reading in a Foreign Language, 13(1),* 403–430.

Jenkins, J. R., Stein, M. L., & Wysocki, K. (1984). Learning vocabulary through reading. *American Educational Research Journal, 21(4),* 767–787.

Kingsbury, A. (2007, August 28). SAT scores drop for the second year in a row. *U.S. News & World Report*. Retrieved from *www.usnews.com*.

Kutner, M., Greenberg, E., Jin, Y., Boyle, B., Hsu, Y., & Dunleavy, E. (2007). *Literacy in everyday life: Results from the 2003 National Assessment of Adult Literacy* (NCES 2007-480). Washington, DC: National Center for Educational Statistics, Institute of Education Sciences, U.S. Department of Education.

Landauer, T. K. (1998). Learning and representing verbal meaning: The latent semantic analysis theory. *Current Directions in Psychological Science, 7*(5), 161–164.

Landauer, T. K., & Dumais, S. T. (1997). A solution to Plato's problem: The latent semantic analysis theory of acquisition, induction, and representation of knowledge. *Psychological Review, 104*(2), 211–240.

Laufer, B. (1988). What percentage of text-lexis is essential for comprehension. In C. Lauren & M. Nordmann (Eds.), *Special language: From humans to thinking machines* (pp. 316–323). Clevedon, UK: Multilingual Matters.

Lee, J. Grigg, W. S., & Donahue, P. L. (2007). *The nation's report card: Reading 2007* (NCES 2007-496). Washington, DC: National Center for Education Statistics, Institute of Education Sciences, U.S. Department of Education.

Leech, G., Rayson, P., & Wilson, A. (2001). *Word frequencies in written and spoken English based on the British National Corpus*. London: Longman.

Lewin, T. (2006, August 31). Students paths to small colleges can bypass SAT. *The New York Times*. Retrieved from *www.nytimes.com*.

Matthews, J. (2006, August 30). SAT records biggest score dip in 31 years. *Washington Post*. Retrieved from *www.washingtonpost.com/*.

Morrison, L. (1996). Talking about words: A study of French as a second language learners' lexical inferencing procedures. *Canadian Modern Language Review, 53*, 41–75.

Mullis, I. V. S., Martin, M. O., Gonzalez, E. J., & Kennedy, A. M. (2003). *PIRLS 2001 International Report: IEA's Study of Reading Literacy Achievement in Primary Schools*. Chestnut Hill, MA: Boston College. Retrieved July 31, 2008, from *timss.bc.edu/PIRLS2001.html*.

Nagy, W., Anderson, R. C., & Herman, P. A. (1987). Learning word meanings from context during normal reading. *American Educational Research Journal, 24*, 237–270.

Nagy, W. E., Herman, P., & Anderson, R. C. (1985). Learning words from context. *Reading Research Quarterly, 20*, 233–253.

Nassaji, H. (2004). The relationship between depth of vocabulary knowledge and L2 learners' lexical inferencing strategy use and success. *The Canadian Modern Language Review, 61*(1), 107–134.

National Center for Education Statistics. (2007). *Digest of Education Statistics: 2007*. Washington, DC: U.S. Department of Education. Retrieved June 15, 2008, from *nces.ed.gov/programs/digest/d06/tables/dt06_132.asp*.

National Commission on Excellence in Education. (1983). *A nation at risk: The imperative for educational reform*. Washington, DC: U.S. Government Printing Office. Retrieved June 15, 2008, from *www.ed.gov/pubs/NatAtRisk*.

National Institute of Child Health and Human Development. (2000). *Report of the National Reading Panel: Teaching children to read: An evidence-based assess-*

ment of the scientific research literature on reading and its implications for reading instruction (NIH Publication No. 00-4769). Washington, DC: U.S. Government Printing Office.

O'Reilly, T., & McNamara, D. S. (2007). The impact of science knowledge, reading skill, and reading strategy knowledge on more traditional "high-stakes" measures of high school students' science achievement. *American Educational Research Journal, 44*(1), 161–196.

Perfetti, C. A., Wlotko, E. W., & Hart, L. (2005). Word learning and individual differences in word learning reflected in event-related potentials. *Journal of Experimental Psychology: Learning, Memory, and Cognition, 31*(6), 1281–1292.

Price, G. G., & Carpenter, T. P. (1978). Review: On further examination: Report of the Advisory Panel on the Scholastic Aptitude Test Score Decline. *Journal for Research in Mathematics Education, 9*(2), 155–160.

Robbins, C., & Ehri, L. C. (1994). Reading storybooks to kindergartners helps them learn new vocabulary words. *Journal of Educational Psychology, 86,* 54–64.

Rothstein, J. M. (2004). College performance predictions and the SAT. *Journal of Econometrics, 121*(1–2), 297–317.

Seastrom, M., Hoffman, L., Chapman, C., & Stillwell, R. (2005). *The averaged freshman graduation rate for public high schools from the common Core of Data: School years 2001–02 and 2002–03* (NCES 2006-601). Washington, DC: National Center for Education Statistics, Institute of Education Sciences, U.S. Department of Education.

Sereno, J., & Jongman, A. (1997). Processing of English inflectional morphology. *Memory and Cognition, 25,* 425–437.

Shapiro, A. M. (2004). How including prior knowledge as a subject variable may change outcomes of learning research. *American Educational Research Journal, 41*(1), 159–189.

Share, D., & Shalev, C. (2004). Self-teaching in normal and disabled readers. *Reading and Writing: An Interdisciplinary Journal, 17,* 769–800.

Shefelbine, J. (1990). Student factors related to variability in learning word meanings from context. *Journal of Reading Behavior, 22,* 71–97.

Sloman, S. A. (1996). The empirical case for two systems of reasoning. *Psychological Bulletin, 119*(1), 3–22.

Sloman, S. A. (2005). *Causal models: How people think about the world and its alternatives.* Oxford, UK: Oxford University Press.

Stahl, S. A., & Fairbanks, M. M. (1986). The effects of vocabulary instruction: A model-based meta-analysis. *Review of Educational Research, 56,* 72–110.

Stanners, R. F., Neiser, J. J., Hernon, W. P., & Hall, R. (1979). Memory representations for morphologically related words. *Journal of Verbal Learning and Verbal Behavior, 18,* 399–412.

Stanovich, K. E., & Cunningham, A. E. (1992). Where does knowledge come from? Specific associations between print exposure and information acquisition. *Journal of Educational Psychology, 85*(2), 211–229.

Stanovich, K. E., & Cunningham, A. E. (1993). Studying the consequences of literacy within a literate society: The cognitive correlates of print exposure. *Memory and Cognition, 20*(1), 51–68.

Stedman, L. (1993). The condition of education: Why school reformers are on the right track. *Phi Delta Kappan, 75*(3), 215–225.

Stedman, L. C. (1996). Respecting the evidence: The achievement crisis remains real. *Education Policy Analysis Archives, 4*(7), 1–36. Retrieved July 31, 2008, from *epaa.asu.edu/epaa/v4n7.*

Sternberg, R., & Powell, J. S. (1983). Comprehending verbal comprehension. *American Psychologist, 38,* 878–893.

Sum, A., Kirsch, I., & Taggart, R. (2002). *The twin challenges of mediocrity and inequality: Literacy in the U.S. from an international perspective.* Princeton, NJ: Educational Testing Service.

Turnbull, W. W. (1985). *Student change, program change: Why the SAT scores kept falling* (ETS RR No. 85-28). New York: College Entrance Examination Board.

West, R. F., & Stanovich, K. E. (1991). The incidental acquisition of information from reading. *Psychological Science, 2,* 325–330.

Wolfe, M. B. W., Schreiner, M. E., Rehder, B., Laham, D., Foltz, P. W., Kintch, W., et al. (1998). *Discourse Processes, 25*(2–3), 309–336.

Zipf, G. K. (1935). *The psycho-biology of languages.* Boston: Houghton Mifflin.

9

Increasing Reading Opportunities for English Language Learners

Elizabeth Bernhardt

Misconceptions about second-language learners abound in the literacy research and practice arena. Many of these misconceptions are seated in the linguistic egocentrism that makes Americans incapable of appreciating the utility and applicability of any language other than English. This self-perception feeds the xenophobia that characterizes much of the controversy over immigration reform as well as the English-only movement. It has been reinforced, in addition, by several influential documents developed by literacy specialists. This chapter devotes some thought to exploring how major federal reports and publications in highly visible research journals portray learning to read in a second language (i.e., English). But, far more important, this chapter describes the process of second-language reading, or learning to read in a second language, in classrooms—a process that is often invisible to teachers—in order to embody the spirit aspired to in this volume of ensuring that students get the "right stuff." This chapter focuses on three principles that need to be infused into classrooms that include students who take on the challenge of learning to read and reading to learn in a second language. First, teachers need to understand the influence and importance of first-language literacy and place their formative assessments against this backdrop when diagnosing individual students. Second, teachers need to acknowledge and account for the role of the language structure from which students come in order to figure it, too, into the assessment scheme as a source of potential support as well as possible interference. Third, teachers need to increase the volume of reading materials that contain content with which students might be familiar, namely, informational text, and understand that what students might *understand* about that content and what students can *say* about that content are very different things.

The Influence and Importance of First-Language Literacy in Learning to Read and Speak a Second Language

Pinpointing the exact instant in time when a field turns its attention to a particular educational flashpoint is difficult. Interestingly, though, the field of literacy was an early player in examining second-language reading for its insights into the reading process in general. Both Javal (1879) and Cattell (1885) commented on the differences between readers reading in a first and then a second language, as did Huey (1909) subsequently. Some awareness of second-language reading was also extant during the early years of intelligence testing, but by and large a recognition of the unique process of second-language reading remained dormant for most of the 20th century. Goodman (1968) helped to refocus attention on the concern of second-language reading when patterns of immigration made it clear that American classrooms would soon be populated by students, adolescents, and adults who were entering schooling with a home oral language that did not match the oral language in which literacy instruction would be rooted. Subsequently, the 1980s witnessed patterns of increased interest in second-language reading that were clearly identifiable among professional groups such as the International Reading Association, the National Reading Conference, and the National Council of Teachers of English. A review of the nature of papers on these groups reveals a focus on cultural matters, arguing for inclusiveness and egalitarianism. Little instructional assistance was offered. Articles in professional journals as well as materials for the preparation of literacy teachers offered little in the way of specifics for differentiated instruction (Bernhardt, 1994).

The late 1990s witnessed a sea change in the amount of attention that literacy educators gave to matters of second-language reading. An influential review article by Fitzgerald (1995) is important in this regard. Based on her review, restricted to work done with students learning to read in English, Fitzgerald (2000) ultimately argued that "there is little *evidence* to support the need for a special vision of second-language reading instruction" (p. 520, emphasis added). Writings such as these led the field to ignore the concept of evidence and to create the comfortable philosophy that there was "little need for a special vision of second-language reading instruction." What Fitzgerald and others had actually focused on was *a lack of evidence* about child second-language readers as well as about the procedures of literacy instruction. True enough, at the procedural level little can be different when teaching second-language learners to read. Similar to the learning to read process of native English speakers, second-language learners need to practice word recognition and fluency and to have opportunities for practice; good and interesting materials need to be available; teachers need to spend one-on-one time with individuals as well as with small groups of readers; readers need to be given opportunities to write and to talk about what they read; and so on and so forth. Indeed, these are procedures one would expect to find in use in all classrooms. To argue that instruction within its broadest parameters would somehow appear to be different for second-language students is missing the point.

While there are similarities, there are also differences in the processes for students learning to read in English as native English speakers or as second-language learners, as acknowledged by the National Literacy Panel report (August & Shanahan, 2006). The panel concluded that "second-language learners differ in some significant ways from first-language learners in literacy learning because they bring to this challenge an additional and different set of language resources and experiences" (p. 14). Indeed, it is not the literacy procedures that are and might be different but rather *the nature of the language resources and experiences* that renders the process different for second-language readers. In other words, it is at the level of diagnosis and assessment where the differences are at work. Yet, ironically, the panel report falls into the same illogic as previous publications. It perpetuates the view that research findings (or lack thereof) describe a process rather than acknowledging that research findings merely portray answers to questions as asked. If questions are asked in univariate, isolated ways disregarding context, then univariate-isolated answers are revealed. These answers might provide some insight, but they do not necessarily reveal the process itself and most certainly offer little to teachers who are focused on accommodating and assisting all students, each of whom comes to school with a unique set of *language resources and experiences*.

Restricting itself to analyzing studies almost exclusively involving preadult second-language readers, the panel drew a number of generalizations about second-language reading. It concluded, for example, that the most consistent finding is that English language learners (ELLs) "achieve adequate word reading" (Snow, 2006, p. 633). In her synthesis of the panel's findings, Snow (2006) is quick to add that in most studies students were not reading extended text and were rarely assessed in their fluency and comprehension. In studies that were examined on the topic of comprehension the hardly surprising conclusion drawn by the panel was that "comprehension performance falls well below that of native-speaking peers" (p. 633). The panel also indicated that the "same social factors" (p. 634) for ELLs as for native English readers are at play in the literacy process—such factors as poverty level, parental involvement, educational level, and the like. The panel found little if any evidence on what kind of instruction is effective and provided only "limited guidance" about how good instruction for second-language speakers differs from that for first-language speakers (p. 638). In fact, only one accommodation seemed to be of great assistance—developing English oral proficiency in the context of literacy instruction (p. 639). Nothing in the professional development of teachers seemed to be unique for English language learners. Features of professional development such as hands-on, field-based experiences were found to be useful. The only area of the panel's work that acknowledged the *language resources* of second-language learners in a serious manner was the section on cross-linguistic relationships. Snow acknowledges how important the notion of these relationships has been historically in the second-language acquisition literature. She does, however, by and large dismiss any findings from this arena as inconclusive because of the correlational nature of most of the studies. In other words, in spite of the significant relationships between first and second languages found on most language tasks, it is unclear whether being able to do a task in language 1 actually *causes* the ability to conduct the task in language 2.

Ultimately, Snow's (2006) synthesis points to the tautological nature of much of what was indicated in the report:

> Thus, it is not surprising that the individual skills that predict good reading for English-learning versus monolingual readers are so similar—they are the skills that help children solve the particular challenges of reading English. Nor is it surprising that features of

> instruction that work well for English monolingual children also work for English-learning children, who must learn the same skills because they are ultimately faced with the same task. (p. 645)

In other words, when learning to read a given language, achievement is linked to procedures known to be effective for that particular language. There is hardly any wonder at how such an analysis leads educators to the conclusion that instructing ELLs is an identical process for all students; there is even less wonder at why teachers then become so frustrated with ELLs who are often stymied in instruction.

Admittedly, the task of the National Literacy Panel was to review the research about all dimensions of preadult second-language reading even though an accepted subtext of all such work is to guide the improvement of practice. In fact, the Institute of Education Sciences practice guides take up the mission of improving practices in many educational areas. The intention behind the guides is to base advice for instruction on both research and field-based expertise. The practice guide most relevant to this chapter is *Effective Literacy and English Language Instruction for English Learners in the Elementary Grades* (Gersten et al., 2007), whose authors note:

> Our goal is to provide guidance for all English learners, whether they are taught to read in their home language, in English (by far the most prevalent method in the United States), or in both languages simultaneously. The recommendations are relevant for students regardless of their language of reading instruction. (p. vii)

The attitude portrayed in this statement is one of perceiving no difference between first- and second-language readers. In fact, the five recommendations listed in the practice guide hold true to the concept of *all* students being ELLs, arguing that the same assessment mechanisms can be employed (recommendation 1); the same kinds of small-group reading interventions can be implemented (recommendation 2); and the same focus on academic English is at hand (recommendation 4). Only two of the recommendations provide any special advice regarding ELLs. Recommendation 3, regarding vocabulary instruction, emphasizes "the acquisition of everyday words that native speakers know and that are not necessarily part of the academic curriculum" (p. 4). And recommendation 5, concerning leveled group learning, acknowledges that "different English language proficiencies" (p. 2) are at play. Beyond these latter two recommendations, no distinction between native and nonnative is drawn in the practice guide's recommendations. These principles may confuse one through oversimplification in that they emphasize the hyperprocedural level, which suggests that literacy instruction in all languages shares many things in common. Hyperprocedurally, instruction in any language involves books, teachers, classrooms, and such things as group work, assessment, and notions of academic vocabulary. Yet, how all of these features develop into a sustainable literacy program for students who do not come to school speaking English is an entirely different matter.

Focusing on research studies that fit the requirements set forth by federally funded panels seeking "scientifically based" guidance is laudable. Yet, it is critically important to understand that reviewing and citing research without regard to the fundamental contextual factor in second-language reading—namely, the dimension of *second* and all that *second* entails—is potentially fatally flawed. While it might appear that every conclusion or guideline cited above reflects the general reading process, there are critical features that *distinguish* ELLs as they go through the learning-to-read process that must be at the forefront of all instruction. First, traditional instruction tends to suppress or ignore the first-language literacy of ELLs because either state policy discourages the recognition of languages other than English or teachers are unaware of languages other than English. Second, while admitting that ELLs come to school with different levels of oral language proficiency in English, the depth of the differences has to be understood. The levels are far more diverse and grammatically marked than that of their English-speaking counterparts. Third, the background knowledge that ELLs bring to school is more often than not invisible because it is housed in a language other than English. In other words, ELLs, like their English-speaking counterparts, might know a lot about their pets at home, but unlike those counterparts they are not able to articulate that knowledge in English. This circumstance means that ELLs are in triple jeopardy in that (1) they have to learn to read; (2) they have to learn the content from reading; and (3) they have to learn the language fluently to express the content of their reading. While all students have to *learn to read* and *read to learn*, ELL students must also learn the language of learning to read *and* they must understand the sociocultural nature of any given text for learning. Teachers charged with guiding learners through this complex and difficult terrain find little assistance in large-scale research and applied syntheses, most of which are superficial and fundamentally misguided.

What ELLs Know and What They Need to Learn: The Role of Language Structures

The second-language acquisition literature is fairly consistent in the finding that, even though adults are far more cognitively developed and metalinguistically "aware" child and adult second-language learners proceed through similar developmental processes in their learning of second languages (Hawkins, 2001). This finding is particularly stark in the development of syntax. The classic example illustrating this research-driven insight is the development of questions across languages. Intonation while maintaining canonical word order is always the first question form; then verb inversion; next, the acquisition of question words (*who, where, why,* and so forth); embedded questions (*Do you know what time it is?*); and so forth. Adults may go through these stages more quickly than students, but the fact remains that the stages seem to be parallel. Adults often "know" a grammatical rule such as "In English, the verb comes first in a yes–no question." Yet, in speech, similar to students who may not have much metalinguistic awareness, adults pose a question such as "You coming to my party?" Findings such as these that examine different morphosyntactic structures as well as some semantic features (*buy/sell, give/take,* and so forth) provide convincing evidence that the second-language process is indeed a *route* that any learner moves through, albeit at different *rates* (Ellis, 1994).

Ironically, the literacy field, with its very public syntheses about second-language reading, seems not to take any of this literature into account. In fact, it deliberately ignores it by sidelining most of the research about adult readers of second languages. The argument is put forth in this chapter that ignoring what is known about second-language acquisition and about adult second-language reading is misguided. It buries insights and a significant knowledge base for teachers that can assist them in working with students who are ELLs *and* literacy learners *and* content learners all at the same time.

Every teacher, researcher, and theorist from behaviorist to cognitivist to Vygotskian knows that what the learner brings to the learning environment is absolutely critical. The learner context is arguably the most critical factor for teachers to comprehend and the most secure foundation from which to launch their instruction. Whether this contextual principle is couched in the rubric of *background knowledge, prior knowledge, known to the new, new learning based on previous learning,* or *the more knowledgeable other,* it focuses on what the learner already possesses internally as the soil in which new learning will take root. Often this soil is absolutely compatible with the learning that is to take root, but at other times it may well be like trying to plant corn in sand or a cactus in a bog. The task for teachers is to change the nature of the environment by making it more flexible, hospitable, or welcoming. Whatever metaphor one chooses, the irony is that key literacy policy statements on second-language reading seem to ignore this fundamental concept.

The remaining pages of this chapter examine second-language reading within the context of what learners bring to the process and provide teachers with usable guidelines when assessing and assisting ELLs. The model in Figure 9.1 attempts to vivify the research data that we have within a convenient and helpful thumbnail conceptualization (Bernhardt, 2005). Broadly speaking, research indicates that learning to read in a second language relies on these critical components: *first-language literacy knowledge* (represented by the light gray bottom arc) and captured in the middle; and slightly grayer area *second-language knowledge*, meaning a knowledge of second-language forms (grammatical knowledge) and word knowledge. These two components—*literacy knowledge and language knowledge*—seem to interact against the backdrop of *world knowledge*. Effective second-language reading is dependent upon a reader's using these three knowledge sources in a *compensatory* fashion. The model attempts to capture compensation in its three-dimensional form. What does *compensation* mean? It means that at times a knowledge of how literacy works helps the reader compensate for a lack of word knowledge; sometimes grammatical ability can override a background knowledge deficit to help a reader decode a word; sometimes knowing the content arena of a text can help readers to both understand a word and to figure out its syntactic properties; and so forth. The following unpacks each of these concepts in more detail.

Literacy Knowledge

Using literacy knowledge means applying what a reader already knows about written language to understand other written language. Teachers of young students are, of course, hardly strangers to this concept, but a key feature for second-language students is this: how literacy is realized in their mother tongue may be on some levels quite different from the way it is realized in the English-speaking world. The first two examples in Spanish in Table 9.1 illustrate a literacy perception that would be immediately transferable, whether in Spanish to English or in English to Spanish. The first example row is easily recognizable as a paragraph. Familiarity with written language signals that this paragraph (whether or not one knows any Spanish) likely has a central idea, is not emotionally laden (note the absence of exclamation points), and is about something in Latin America relating to anthropology. The material in the second example in Table 9.1 is an easily recognizable list. On first glance, it appears to contain key points that a reader should remember for future use. One could probably go on, listing assumptions about each text, perhaps even discovering that example 2 in Table 9.1 contains the *same* text as in example 1 (thus, nonsensical as a "list"). The point to comprehend is that the outward features of a passage may bring with them sets of assumptions about what is and is not signaled by the text.

The third example in Table 9.1 consists of text in German. Whether one knows German or not, the text layout appears to signal that language is missing or that the words might be in a random order, given the different types of fonts with lots of words capitalized. These assumptions, which are reasonable for English and Spanish literate readers, turn out to be inaccurate. All nouns in German are capitalized. And it is merely the type faces and fonts and spacing that signal incoherence; the text itself is a perfectly normal German sentence. In fact, had the reader seen the sentence in a normal configuration—*Selbst in Hannover, wo er immerhin 40 Jahre lang gelebt hat, wissen die Meisten wenig mit Gottfried Wilhelm Leibniz anzufangen* (Most people who lived in Hannover, where Gottfried Wilhelm Leibniz lived for 40 years, didn't know what to make of him)—an entirely different set of assumptions might have come into play.

The point of these illustrations is that, whether one "knows" a particular language or not, a literate person comes to the reading process with a set of assumptions about what one might find in written language. Other examples in this regard are such features as color, print size, and typography. The public outcry attending the introduction of color photos into the *New York Times* is one example: that outcry was not based on the use of color per se, but rather on equating the subsequent quality of the text with "McNews" even before any of the articles were read. Similarly, the use of "thick print" or sans serif typefaces connotes nonserious or nonintellectual content (Bernhardt, 1991). While these examples might be a bit too sophisticated in discussions with young students, we know that students are very early on deliberately sensitized to the print environment around them. That print environment sends significant messages to them regardless of the specifics of the language in print.

Beyond the specifics of print configuration and beliefs about con-

TABLE 9.1. Illustrations of Conventions and Content in Spanish, German, and Urdu

Example	Illustration
1	Así como el médico toma una radiografía para analizar internamente el organismo, los antropólogos, mediante el único laboratório de prospección arqueológica de América Latina, analizarán en marzo un sitio preolmeca del año 3000 AC, ubicado en la costa del Pacífico. El objetivo es identificar con precisión asentimientos humanos utilizando imágenes satelitales y fotografías aéreas a color de alta resolución.
2	• Así como • el médico toma una radiografía para analizar internamente el • organismo, los • antropólogos, mediante el • único laboratório de • prospección arqueológica de América • Latina, analizarán • en marzo un sitio preolmeca del año • 3000 AC, ubicado en la costa del Pacífico
3	Selbst in Hannover, wo *er immerhin* 40 Jahre land gelebt hat, **wissen die** Meisten wenig mit Gottfried Wilhelm Leibniz **anzufangen**.
4	

tent based on it, the knowledge of what words look like and "should" look like and should sound like are also at play. The expectations set up by sound–symbol correspondences as well as the prosodic features of language play an important role. The early stages of literacy learning always involve understanding *concepts of oral language written down*. For second-language learners, the issue will be that *the oral language they possess and the one that is written down are different*. Even though there is no match between the oral language they bring and the one they see in print, they will, nevertheless, impose those known oral language forms on the new written language.

One could spend an infinite amount of time teasing out hundreds of these kinds of comparisons. The point remains that the reader, no matter how young, will bring a set of expectations based on prior literacy experiences that will not match the target's literacy most of the time. In fact, research indicates that literacy knowledge tends to account for about 20% of comprehension performance among second-language readers (Bernhardt & Kamil, 1995). Being able to account for this much of the process, based on literacy knowledge alone, is critical. A convenient image to use is that second-language readers have a leg up on the second-language process. They are not blank slates; upwards of 20% of their slate is already colored in. Or another way of thinking about this is that on a 100-point test, a second-language reader might be able to answer upwards of 20 questions based on his or her knowledge of how literacy works. We will put this metaphor to the test in a few pages.

Language Knowledge

The next dimension illustrated in Figure 9.1 is language knowledge. In contrast to literacy knowledge, language knowledge appears to account for about 30% of the process of second-language reading. As noted earlier, language knowledge entails grammatical form, vocabulary, cognates, and concepts of linguistic distance. *Grammatical form* refers to linguistic features such as morphology and syntax that entail inflections and endings, case markings, and features such as mood. Grammatical form itself presents text that is far less ambiguous, for example, in Spanish than it is in English because Spanish overspecifies while English underspecifies. For example, regular present tense verbs in English inflect only for the third person (I, you, we, they *sing*; he/she *sings*), while in Spanish separate inflections exist for all three persons and in both the singular and plural forms. Similarly, Spanish distinguishes between direct objects (*lo, la, los, las*) and indirect objects (*le, les*), while English does not (*him, her, it, you, them*) in both cases. The additional specifications on the part of Spanish offer the reader a grammatical signal about word relationships that helps to disambiguate sentences. English, in contrast, offers little grammatical signaling here. Generally speaking, it is only through word order that one can disambiguate in English. Another convenience that Spanish offers that English does not is the explicit signaling of mood—language that expresses attitudes or feelings such as a wish, or a doubt, uncertainty, advice, or an emotion.

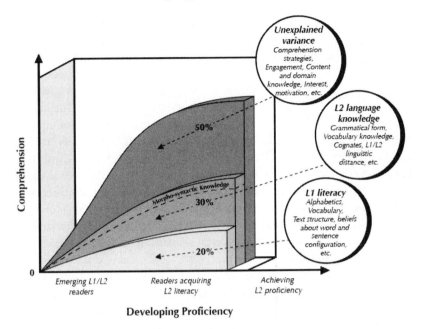

FIGURE 9.1. A compensatory model of second-language reading. From Bernhardt (2005). Copyright 2005 by Cambridge University Press. Reprinted by permission.

For English to express attitude or feeling, additional words or expressions have to be added to the discourse. One has to read and process more words to get the same effect. In other words, language users are conditioned by their native language to expect certain grammatical signals. This expectancy grammar is based on individual-languages and is in no way universal.

An illustration within the domain of syntax illustrates this point. The answer to the English language question *Shall I give you the information?* might have the response *Yes, I want you to give it to me* or *Yes, I want you to give me it.* That same question posed in Spanish—*Te doy la información?*—and its comparable response—*Sí, quiero que me la des*—is far more restrictive syntactically and morphologically. The pronouns do not move around the way they can in English. Of course, in other situations the reverse may be true; that is, in other configurations, English may be more restrictive than Spanish. Consider two Spanish sentences that exhibit a flexibility in word order that English simply does not have: *Se lo voy a escribir. Voy a escribírselo.* English does not permit either of the direct translations of these sentences: *To them I'm going to write it* or *I'm going to write to them it.* What do these linguistic phenomena mean for the reader? In learning fluency, one learns to anticipate what might come next in a text. In fact, miscue analysis is based precisely on this principle. For the second-language reader, this ability to anticipate accurately is suspended and must be relearned. Critically, at least in the Spanish—English situation, there is indeed substantial anticipatory overlap. Yet, *substantial* does not mean *exclusive.* It is precisely in those areas of nonoverlap that teachers must become vigilant. Admittedly, even though there are very real differences in language forms for all readers, texts for younger students tend to incorporate a relatively simple syntax. In actuality, the challenges posed by syntax crosslingually actually become more demanding as texts become more demanding. Syntax becomes more confounding as second-language readers mature and tackle more demanding texts.

The model in Figure 9.1 indicates that a knowledge of vocabulary is a more substantial language knowledge component in second-language reading than morphosyntax (Brisbois, 1995). In this regard, the concept of *cognate* is absolutely critical, both in teaching second-language readers and in helping them to achieve greater fluency. A cognate is a word related to another word through derivation or borrowing. *Cognate* literally means "born in similarity," most assuredly reflecting the notion of prior knowledge. Cognates are in some sense words that the learner already possesses.

Consider these examples of German words: *Computer, Museum, Video, Stereo, intelligent, Buch, alt, machen, Welt, Umwelt.* Since German and English are Germanic languages, the cognate overlap is significant. Within this group of words, cognates range from outright word adoptions such as *Computer* and *Museum* (the only distinction being that all nouns are capitalized in German) to more distant cognates such as *alt* (old), *Welt* (world), and *Umwelt* (environment), the latter demonstrating that cognates are sometimes not very transparent.

Because of the historical roots of English in French and Latin, there is an overlap in cognates between Spanish and English as well. A minimal overlap of 30%, according to Nash (1997), indicates that Spanish speakers learning English are at a substantial advantage in their learning of content words in English. Transparency can at times be an issue on both the learner's side and the teacher's. If the teacher does not know Spanish, it may be difficult to perceive the areas of assistance for learners; if learners do not appreciate the strategy that words are related to one other, they may not perceive the huge knowledge store that they already have at hand. Both teachers and learners need to heighten their metalinguistic knowledge in this regard. For example, knowing that regular word endings such as *-dad, -ión, ía, -or,* and *-encia* that Spanish speakers have minimally in their oral vocabulary (if not also in their literacy vocabulary) enables a transition into English nouns ending, respectively, in *-ty, -tion, -sion, -y, -er, -or, -ence,* and *-ency.* Or knowing that words that can describe nouns, such as words ending in *-ico, -ica, oso, -osa, -ado,* and *-ido* in Spanish become English language adjectives ending, respectively, in *-ic, -ical, -ous, -ed,* and *-ing,* can significantly enhance active vocabulary knowledge. There are also regularities in spelling and sound that can be helpful to crosslingual readers such as the elimination in English of the initial *e* on many Spanish words (e.g., *escriba/scribe, escolar/scholastic*). Fundamentally, teachers need to understand these relationships for diagnostic purposes, and learners should be explicitly taught these relationships. We explain to monolingual students how to figure out words, and we should do the same for ELLs; it is the content of the explanation that is different.

World Knowledge

The third element in second-language reading that is intuitively critical is world knowledge. The concept *intuitive* is employed because it is far less concrete and far more expansive than the former two factors, for which we have substantially greater evidence. We do indeed have evidence within adult second-language readers that a knowledge of topic can override grammatical deficiencies (Bernhardt, 1991). In other words, if a reader knows much about a topic, the topic knowledge can assist in decoding difficult, low-frequency, or technical vocabulary. In other words, adult readers reading within high-knowledge domains are able to use strategies to decide that "this is a text about a coal mining disaster." Therefore, the text probably has such words or phrases in it as *mine shaft, oxygen, life line, carbon monoxide, rescuer,* and the like. Research also indicates that the converse may also be true: that background knowledge can mask or depress language knowledge. If one is familiar, for example, with the traditional conflict between environmentalists and golfers (due to the high environmental costs of golf course maintenance), reading a headline about an environmentalist–golfer coalition might lead to the reaction "I must have misread that." In other words, readers may use knowledge to overcompensate. Within second-language contexts in which readers are already insecure about their language knowledge but often feel more secure about their world knowledge, they are often ready to dismiss what the language "has told them" in favor of a more "reasonable" interpretation based on their version of the "real world." This is the instance where literacy knowledge, language knowledge, and world knowledge collide.

Cultural beliefs undoubtedly enter into the concept of world knowledge. The text in example 4 of Table 9.1 is written in Urdu. Whether one can recognize the language or not, in applying general principles of literacy, one recognizes the text as a text, assumes that it contains a coherent message and that it is not a story (note the telephone numbers that are listed) and that it is perhaps an ad of some sort because of the three identical words across the top, much like "attention, attention, attention" or "closeout, closeout, closeout." In fact, the three words are "good news, good news, good news." The back of the card appears alongside the front. It has a space for the listing of names, an address, and a dollar amount. This configuration seems to be curious and one might respond with "I have no idea of what this card is about. Somebody wants money for sure." Yet, if one then instantiates a religious notion, the card can become suddenly an indulgence or prayer card. It is cultural or, better said, *subcultural* information that enables comprehension. In fact, the solicitation is for money to pay pilgrims to visit a shrine and to return with a souvenir, a relic of sorts. A person who has that subcultural knowledge can understand at some level *without* linguistic knowledge, and a person without that subcultural knowledge who may have *linguistic* knowledge may fail to understand.

A key point is that world knowledge is often invisible. Figure 9.2 depicts an instance of invisible background knowledge and helps us to transition to the final portion of this chapter. The teacher and her student each display very positive literacy instincts. The teacher has taken her students on a very interesting field trip to the Monterey Aquarium. She expects her pupils to then talk about their experience, share the facts that they learned, probably read more about those facts, and then write about them, all of which are excellent examples of a balanced and diverse literacy program. Her pupil was fascinated by the field trip. He is excited about the new information he learned about sharks. He is poised more than likely to read more about sharks since he already knew some facts and he learned some more details. The problem is not the procedures of literacy, or motivation, or interest. The problem is the inability of the pupil to communicate his excitement, knowledge, and readiness for more learning in a language the teacher understands. Second-language speakers may not be able to *articulate* their background knowledge. But being unable to articulate does not mean that a person does not have background knowledge. It means that he

FIGURE 9.2. Interpretations and misinterpretations in classroom talk. From Graves, Juel, and Graves. *Teaching Reading in the 21st Century, 1st edition.* Published by Allyn & Bacon, Boston, MA. Copyright 1998 by Pearson Education. Reprinted by permission of the publisher.

or she might not be able to display it comfortably and therefore keeps it hidden. Imagine the previous example of Urdu. Depending on the reader, there is probably more or less understanding of the content of the language in the two figures. Describing that content in a native language is one thing; describing it in the second language may be nearly impossible. Monolinguals tend to be extremely insensitive to second-language speakers, believing that oral speech is somehow synonymous with understanding. If teachers believe that fluent oral speech is the primary and possibly only indicator of comprehension, they will never be able to perceive the genuine abilities of the second-language students in their classrooms. In fact, research repeatedly indicates that readers able to display their comprehension in the stronger (i.e., native) language achieve much higher comprehension ratings than those forced to both understand and display understanding in a second language (Shohamy, 1982, 1984).

In summary, second-language readers must be viewed from a variety of perspectives. First, teachers must get a sense of students' *literacy* abilities *in whatever language* they bring with them to school. It is simply not good enough to accept that students come from "low-literacy, high-poverty areas." Most ELLs in the United States come from cultures that have a long literate tradition, and they come from print environments. In large sectors of the United States, one sees signs written in languages other than English every day; one can walk into almost any bookstore and find a section devoted to languages other than English, and virtually any ethnic or cultural event has print in languages other than English. To fail to perceive that many students come to school with a print awareness is to ignore a genuine strength. Further, teachers must be aware of how to access the *language knowledge* that students bring. Undoubtedly, students will use the knowledge of language that they have. If they believe that one does not need to mark the subject with anything but a verb ending, they will misconstrue that knowledge. This lack of awareness may cause difficulty in their learning of a language that also requires a subject and that may signal grammatical relationships through particular inflections. Teachers need to diagnose students' performances in terms of the linguistic and metalinguistic knowledge that they bring to the task. Finally, teachers need to empower students to use the world knowledge that they already possess. They need to find ways of helping students to make their comprehension visible in ways not completely and exclusively reliant on use of a second language.

Increasing the Volume
of Reading Informational Text

The challenge for students is this: they have to use what they know about literacy and have to rework what they know about language while they are learning new content material and how to express that content in English. This is a tall cognitive order. The challenge for teachers is this: to try to lessen the cognitive burden on students by enabling them to be assessed on these varying dimensions separately and not conflating their performances across the dimensions. One of the most discussed notions about lessening cognitive burdens is within the framework of the materials that students are asked to read. Ironically, teachers often turn to stories, believing in their universality and engaging nature. There are several dimensions to *story* text that often make them more difficult than they would appear to be. First of all, stories are deliberately cultural. While it might be true that the genre of "folk tale" is universal, the structure, the value system, the level of fantasy, and so forth are clearly *not* universal; that is what makes them reflections of culture. Most stories that would be recognized as "North American," for example, come from the German tradition of Grimm's fairy tales (often "Disney-fied" for the large screen) or from such legends as Johnny Appleseed or Paul Bunyan and Babe the Blue Ox—stories that reflect a North American tradition. Other folk tales such as those from South Asia or the Middle East are not set in similar geographic settings and use animal-like characters specific to the region. Folk tales in the American tradition feature blue oxen and superhuman strength; those from the Middle East, flying carpets; and those from Asia, snakes that talk. None of these types of fantasies contains images that are part of the real-world knowledge store. Using this type of text forces students to rely almost exclusively on linguistic knowledge for comprehension. Another characteristic of story text is that it is often intentionally ambiguous. The quality of a good story is found in its ability to sustain multiple interpretations. This makes stories intriguing; we can turn them around and find different "secret" messages in them; the question *Are things really what they appear to be?* is a foundational question in any analytic approach to stories. For second-language readers, this dimension of story is unnerving. Second-language readers tend to be happy if they know the foundational vocabulary; they are not engaged by having to maintain a flexibility of thought for which they have few if any cognitive resources left over. Finally, stories often use extremely economical language. Good stories are often carefully structured, demanding that the reader rely on *all* of the words that carry the story forward. While children's books tend to have pictures, the pictures illustrate something mentioned in the text and do not necessarily propel the story forward. They *illustrate* the language; they do not *add* to the content of the story. In this case, students are often forced into a word-based strategy.

All of these features can combine to undermine the confidence of ELLs. If the story line does not match the knowledge store or fails to reflect the cultural value system the learner has been taught and moreover is ambiguous, the second-language reader may be floundering in a sea of words and concepts that do not exist in any *real* world the second-language learner inhabits.

A resolution for teachers lies in the use of information text for ELLs. An information text can focus on a topic that might be in the knowledge store (such as what to feed puppies versus older dogs, or how light affects plant growth, or how sea animals propel themselves through water, or how sharp the teeth of sharks really are). Information text potentially taps into the invisible—that information that the student in Figure 9.2 has, that the student cannot articulate and the teacher cannot access. Knowing about a topic can lighten both the grammatical load and the content load of a second-language text, allowing the English language learner to actually read the text. Admittedly, the vocabulary load in such texts can appear to be more demanding than perhaps in story text. Yet, it is indeed often this low-frequency academic vocabulary that might contain recognizable cognates and further might be vocabulary for which readers already encountered related concepts. In other words, students may already be prepared to learn the words due to their knowledge store—a far more comfortable position to be in than trying to understand words for which there is no immediate knowledge store. Information text is often redundant. The text often contains charts, figures, subheadings, and the like that repeat verbal information and provide additional signals of importance. The scaffolded nature of information text can be invaluable for second-language readers. They are not necessarily left to flounder in a sea of words.

Perhaps most importantly, using information text potentially equalizes learners in classrooms. ELLs could potentially have a greater knowledge store on particular topics that their native English-speaking peers, allowing the ELLs to be more knowledgeable and to participate more confidently than otherwise. Especially for learners who have felt unwelcome in schools or have been made to feel less intelligent because they are not fluent or use a grammatically marked or phonetically marked English, the possibility of being the achiever in a class, the child to whom others can turn as the expert, is an opportunity that teachers should not overlook or bypass.

Making sure that ELLs are getting the "right stuff" means that teachers must individually diagnose them and assess them within their unique set of strengths. These strengths tend to be housed in their native language, not in English. While it may be somewhat difficult for teachers to cope with a language other than English, knowing how powerful and useful that second language and literacy knowledge are and can be will support teachers in the long run in making better assessments and creating a more positive classroom experience for all learners.

References

August, D., & Shanahan, T. (Eds.). (2006). *Developing literacy in second-language learners: Report of the National Literacy Panel on Language-Minority Children and Youth.* Mahwah, NJ: Erlbaum.

Bernhardt, E. B. (1991). *Reading development in a second language: Theoretical, research, and classroom perspectives.* Norwood, NJ: Ablex.

Bernhardt, E. B. (1994). A content analysis of reading methods texts: What are we told about the nonnative speaker of English? *Journal of Reading Behavior, 26,* 159–189.

Bernhardt, E. B. (2005). Progress and procrastination in second-language reading. In M. McGroarty (Ed.), *Annual review of applied linguistics* (pp. 133–150). Cambridge, UK: Cambridge University Press.

Bernhardt, E. B., & Kamil, M. L. (1995). Interpreting relationships between L1 and L2 reading: Consolidating the linguistic threshold and the linguistic interdependence hypotheses. *Applied Linguistics, 16*(2), 16–34.

Brisbois, J. (1995). Connections between first- and second-language reading. *Journal of Reading Behavior, 24*(4), 565–584.

Cattell, J. M. (1885). The inertia of the eye and the brain. *The Brain, 8,* 295–312.

Ellis, R. (1994). *The study of second-language acquisition.* Oxford, UK: Oxford University Press.

Fitzgerald, J. (2000). How will bilingual/ESL programs in literacy change in the next millenium? (RRQ Snippet). *Reading Research Quarterly, 34*(4), 520–521.

Gersten, R., Baker, S. K., Shanahan, T., Linan-Thompson, S., Collins, P., & Scarcella, R. (2007). *Effective literacy and English language instruction for English learners in the elementary grades: A practice guide* (NCEE 2007-4011). Washington, DC: National Center for Education Evaluation and Regional Assistance, Institute of Education Sciences, U.S. Department of Education. Retrieved from *ies.ed.gov/ncee.*

Goodman, K. (Ed.). (1968). *The psycholinguistic nature of the reading process.* Detroit, Ml: Wayne State University Press.

Graves, M. F., Juel, C., & Graves, B. B. (1998). *Teaching reading in the 21st century.* Boston: Allyn & Bacon.

Hawkins, R. (2001). *Second language syntax: A generative introduction.* Malden, MA: Blackwell.

Huey, E. B. (1909). *The psychology and pedagogy of reading.* New York: Macmillan.

Javal, E. (1879). Essai sur la physiologie de la lecture. *Annaels d'oculistique, 82,* 242–253.

Nash, R. N. (1997). *NTC's dictionary of Spanish cognates.* Lincolnwood, IL: NTC Publishing Group.

Shohamy, E. (1982). Affective considerations in language testing. *Modern Language Journal, 66,* 13–17.

Shohamy, E. (1984). Does the testing method make a difference? The case of reading comprehension. *Language Testing, 1,* 147–170.

Snow, C. (2006). Cross-cutting themes and future research directions. In D. August & T. Shanahan (Eds.), *Developing literacy in second-language learners: Report of the National Literacy Panel on Language-Minority Children and Youth* (pp. 631–651). Mahwah, NJ: Erlbaum.

10

TEXT READING AND STUDENTS WITH LEARNING DISABILITIES

ELIZABETH A. SWANSON
JADE WEXLER
SHARON VAUGHN

W hile the National Reading Panel (National Institute of Child Health and Human Development [NICHD], 2000) recognized that several critical elements of reading were necessary to promote successful outcomes for beginning readers (e.g., fluency, phonological awareness, comprehension), critical to effective instruction for students with reading difficulties is the inclusion of other features of effective instruction such as modeling, corrective feedback, and pacing of instruction. To maximize the benefits of available instructional time, students benefit when teachers are mindful of how they can make the best use of the available instructional time.

In an observational study in 1975, Stallings confirmed that time spent in content-area related activities and time working with textbooks were related to achievement in reading and math. Another study conducted in secondary remedial classrooms confirmed that the amount of time dedicated to reading activities did indeed affect reading levels (Stallings, Needels, & Stayrook, 1979). Researchers also found that low-achieving students who made above-average gains in reading were engaged in interactive academic-related activities such as practicing reading connected text orally (with feedback) for a majority of their available instructional time. Therefore, in addition to making sure that students are on task and engaged in academic-related instruction/ activities in general, instruction should be distributed purposefully in the academic areas needed to improve student achievement.

One element of instruction necessary to make progress in reading achievement is time for students to read text, including opportunities to *practice* applying the key elements of reading as well as reading for understanding and interest. It is difficult to imagine students with reading difficulties becoming better readers without appropriate instruction; however, it is also difficult to imagine these students profiting adequately from instruction without extensive time to read purposefully and with guided feedback.

While it may seem obvious that time spent reading connected text with guidance and feedback from the teacher can lead to success, it is surprising how this element of instruction is often neglected. Observational studies have confirmed that for our most struggling readers oral reading practice opportunities are often limited (Haynes & Jenkins, 1986; Leinhardt, Zigmond, & Cooley, 1981) and further complicated by large class sizes (Chard & Kame'enui, 2000). Even when teachers are dedicated to maximizing instructional time, often they spend a majority of instructional time providing instruction in the form of excessive "teacher talk," neglecting to provide students with opportunities to practice the skills being taught. Therefore, teachers must balance explicit instruction with time for students to practice what they have been taught through reading. This practice time allows not only student practice time but also opportunities for teachers to provide corrective feedback.

The importance of providing time for text reading practice is evident in a study conducted by Vadasy, Sanders, and Peyton (2005) where they assigned 57 struggling first-grade readers to either word study tutoring or word study tutoring combined with text reading practice. Treatment students made significant progress as compared to nontutored peers, and both groups performed comparably on most measures. One difference, however, was that the group that practiced reading connected text in addition to having word study instruction made significant gains in their reading fluency rate and passage reading accuracy, two elements of reading necessary for good comprehension (Chard, Vaughn, & Tyler, 2002). They also outperformed the word study only group on measures of spelling accuracy. Therefore, in addition to providing explicit *instruction* in the key elements of reading such as word study, there is evidence that there are advantages for teachers to devote a sufficient amount of time to *practice* applying these skills through guided instruction in text reading.

The purpose of this chapter is to synthesize findings from previous observational studies that investigated teachers' use of text reading for students with learning disabilities (LD) and to present findings from a recent observational study that examined the amount and purpose of text reading for students with LD in the resource room as well as types of text used.

Observational Studies of Reading Instruction for Students with LD: Previous Syntheses

Two syntheses of observational studies that reported general traits of reading instruction in special education settings have been conducted in the past decade (Swanson, 2008; Vaughn, Levy, Coleman, & Bos, 2002). The first (Vaughn et al., 2002) examined reading instruction provided to elementary school students with LD or emotional or behavior disorders. The authors concluded that within special education settings students were more often provided whole-group instruction with little individualization or differentiation, while remedial reading teachers spent more time on individual instruction. Instructional quality was reported as low overall, with a large amount of time dedicated to independent seatwork and completion of worksheets and with little time allocated to text reading.

Swanson's recent synthesis (2008) examined a wider breadth of studies that included observation of reading instruction provided to students with LD in any elementary, middle, and high school setting where reading was taught (e.g., a general education setting and/or a special education setting). Generally, resource room teachers spent only 44% of the allocated time focused on reading activities (Haynes & Jenkins, 1986), with as much as 26% of students' time spent outside of the classroom or engaged in off-task behavior, waiting, or classroom management (Leinhardt et al., 1981). Of the few studies that reported time engaged in one of the essential components of reading instruction (phonological awareness, phonics, fluency, vocabulary, and comprehension; NICHD, 2000), findings converge toward relatively small amounts of low-quality explicit instruction in each of the components.

Little to no explicit instruction in word study phonics was reported in either elementary (Gelzheiser & Meyers, 1991; Meents, 1990; Moody, Vaughn, Hughes, & Fischer, 2000; Schumm, Moody, & Vaughn, 2000; Vaughn, Moody, & Schumm, 1998) or middle school (Kethley, 2005) general education or resource room settings (Gelzheiser & Meyers, 1991). Comprehension instruction was lacking as well. Most studies reported low-quality instruction such as students or teachers reading a story followed by teacher questioning that was largely factual and literal in nature (Kethley, 2005; Rieth et al., 2003; Vaughn et al., 1998). Reports of vocabulary and fluency instruction were few, with vocabulary instruction being mentioned by middle school resource room teachers during interviews (Kethley, 2005) but never observed. No studies reported evidence of explicit instruction in reading fluency.

Reported text reading estimates were low, with students engaged in oral or silent reading from 0 to 17.4 minutes per day. Of particular note is that this limited amount of time reading was with students who had identified learning disabilities and were very low ability readers. While Haynes and Jenkins (1986) reported that students with LD spent a greater number of minutes reading in the general education classroom than in the special education resource room, others reported conflicting findings. For example, O'Sullivan, Ysseldyke, Christenson, and Thurlow (1990) and Thurlow, Graden, Greener, and Ysseldyke (1983) reported that students with LD spent between 12.8% and 34.8% of their time in the resource room engaged in silent or oral reading, whereas in the general education classroom this percentage dropped to between 2.5% and 17.7%. When students with and without LD were compared across all instructional settings, the difference was less evident—students with LD engaged in oral or silent reading 12.1% of the time as compared to students without LD, who engaged in oral or silent reading 13.5% of the time.

The focus of the remainder of this chapter is twofold. First, while previous syntheses have investigated the amount of reading instruction provided to students with LD and one briefly summarized the amount of text reading observed (Swanson, 2008), none has conducted an in-depth analysis of the amount of time students with LD have been engaged in text reading. Therefore, a review of the existing literature was conducted to determine the extent to which students with LD are engaged in text reading during reading instruction as well as the instructional purpose of text reading. Second, because previous observational studies placed minimum focus on reporting the use of text reading, analysis of data from a recent observational study provides a more detailed account of text reading practices for students with LD who are served in resource rooms.

Review of the Existing Literature on Text Reading

For this review, all studies included by Swanson (2008) were compiled, representing all observational studies conducted on reading instruction for students with LD in grades kindergarten through 12 that were published between 1980 and 2005. This corpus consisted of 21 studies. Using Swanson's search terms, we conducted an electronic and hand search of peer-reviewed journals to locate additional studies published between 2005 and 2007. This search resulted in the identification of 110 abstracts. Swanson's selection criteria were used to identify additional articles. No additional articles that met selection criteria were located. To narrow the focus, the 21 studies were examined for reports of student oral or silent text reading, resulting in eight studies identified for inclusion in the current synthesis (Gelzheiser & Meyers, 1991; Haynes & Jenkins, 1986; Kethley, 2005; Leinhardt et al., 1981; O'Sullivan et al., 1990; Thurlow, Graden, et al., 1983; Thurlow, Ysseldyke, Graden, & Algozzine, 1983; Zigmond & Baker, 1994).

Findings

The eight studies included in this synthesis were conducted between 1981 and 2005. Studies explored reading instruction in all settings where students with LD received reading instruction—general education (Haynes & Jenkins, 1986; O'Sullivan et al., 1990; Thurlow, Graden, et al., 1983; Thurlow, Ysseldyke et al., 1983; Zigmond & Baker, 1994), special education (Haynes & Jenkins, 1986; Kethley, 2005; Leinhardt et al., 1981; O'Sullivan et al., 1990; Thurlow, Graden, et al., 1983; Thurlow, Ysseldyke, et al., 1983; Zigmond & Baker, 1994), and other remedial instruction classrooms (e.g., Title I; Gelzheiser & Meyers, 1991). Students' grade levels ranged from second through eighth grade, with most studies ($n = 7$) conducted in the elementary setting. Only one study (Kethley, 2005) was conducted at the middle school level. The number of observations per study ranged from 1 (O'Sullivan et al., 1990) to 33 (Gelzheiser & Meyers, 1991), with the length of the observation ranging from 50 minutes (Kethley, 2005) to the entire school day (e.g., Haynes & Jenkins, 1986). The number of student participants ranged from 1 (Zigmond & Baker, 1994) to 178 (Haynes & Jenkins,

1986). Table 10.1 provides participant information and a summary of text reading findings for each study included in the synthesis.

Time Spent Text Reading

Five studies reported oral reading time in either the resource room (Haynes & Jenkins, 1986; Leinhardt et al., 1981) or both general education and resource rooms (Gelzheiser & Meyers, 1991; O'Sullivan et al., 1990; Thurlow, Ysseldyke, et al., 1983). In the general education classroom, students with LD were engaged in oral reading from between 1.1 minutes (3.5% of reading instruction) and 7.47 minutes (16% of reading instruction). The range is only a bit higher in the resource room, with oral reading ranging from 4.4 minutes (25.1% of reading instruction) to 13.4 minutes (proportion not reported).

Four studies reported silent reading time in either the resource room (Haynes & Jenkins, 1986; Leinhardt et al., 1981) or both general education and resource rooms (O'Sullivan et al., 1990; Thurlow, Ysseldyke, et al., 1983). In the general education classroom, students with LD were engaged in silent reading 4.7 minutes per day (14.2% of reading instruction). In the resource room, a range of silent reading was reported as between 2.6 minutes (9.70%) and 13.68 minutes (proportion not reported).

Two studies reported oral plus silent reading in either the resource room (Haynes & Jenkins, 1986) or both settings (Zigmond & Baker, 1994). Zigmond and Baker's report (1994) of one student with LD indicated that he was engaged in silent or oral reading for 12.6 minutes per day in the general education setting. In the resource setting, silent plus oral reading time was reported as lower than in the general education setting (10.01 minutes versus 12.42 minutes). Another study investigated text reading time across the entire school day and did not disaggregate by instructional setting (Thurlow, Graden, et al., 1983). The researchers reported 3.7 minutes of oral reading and 8.4 minutes of silent reading. The most obvious summary statement from these studies is that the amount of reading per day was exceedingly low and unlikely to provide adequate time for students to practice discrete reading skills.

Instructional Purpose for Text Reading

While Kethley (2005) did not report the number of minutes or the proportion of time spent engaged in oral or silent text reading, she did describe oral reading fluency instruction. During interviews of four

TABLE 10.1. Characteristics of Studies Included in Synthesis

Study	No. of student participants	Age/grade	No. of teacher participants	No. of observations	Length of observations	Observation setting	Findings
Gelzheiser & Meyers (1991)	Not reported	Grades 2–5	31 general ed., 7 special ed., 10 remedial reading	4–33 per teacher	Not reported	General ed., resource, and remedial reading	Classroom: M = 448 sec; 16% Remedial: M = 274 sec; 16% Resource: M = 438 sec; 19%
Haynes & Jenkins (1986)[a]	178 total; 114 LD	Grades 4–6	7 general ed., 23 special ed.	5–8 times per student	General ed.: entire school day Resource room: reading period	General ed.: all academic settings Resource: reading only	Range: 5.42 min–22.04 min/day Classroom: M = 17.44 min Resource: M = 13.08 min
Kethley (2005)	Not reported	Grades 6–8	4 special ed.	7 times per teacher	50–90 min	Resource	Range: 1–36% of instructional time
Leinhardt, Zigmond, & Cooley (1981)	105 total; 105 LD	Ages 6–12 years	Not reported	30 times per student and teacher	1 hour	Resource	Oral reading: M = 13.40 min (5%) Silent reading: M = 13.68 min (5%)
O'Sullivan, Ysseldyke, Christenson, & Thurlow (1990)	77 total; 21 LD	Grades 2–4	Not reported	1 per student	Entire school day	All academic settings	*Classroom* Oral: M = 1.1 min (3.5%) Silent: M = 4.7 min (14.2%) *Resource* Oral: M = 4.4 min (25.1%) Silent: M = 2.6 min (9.7%)

Study	Sample	Grade		Observations		Setting	Results
Thurlow, Graden, Greener, & Ysseldyke (1983)	34 total; 34 LD	Grades 3–5	12 general ed.	2 per student	Entire school day	All academic settings	Oral: M = 3.7 min (2.1%) Silent: M = 8.4 min (8.4%)
Thurlow, Ysseldyke, Graden, & Algozzine (1983)	8 total; 8 LD	Grades 3–4	8 general ed.	2 per student	Entire school day	All academic settings	*Classroom* Oral: 0.6% Silent: 1.9% *Resource* Oral: 6.5% Silent: 6.3%
Zigmond & Baker (1994)	Year 1: 6 LD; Year 2: 12 total, 6 LD	Grade 4	Not reported	4 per student each year (total = 8)	Not reported	General ed.	Classroom: oral or silent reading 63 min/week (21%) Resource: oral or silent reading 62.1 min/week (9%)

middle school teachers, each reported a form of repeated reading as the method used to improve fluency in reading sight words or connected text. Three of the teachers were observed using repeated reading of connected text to improve reading fluency. No other study reported the instructional purpose for text reading.

Additional Information Needed

Limited information regarding text reading practices is available among the existing literature published between 1985 and 2007. In fact, there is scant reporting of the instructional purpose for text reading or the types of text used for students with LD. This information would be helpful in determining the current use of text reading. Recently, an observational study was conducted in 10 elementary school resource rooms that served students with LD to determine the amount and proportion of time engaged in components of effective reading instruction and grouping strategies (Swanson, in press). An analysis of a subgroup of data from this study was conducted to investigate the amount of and purpose for text reading in special education resource rooms that serve students with LD.

Subanalysis of Larger Study

Ten participating resource room teachers were asked to identify all reading instructional periods that met the following criteria: (1) at least 50% of the students assigned to the group are second- through fifth-grade students, (2) at least 50% of the students in the identified group are identified as having an LD, and (3) the reading instructional period lasts at least 45 minutes per day (Swanson, in press). Of the identified instructional periods, one was randomly chosen for inclusion in the study. Teachers were observed during the target reading instructional time over a period of 3 days. A total of 2,178 minutes of reading instruction was observed. Observed class periods ranged from 41 to 90 minutes, with a mean of 59.5 (SD = 13.5) minutes. The class size ranged from one to seven students, with an average class size of 3.9 (SD = 1.54).

Methodology of the Study

Teachers and Students

All teachers held a bachelor's degree. Two teachers earned a master's degree. Three teachers were alternatively certified, while seven secured teaching certification through a 4-year university program. Students were in grades 2–5, with a mean age of 10.5 years. Most students (56.3%) were identified with an LD as their primary disability, followed by other health impairment (34.4%), speech impairment (6.3%), or emotional disturbance (3.1%).

Description of Observation Instrument

Observers recorded each instructional activity and coded the content, using the Instructional Content Emphasis—Revised (ICE-R; Edmonds & Briggs, 2003) observation instrument. Data yielded by the ICE-R included (1) multidimensional descriptions of reading and language arts instruction, (2) the amount of time allocated to instructional components, (3) student grouping patterns, (4) the types of materials utilized by teachers and students, (5) the levels of student engagement, and (6) the quality of instruction. Only data related to the amount and proportion of text reading, the instructional purpose for text reading, and materials used for text reading are included in the current report.

Text reading was captured in two unique ways using the ICE-R coding system. First, text may be used within the context of activities that are aimed at other goals such as comprehension or fluency building. In these cases, text reading is a vehicle for reaching a separate instructional goal. To capture text reading for this purpose, during every event, the coder recorded the number of minutes the teacher or student(s) spent reading connected text. The number of minutes was categorized as student text reading if (1) students read orally, (2) students read silently, or (3) the teacher read aloud and the students followed along in their own copy of the text. The number of minutes is categorized as teacher text reading if the teacher is reading aloud and students have no text to read simultaneously.

Second, students may read text for enjoyment or to fill extra time during a lesson. In these cases, text reading does not serve a separate instructional goal. This type of text reading received its own code if text reading was not used as a vehicle for any other objective. For example, if students were reading text repeatedly with the purpose of fluency building, the event is coded as "fluency." On the other hand, if students were engaged in sustained silent reading with the purpose of simply reading text for no other reason, the event was coded as "text reading." Figure 10.1 provides a decision tree that was used to assist observers in coding this component.

Following is a description of text reading that considers text reading across all components. Then, we will focus on text reading dur-

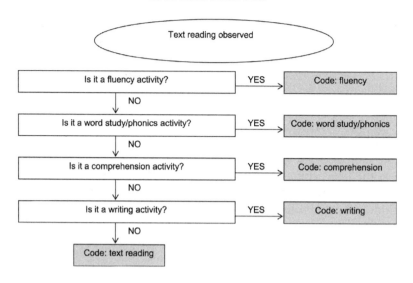

FIGURE 10.1. Decision tree for determining how to code text reading events.

ing fluency, comprehension, and word study/phonics instruction. This will be followed by a report of the amount of text reading conducted with no other associated instructional goal. Finally, we will report on the types of text used during instruction.

Text Reading across All Components of Reading Instruction

During the 2,178 minutes of reading instruction observed, students were engaged with text for a total of 520 minutes, representing 23.88% of the total instructional time. Teachers spent an additional 40 minutes reading text aloud to students (1.84%). Across all 30 observations, average student text reading was 17.33 minutes per observation. Among the 10 classrooms observed, student text reading ranged from 0 to 137 total minutes, constituting between 0% and 62.56% of instructional time. Table 10.2 provides additional information on student reading time and the proportion for each teacher. The amount of text reading represented in this more recent observational study compares favorably with previous studies (see Swanson, 2008) and suggests that teachers may be increasing the amount of time that students with learning disabilities are engaged in text reading. Of course, this finding is speculative because teachers in the more recent study can not be compared directly with teachers from previous studies.

TABLE 10.2. Student Text Reading by Observation

Teacher	No. of minutes observation 1	No. of minutes observation 2	No. of minutes observation 3	No. of minutes total	% of observed time[a]
Bailey	0	0	9	9	7.56%
Cox	32	15	34	81	26.47%
Davis	9	13	5	27	16.98%
Goodwin	11	10	4	25	17.24%
Gold	0	0	0	0	0.00%
Hill	37	63	37	137	62.56%
Jones	11	19	31	61	19.43%
Mack	11	10	14	35	20.59%
Robertson	0	26	10	36	16.74%
Wilson	32	41	36	109	42.08%

[a]Total time observed in minutes: Bailey = 119; Cox = 306; Davis = 159; Goodwin = 145; Gold = 131; Hill = 219; Jones = 314; Mack = 170; Robertson = 215; Wilson = 259.

Text Reading during Word Study/Phonics, Fluency, and Comprehension

It is expected that teachers use text during application of letter–sound knowledge to reading (one component of word study/phonics), fluency, and comprehension instruction. Therefore, text reading as a vehicle for delivery of instruction in these areas is important to note. Table 10.3 details the amount of time spent in each instructional component and how much text reading occurred during each component.

One purpose for text reading is to apply skills learned during word study/phonics to reading connected text. In fact, Chard and Osborn (1999) suggest that it is of great importance for students to learn letter–sound correspondences in such a manner that allows word and text reading as early as possible. How did teachers in this study fare in providing students opportunities to apply word study/phonics skills to reading connected text? These teachers spent 481 minutes (22.08% of the total observed time) having students apply word study/phonics skills to reading, writing, or spelling. However, for only 38 of these 481 minutes were students engaged in reading connected text, leading us to assume most of the application work was conducted through writing or spelling. While this type of practice is important, teachers missed key opportunities to provide students with word study/phonics practice embedded within text reading experiences.

TABLE 10.3. Text Reading That Occurred during Instructional Components

Instructional component	No. of minutes observed	No. of minutes of student text reading	Text reading as % of time observed in each component
Phonological awareness	60	0	0.00%
Word study/phonics	696	38	5.46%
Fluency	193	149	77.20%
Comprehension	557	61	10.95%
Vocabulary	209	0	0.00%
Spelling tests	73	0	0.00%
Text reading[a]	241	241	100.00%
Writing	149	0	0.00%

[a]Includes the reading of text with no accompanying comprehension, vocabulary, or fluency activity.

During the 193 minutes of fluency instruction, students read text 77.20% (149 minutes) of the time, indicating the existence of other types of fluency instruction such as word reading or letter naming fluency. During 557 minutes of comprehension instruction, students were engaged with text for 61 minutes (10.95% of comprehension time). During an additional 146 minutes (26.21% of comprehension time), students used workbooks or worksheets. It is unclear from field notes as to whether these worksheets included text. Therefore, the amount of text reading accomplished during comprehension instruction may actually be a bit higher.

Text Reading with No Other Associated Instructional Goal

The "text reading" code was assigned only if text reading was not used as a vehicle for another instructional component. The "text reading" code included (1) supported oral reading, where student(s) engaged in reading with guidance from a teacher, peer, or parent but with no explicit instruction provided; (2) choral reading, where the class or a group reads aloud simultaneously; (3) independent silent reading; (4) independent oral reading; or (5) other forms of text reading such as students listening to a book on tape, with minimal emphasis on instruction.

Students were engaged in a total of 241 minutes of "text reading," representing 11.07% of the total observed time. The most common type of "text reading" activity was independent silent reading, followed by supported oral reading. The details on time spent engaged in all "text reading" activities are provided in Table 10.4.

One teacher engaged her students 97 of the minutes coded as "text reading" across all three observations, representing 40.42% of the sum (241 minutes) of "text reading" instruction across all teachers. Therefore, a large portion of "text reading" can be attributed to one teacher whose students were engaged in either supported oral reading or independent silent reading. This leaves 144 minutes of "text reading" spread among the remaining 27 observations of 9 teachers, for an adjusted average of 5.33 minutes of "text reading" per observation.

Types of Text Used

For each instructional event (186 events total), materials were listed and coded. Codes for six types of text were available. Each text type is defined in Table 10.5. Text was used as a material in 72 different coded activities. Authentic (i.e., trade book) texts were used in 40 of these events, making them the most frequently chosen type of text. In fact, authentic text was used during 23% of all instruction observed. The second most common type was decodable text, used during 27 events and 18.6% of

TABLE 10.4. "Text Reading" Instruction

Type of text reading instruction	No. of minutes	% of text reading instruction[a]	% of total instructional time[b]
Supported oral reading	64	26.56%	2.94%
Choral reading	0	0.00%	0.00%
Independent silent reading	147	61.00%	6.75%
Independent oral reading	9	3.73%	0.41%
Teacher reads aloud	7	2.90%	0.32%
Teacher reads aloud while students read along	14	5.81%	0.64%
Total	241	100.00%	11.07%

Note. This text reading category includes the reading of text with no accompanying comprehension, vocabulary, or fluency activity.

[a]Calculated based on 241 minutes of text reading time.

[b]Calculated based on 2,178 minutes of total instructional time.

TABLE 10.5. Types of Text Defined

Type of text	Definition
Basal text	Basal text is found in the school district-adopted text book. It varies in characteristics according to the particular grade level.
Trade book text	In trade books, also known as "authentic literature," word choice is not controlled for beginning reader accessibility. The plot is often complex, and there is usually more text per page than in pattern or decodable text (Brown, 1999).
Decodable text	Decodable text contains a simple story line with simple sentence structure and a restricted amount of text per page. This type of text is controlled to emphasize letter–sound relationships, spelling patterns, and irregular word use (Brown, 1999).
Pattern text	Pattern text is controlled to emphasize repetition, rhythm, and rhyme. Simple sentence structures are used, and illustrations support text (Brown, 1999). A classic example of pattern text is *Brown Bear, Brown Bear, What Do You See?* (Martin & Carle, 1995).
Unknown text	When the observer could not tell what type of text was used, even after viewing the text itself, it was coded as "unknown text."
Student- or teacher-made text	This code was used when students read connected text that either he or she or the teacher wrote. The complexity of this text depends upon the grade and ability level of the student writer.

all instruction, followed by unknown types of text (4 events; 2.8% of all instruction), and finally basal text (1 event; 1.2% of all instruction). No pattern or teacher/student-made text was used.

Different types of text should be used for different purposes. Indeed, text designed for word study/phonics practice is different from text designed for comprehension development (Menon & Hiebert, 2005). In particular, features of text such as repetition of words and sentence structure can influence student performance on tasks such as reading fluency (Hiebert & Fisher, 2005; Menon & Hiebert, 2005). Therefore, text type is of particular interest when considering applications for word study/phonics and fluency instruction. In the current study, teachers engaged students in fluency instruction for a total of 193 minutes. During this time, decodable text was used for 100 minutes, and trade books were used for an additional 33 minutes. Teachers also engaged students in applying word study/phonics skills to reading, writing, and spelling for a total of 448 minutes. During this time, decodable text was used for 48 minutes (by two teachers). Trade books were used for an additional 46 minutes (by one teacher) and basal text was used for 25 minutes (by one teacher). Seven teachers did not use any type of text for student application of word study/phonics skills.

Summary

This chapter reviews the existing literature on observational studies examining the amount and types of text reading used in classrooms that serve students with learning disabilities. It also provides a report on a recently conducted study further examining the amount of time students with LD spent engaged with text and the types of text read (Swanson, in press). An essential assumption in these syntheses is that students with significant reading problems require opportunities for time to read and to respond to text. Furthermore, opportunities for text reading while teaching particular elements such as vocabulary and fluency is also essential. It is also valuable to choose text appropriate to the activity at hand and embed a sufficient amount of teacher support when students interact with text such as opportunities for feedback. Each of these issues will be discussed below.

Optimal Amount of Text Reading

The data reported here indicate that students spend a range of time reading during observed classes. While there is evidence that this amount of time is increasing, the amount may still be considered low, with student text reading averaging 17.33 minutes per observation. One must be cautious, however, in overanalyzing the limited observation data available here (10 teachers with 30 total observations). Although one must be cautious in overanalyzing the limited observation data, we can still suggest a few trends. For example, if we extrapolate an average of 17.33 minutes of daily reading time over a 180-day school year, students may read approximately 52 hours annually while in school.

Still the question remains: Is this enough text reading to effect real change in reading achievement? The fact is that data on the amount of reading time required to attain particular levels of proficiency among students in general—much less students with LD—are not readily available. We believe that the answer to this question depends on the purpose for text reading. For example, the amount of text exposure for the development of decoding skills is probably different from the amount of text exposure needed to increase vocabulary and comprehension knowledge. Some research evidence can help us determine whether observed teachers provided enough text engagement.

Let us consider text reading for the purpose of practicing word study/phonics skills. First, Chard and Osborn (1999) suggest that students learning letter–sound correspondence should apply this knowledge to text as early as possible. In addition, exposure to print is related to spelling ability—children who read more text are better spellers (Cunningham & Stanovich, 1990; Stanovich & West, 1989). While it is still unclear what proportion of word study/phonics instructional time should be dedicated to text reading, we can confidently assert that the 38 minutes observed over the course of 30 observations dedicated to applying word study/phonics skills to reading connected text is simply not enough. This insufficiency is not new. In fact, Allington (1984) studied a first-grade sample where the average skilled reader read approximately three times as many words as the average struggling reader. This type of situation creates what Stanovich (1986) refers to as the Matthew effect, wherein skilled readers will naturally read more, learn more word meanings, and as a result read even better. Conversely, struggling readers will read slowly and without enjoyment; thereby reading less and experiencing slower development of vocabulary. This cycle continues over time, thus inhibiting growth in reading skills. Twenty-five years have passed since Allington's (1984) observation that struggling readers read only one-third as many words as average readers, and the latest evidence still points to inadequate reading time for students with LD.

Choosing Appropriate Text Types

While research findings have not fully informed the field regarding the optimal *amount* of text engagement for word study/phonics development, we are more informed about the *types* of text best used for this purpose. Here the goal is to provide a text that contains multiple opportunities to practice newly learned word study/phonics skills. When choosing text for this purpose, teachers should consider the following (see Foorman, Francis, Davidson, Harm, & Griffin, 2004; Hiebert, 2002). First, consider spelling. Choose text that contains common spellings of the phonics elements previously taught. Second, consider the frequency with which words containing the target word study/phonics element are presented. Students with LD require extensive practice with new phonics concepts. Third, consider the vocabulary level of words. Because oral vocabulary contributes to word reading, teachers should avoid texts with high numbers of uncommon or difficult-to-understand words.

It is important for teachers to become aware of the ways in which text can be controlled to provide effective practice in word study/phonics, because there is strong evidence that early elementary basal-level texts do not provide a strong match between letter–sound correspondences taught and the accompanying text. Stein, Johnson, and Gutlohn (1999) reviewed seven basal series submitted to the California textbook adoption program. One of the basal series provided text in which 52% of the included words could be decoded, based on the skills learned. In the other six series, only 15% of the words in the student reader selections could be decoded, based on the skills learned. Foorman et al. (2004) recently conducted a more detailed analysis of text features included in six basal series submitted to the Texas textbook adoption program. Remember that vocabulary level is important in determining the appropriate text for practicing word study/phonics skills. Foorman et al. (2004) found that, while a greater number of words were decodable based on phonics skills taught (the range of decodable words was from 19.0% to 84.6%), the majority of words used in student reader selections were above the oral vocabulary level of many first graders and thus would require vocabulary instruction prior to reading. In sum, teachers should be aware of the text characteristics that are conducive to practicing word study/phonics skills as well as the need to develop vocabulary and background knowledge before students read.

Teacher Support during Text Reading

Of course, text alone does not account for progress in word and text reading. So, what type of teacher support is needed to best develop word and text reading? First, teachers play a particular role during text reading in developing students' vocabulary and comprehension skills. We recommend that teachers embed strategy instruction within an intensive focus on text engagement. In this model, teachers provide instruction in discrete vocabulary and comprehension strategies, but they spend the bulk of their time modeling and guiding students in how to use these strategies within text. Thus, the strategy itself is not the goal of instruction, but rather, content learning is the goal—the strategy becomes the tool.

Second, instruction and practice incorporating text reading must be supported with extensive opportunities for students to receive feedback. Two recent syntheses provide guidance about the appropriate use of feedback. Hattie and Timperley (2007) synthesized findings from 12 meta-analyses on feedback and identified several levels of feedback. Shute (2008) also summarized the research on feedback. Both agree that effective feedback is characterized by several components that have as their goal enhancing learning. First, feedback should focus on the specific behaviors needed to complete the task, not on the student. In this way, the teacher avoids identifying a personal flaw (e.g., "You didn't do this correctly") and instead is focused on the specific task (e.g., "Reread the paragraph and make a list of all of the characters the author mentions; then decide who the most important character is"). Second, the teacher should provide feedback in as simple and focused a manner as possible, thereby promoting goal-oriented learning. In short, teachers should provide feedback, give the learner an opportunity to address the issue, and then provide guidance and feedback once again.

Both earlier reports of the amount of text reading and our most recent investigation expose a need to inform teachers of the importance of and the instructional skills needed to engage students with LD in text reading activities. In summary, students with learning disabilities and reading difficulties who are provided extensive opportunities to read with teacher support, feedback, and opportunities to respond to the text are more likely to learn to read proficiently than students who are provided significantly less time to engage in these practices.

References

Allington, R. L. (1984). Content coverage and contextual reading in reading groups. *Journal of Reading Behavior, 16,* 85–96.

Chard, D. J., & Kame'enui, D. J. (2000). Struggling first-grade readers: The frequency and progress of their reading. *The Journal of Special Education, 34,* 28–38.

Brown, K. (1999). What kind of text—For whom and when? Textual scaffolding for beginning readers. *The Reading Teacher, 53,* 292–307.

Chard, D. J., & Osborn, J. (1999). Phonics and word recognition instruction in early reading programs: Guidelines for accessibility. *Learning Disabilities Research and Practice, 14,* 107–117.

Chard, D. J., Vaughn, S., & Tyler, B.-J. (2002). A synthesis of research on effective interventions for building reading fluency with elementary students with learning disabilities. *Journal of Learning Disabilities, 35,* 386–406.

Cunningham, A. E., & Stanovich, K. E. (1990). Assessing print exposure and orthographic processing skill in children: A quick measure of reading experience. *Journal of Educational Psychology, 82,* 733–740.

Edmonds, M., & Briggs, K. L. (2003). The instructional content emphasis instrument: Observations of reading instruction. In S. Vaughn & K. L. Briggs (Eds.), *Reading in the classroom: Systems for the observation of teaching and learning* (pp. 31–52). Baltimore: Brookes.

Foorman, B. R., Francis, D. J., Davidson, K. C., Harm, M. W., & Griffin, J. (2004). Variability in text features in six grade 1 basal reading programs. *Scientific Studies of Reading, 8,* 167–197.

Gelzheiser, L. M., & Meyers, J. (1991). Reading instruction by classroom, remedial, and resource room teachers. *The Journal of Special Education, 24,* 512–526.

Hattie, J., & Timperley, H. (2007). The power of feedback. *Review of Educational Research, 77*(1), 81–112.

Haynes, M. C., & Jenkins, J. R. (1986). Reading instruction in special education resource rooms. *American Educational Research Journal, 23,* 161–190.

Hiebert, E. H. (2002). Standards, assessments, and text difficulty. In A. E. Farstrup & S. J. Samuels (Eds.), *What research has to say about reading instruction* (pp. 337–391). Newark, DE: International Reading Association.

Hiebert, E. H., & Fisher, C. W. (2005). A review of the National Reading Panel's studies on fluency: On the role of text. *Elementary School Journal, 105,* 443–460.

Kethley, C. I. (2005). *Case studies of resource room reading instruction for middle school students with high-incidence disabilities.* Unpublished doctoral dissertation, University of Texas, Austin.

Leinhardt, G., Zigmond, N., & Cooley, W. (1981). Reading instruction and its effects. *American Educational Research Journal, 18,* 343–361.

Martin, B., & Carle, E. (1995). *Brown bear, brown bear, what do you see?* New York: Holt.

Meents, C. K. (1990). *Literacy instruction in high school resource rooms.* Unpublished doctoral dissertation, State University of New York, Albany.

Menon, S., & Hiebert, E. H. (2005). A comparison of first graders' reading with little books or literature-based basal anthologies. *Reading Research Quarterly, 40,* 12–38.

Moody, S. W., Vaughn, S., Hughes, M. T., & Fischer, M. (2000). Reading instruction in the resource room: Set up for failure. *Exceptional Children, 66,* 305–316.

National Institute of Child Health and Human Development. (2000). *Report of the National Reading Panel. Teaching children to read: An evidence-based assessment of the scientific research literature on reading and its implications for reading instruction* (NIH Publication No. 00-4769). Washington, DC: U.S. Government Printing Office.

O'Sullivan, P. J., Ysseldyke, J. E., Christenson, S. L., & Thurlow, M. L. (1990). Mildly handicapped elementary students' opportunity to learn during reading instruction in mainstream and special education settings. *Reading Research Quarterly, 25*, 131–146.

Rieth, H. J., Bryant, D. P., Kinzer, C. K., Colburn, L. K., Hur, S., Hartman, P., et al. (2003). An analysis of the impact of anchored instruction on teaching and learning activities in two ninth-grade language arts classes. *Remedial and Special Education, 24*, 173–184.

Schumm, J. S., Moody, S. W., & Vaughn, S. (2000). Grouping for reading instruction: Does one size fit all? *Journal of Learning Disabilities, 33*, 477–488.

Shute, V. J. (2008). Focus on formative feedback. *Review of Educational Research, 78*(1), 153–189.

Stallings, J. (1975). Implementation and child effects of teaching practices in Follow Through classrooms. *Monographs of the Society for Research in Child Development, 40* (Serial No. 163).

Stallings, J., Needels, M., & Stayrook, N. (1979). *The teaching of basic reading skills in secondary schools, Phase II and Phase III.* Menlo Park, CA: SRI International.

Stanovich, K. E. (1986). Matthew effects in reading: Some consequences of individual differences in the acquisition of literacy. *Reading Research Quarterly, 21*, 360–380.

Stanovich, K. E., & West, R. F. (1989). Exposure to print and orthographic processing. *Reading Research Quarterly, 24*, 402–433.

Stein, M. L., Johnson, B. J., & Gutlohn, L. (1999). Analyzing beginning reading programs: The relationship between decoding instruction and text. *Remedial and Special Education, 20*, 275–287.

Swanson, E. A. (2008). Observing reading instruction for students with LD: A synthesis. *Learning Disability Quarterly, 31*, 115–133.

Swanson, E. A. (in press). Observing reading instruction for elementary students with learning disabilities served in resource rooms. *Psychology in the Schools.*

Thurlow, M., Graden, J., Greener, J., & Ysseldyke, J. E. (1983). LD and non-LD students' opportunities to learn. *Learning Disability Quarterly, 6*, 172–183.

Thurlow, M., Ysseldyke, J. E., Graden, J. L., & Algozzine, B. (1983). What's special about the special education resource room for learning disabled students? *Learning Disability Quarterly, 6*, 283–288.

Vadasy, P. F., Sanders, E. A., & Peyton, J. A. (2005). Relative effectiveness of reading practice or word-level instruction in supplemental tutoring: How text matters. *Journal of Learning Disabilities, 38*, 364–380.

Vaughn, S., Levy, S., Coleman, M., & Bos, C. S. (2002). Reading instruction for students with LD and EBD: A synthesis of observation studies. *The Journal of Special Education, 36*, 2–13.

Vaughn, S., Moody, S. W., & Schumm, J. S. (1998). Broken promises: Reading instruction in the resource room. *Exceptional Children, 64*, 211–225.

Zigmond, N., & Baker, J. M. (1994). Is the mainstream a more appropriate educational setting for Randy? A case study of one student with learning disabilities. *Learning Disabilities Research and Practice, 9*, 108–117.

11

Text Difficulty in Reading Assessment

Barbara R. Foorman

We've moved beyond Flesch's (1955) question of *Why Johnny Can't Read* to questions of whether Johnny, Leroy, Maria, José, and Tran can read grade-level text with accuracy, fluency, and understanding. In this age of increased accountability has come a renewed concern about the validity and reliability of measures of reading comprehension. Are a particular text and its associated questions valid and reliable for determining grade-level standards? How does one match reader ability and interests to text? How does one know if a fourth-grade passage on the National Assessment of Educational Progress (NAEP)—referred to as "the nation's report card"—is equal in difficulty to a fourth-grade passage on a state assessment, or if the fourth-grade passages on two states' assessments are comparable? Answering this question of text difficulty is important if the annual yearly progress (AYP) requirement of No Child Left Behind (NCLB; 2001) is to have comparable meaning across states. Currently there is wide variability in states' performance on NAEP reading and their own standards-based assessments, with Missouri, Wyoming, and Maine having scores of comparable difficulty to NAEP at the fourth- and eighth-grade levels and North Carolina, Georgia, and Texas having the largest score gaps with NAEP at these grade levels (Porter, 2007).

There are many issues to consider when discussing text difficulty in reading assessment. First, an example of a paragraph from literary nonfiction will be presented to frame the discussion of text difficulty. Second, what features of text characterize its difficulty? The approach taken in the 2009 NAEP Reading Framework (National Assessment Governing Board, 2007) will be given as an example. Third, experimental tools will be described that measure features of text difficulty at the sublexical, lexical, semantic, syntactic, and discourse levels. Fourth, procedures for designing comprehension questions and for equating text in terms of difficulty will be examined. Finally, instructional issues regarding text difficulty in assessing reading comprehension will be discussed.

What Makes a Text Difficult?

Consider the opening passage from Barbara Tuchman's (1958) *The Zimmermann Telegram*:

> The first message of the morning watch plopped out of the pneumatic tube into a wire basket with no more premonitory rattle than usual. The duty officer at the British Naval Intelligence twisted open the cartridge and examined the German wireless intercept it contained without noting anything of unusual significance. When a glance showed him that the message was in non-naval code, he sent it in to the Political Section in the inner room and thought no more about it. The date was January 17, 1917, past the halfway mark of a war that had already ground through thirty months of reckless carnage and no gain. (p. 3)

Immediately one notices the demands of vocabulary and prior knowledge. Phrases such as *duty officer, morning watch, non-naval code, German wireless,* and *Political Section* require knowledge of military terminology. Words such as *premonitory, carnage,* and *cartridge* are academically challenging words. Words such as *telegram, pneumatic tube, wire basket,* and *wireless intercept* demand prior knowledge of 20th-century communications. In fact, the entire passage requires an understanding of the war that was going on in early 1917 between Britain and Germany. The author's antiwar sentiment is poignantly expressed in the phrase "past the halfway mark of a war that had already ground through thirty months of reckless carnage and no gain." But questions remain, not answered by this paragraph. Who was Zimmermann, and why was the telegram in non-naval code? Answers are readily available in Barbara Tuchman's book but also on the Internet, where one can find the actual telegram (see Figure 11.1).

Arthur Zimmermann, the foreign secretary of the German Empire, sent the telegram to the German ambassador in Mexico to try to encourage Mexico to ally itself with Germany and to go to war with the United States. Such an action might divert the United States from aiding the Allies in Europe against Germany and offer Mexico the opportunity to recapture the southwestern part of the United States that had been lost during the Mexican-American War. The use of the word *ruthless* in the phrase *ruthless deployment of our submarines* makes one wonder about the accuracy of the translation of the decoded message by British Intelligence.

What do the opening paragraph of Barbara Tuchman's book and the wording of the Zimmermann telegram tell us about the characteristics of text difficulty? The demands of vocabulary and prior knowledge

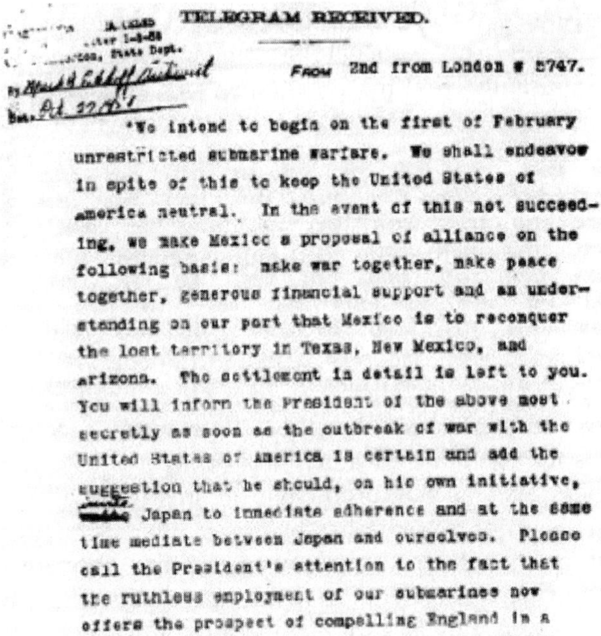

FIGURE 11.1. Zimmermann telegram. Available at *www.ourdocuments.gov/doc.php?doc=60&page=transcript.*

were discussed above. There are also linguistic demands, such as the use of anaphora (e.g., the pronoun *he or him* refers to the *duty officer*), co-reference (e.g., *German wireless intercept* refers to *the message*), and deixis (e.g., *in the inner room*). As readers we bring our general knowledge and linguistic knowledge to the text to extract and construct meaning (RAND Reading Study Group, 2002). In so doing, we build a mental model of the text that represents the situation described by the text (Kintsch & Rawson, 2005). To build an accurate situation model, the reader must draw inferences, and inferences require knowledge. The situation model for the first paragraph of Tuchman's book requires (1) knowledge of the war Britain and Germany were engaged in during early 1917 and (2) the ability to draw inferences about the relevance of a German message intercepted by the British and about the author's antiwar sentiment.

What Features of Text Characterize Its Difficulty?

The 2009 reading framework for the National Assessment of Educational Progress (NAEP; National Assessment Governing Board, 2007) departs significantly from the 1992 framework in its characterization of text difficulty in several ways. First, vocabulary will be reported out separately from comprehension by including sufficient numbers of items that measure word meanings in context. These items go beyond asking for definitions of words to determining the particular meaning of a word used in the text that contributes to comprehending the sentence and paragraph in which it is located. Examples of such academically challenging words from the Zimmermann telegram paragraph cited earlier are *premonitory*, *carnage*, and *cartridge*.

The second way in which the 2009 NAEP reading framework departs significantly from the previous framework in describing text difficulty is that separate subscales will be reported for literary and informational text, as has been done in international assessments of reading. Literary text consists of fiction, literacy nonfiction, and poetry. Informational text consists of exposition, argumentation and persuasive text, and procedural text and documents. The rationale for reporting separate subscales for literary and informational text is that research on text structures indicates that these text types vary in the organizational patterns (or grammars) that signal meaning (e.g., Goldman & Rakestraw, 2000; Graesser, Golding, & Long, 1991; Pearson & Camperell, 1994) and in the construction of mental models to integrate knowledge and inferences (Kintsch & Rawson, 2005). Cognitive targets are distinguished by text type in that locate/recall is appropriate for literary text, critique/evaluate is appropriate to informational text, and integrate/interpret is appropriate to both types of text.

The third way in which the 2009 NAEP reading framework is different is that grade-level standards for literary and informational text have been established. Achievement levels for each text type at grade 8 are provided in Table 11.1. The NAEP achievement levels are divided into three levels of proficiency: advanced (i.e., superior performance); proficient (i.e., solid academic performance for the grade level assessed); and basic (i.e., partial mastery of prerequisite knowledge and skills necessary for proficiency at the grade level assessed). Since 1992, when the previous reading framework was published, proficiency levels have improved for both fourth and eighth graders, particularly among students at or above the basic level, and in the fourth grade at the proficient level as well. In 2007, 33% of fourth graders and 26% of eighth graders performed *below* the basic level on NAEP reading, which means that they lacked the skills to access grade-level text (National Center for Education Statistics, 2007). Among minorities the percentages below basic have dropped since 1992 but remain substantial: for blacks, the percentage below basic in grade 4 declined from 67% in 1992 to 53% in 2007. The corresponding decline in grade 8 was from 55% to 45%. For Hispanics, the percentage below basic in grade 4 dropped from 60% in 1992 to 50% in 2007. The corresponding decline in grade 8 was from 51% in 1992 to 42% in 2007.

In examining Table 11.1, one can quickly see why score gaps exist between NAEP and state tests. At the basic level, NAEP expects students in grade 8 to locate the main idea, identify supporting details, identify the author's purpose, make inferences, recognize explicit causal relations, distinguish between fact and opinion, and identify the mood. For many states these are the expectations for proficient readers. As part of the NCLB legislation, states are required to participate in NAEP reading and mathematics exams in grades 4 and 8. States with sufficient score gaps on NAEP will be encouraged to make their standards more rigorous and, hence, their tests more difficult. The rigor of high school graduation standards is hotly debated (Porter, 2007). As part of NAEP's 2009 reading framework, 12th-grade performance represents the reading and analytic skills necessary for success in college and the workplace. Although the majority of states require students to pass an exam before they graduate from high school, these exams typically do not measure college and workplace readiness. Achieve (2004) conducted a

TABLE 11.1. Preliminary Grade 8 Achievement Levels for the 2009 NAEP Reading Assessment

Achievement level	Literacy	Informational
Advanced	Grade 8 students at the *advanced* level should be able to: • Make complex inferences • Critique the point of view • Evaluate character motivation • Describe thematic connections across literary texts • Evaluate how an author uses literary devices to convey meaning	Grade 8 students at the *advanced* level should be able to: • Make complex inferences • Evaluate the author's purpose • Evaluate the strength and quality of supporting evidence • Compare and contrast ideas across texts • Critique causal relations
Proficient	Grade 8 students at the *proficient* level should be able to: • Make inferences that describe the problem and solution, cause, and effect • Analyze character motivation • Interpret the mood or tone • Explain the theme • Identify similarities across texts • Analyze how an author uses literary devices to convey meaning • Interpret figurative language	Grade 8 students at the *proficient* level should be able to: • Summarize major ideas • Draw conclusions • Provide evidence in support of an argument • Describe the author's purpose • Analyze and interpret implicit causal relations
Basic	Grade 8 students at the *basic* level should be able to: • Interpret textually explicit information • Make inferences • Identify supporting details • Identify the character's motivation • Describe the problem • Identify the mood	Grade 8 students at the *basic* level should be able to: • Locate the main idea • Distinguish between fact and opinion • Make inferences • Identify the author's explicitly stated purpose • Recognize explicit causal relations

study of graduation exams in Florida, Maryland, Massachusetts, New Jersey, Ohio, and Texas and found that the tests tended to measure only 8th- to 10th-grade content. In spite of the relatively easy content, a surprisingly percentage of high school students fail the exit exams and have to retake them in order to graduate. In 2006 in Florida, 32% of students passed the state test, the Florida Comprehensive Assessment Test (FCAT), in 10th grade. A norm-referenced test (NRT; a Florida version of the Stanford Achievement Test) is also given in 10th grade, and the *St. Petersburg Times* reported correctly that the passing score on the 10th-grade FCAT was equivalent to the 66th percentile on the NRT (Stein & Tobin, April 15, 2007). In contrast, in 7th grade 62% of students passed the 7th-grade FCAT, and the equivalent on the NRT was the 56th percentile. Thus, the FCAT appears to become exponentially more difficult in 10th grade, with correspondingly more rigorous standards, in an attempt to address college and workplace readiness. In spite of this increasing rigor, the Achieve study indicates that the content falls short of the demands of college and workplace literacy.

Measuring Text Difficulty

According to the 2009 NAEP reading framework, passage selection is based on expert judgment and the use of at least two research-based readability formulas. Readability formulas such as the Flesch–Kincaid and Fry are based on average sentence length (total number of words divided by number of sentences) and average number of syllables per word (the number of syllables divided by the number of words). Other formulas such as the Dale–Chall and Spache are based on average sentence length and word frequency in grade-level corpora. The ATOS for Books formula, used in Accelerated Reader (Renaissance Learning, 2007), adds average word length to the Dale–Chall and Spache approaches. Given such different approaches to measuring text difficulty, it is not surprising that scores for passage difficulty can vary widely, depending on which formula is used. For example, for the earlier passage from Tuchman's (1958) *The Zimmermann Telegram*, the difficulty ranges from 8.4 on the Dale–Chall to 13.3 on the Flesch—Kincaid and the Fry. A newer readability formula called the Lexile framework, described below, puts the Tuchman passage at a grade level above 13.5.

Readability Formulas: Lexiles

The Lexile framework was developed with funds from federal grants during the 1980s. This proprietary software owned by MetaMetrics computes passage difficulty based on word frequency counts in grade-level corpora as a proxy for semantic load and sentence length as a proxy for syntactic load. Precision is improved by breaking passages into 125-word slices and building the variability in word frequency and sentence length across these calibrations into the resulting Lexile score.

Additional precision is provided by the use of disambiguation software that examines the semantic space of neighboring words to determine the exact meaning of a word (e.g., whether *exit* is a verb or noun, or whether *concrete* refers to building material or a nonabstract idea). This computational approach to representation of multiple meanings in semantic space was revolutionized by Landauer (2001) in latent semantic analysis (LSA). LSA constructs a geometric representation of meaning by computing the similarity between millions of words in a large number of texts. The similarity measures of LSA compare favorably to those of human judges and therefore have been used to score essays and constructed responses in reading comprehension tests (Landauer, Laham, & Foltz, 2000).

The Lexile framework, enhanced by its LSA-type semantic judgments, contains a model for linking readers to text. This is done by assigning a reader ability score to the performance associated with answering 75% of the cloze questions correctly on the 125-word calibrations in a text. Thus, based on the percentage of questions answered correctly on a Lexiled passage, the reader can be assigned a Lexile score range. This Lexile ability range can be used to match readers with Lexiled text. MetaMetrics has made arrangements with a large number of educational publishers to Lexile their tradebooks, textbooks, and tests. Moreover, MetaMetrics has automated the construction of multiple-choice cloze responses that behave similarly to human-generated items. This is done by computer selection of target words with Lexile scores within 100 Lexiles of the text. These words are deleted from the text, and readers are presented with the target word and three additional words that are syntactically correct and asked to choose the word that best completes the sentence, given the meaning of the text (Stenner, Burdick, Sanford, & Burdick, 2006).

The automation of cloze items enables MetaMetrics to offer embedded formative assessments in an Internet-based system called *MyReadingWeb*. In this system, students are matched to reading selections at their Lexile level and are asked to read the selections and complete embedded cloze items. In a pilot version with students in grades 1–12, the data look particularly promising for students in grades 4–10, where observed performance on the cloze items approximated expected performance of just under 80% correct (Torgesen, Miller, & Rissman, 2008). Data from this system quantify for each grade the number of articles read at average Lexile levels, the average number of minutes spent reading, the average number of words read silently per minute, and the average number of cloze items answered correctly.

By automating the match of reader to text, the Lexile framework solves one of the challenges of independent reading, namely, that without guidance children often select books that are too easy or too difficult (Carver & Leibert, 1995). Experimental research shows that controlling text difficulty improves oral reading fluency and comprehension (Shany & Biemiller, 1995). Furthermore, the match between reader and text must also consider the reader's interest if motivation to read independently and engagement with the text are to occur (Guthrie & Humenick, 2004). The Lexile framework addresses this issue by allowing readers to select matched text within interest areas such as sports, adventure, biography, etc.

Concerns about Readability Formulas

There are three major concerns about the use of readability formulas, including the Lexile framework. The first is their circular use in defining and measuring grade equivalencies. The second is their focus on the surface features of text. The third is their measurement error in characterizing primary grade text, poetry, or specialized documents such as tax returns or train schedules.

Circular Use

First, readability formulas are often used to assign passages to grade levels, and the assigned passages are then used to determine grade-level equivalencies for texts or grade-level performance on tests. By exchanging words in a passage, writers can manipulate text difficulty. Such manipulations possibly distort estimates of grade equivalencies and, consequently, invalidate predictions relating to the comprehension of authentic text.

Surface Features

The second concern about the use of readability formulas is that their scores are derived only from the surface features of text—word frequency and sentence length. Thus, by exchanging a word with a less frequent word or by shortening a sentence, readability scores can be altered, with corresponding changes in grade-level designations. This process can lead to invalid predictions about comprehension, as described above. To adequately capture the demands of text that affect its comprehensibility, we must go beyond the surface features to include

linguistic, cognitive, and discourse-level features. Linguistic characteristics include such features as the number of anaphora, overlapping
text segments, vocabulary difficulty, concreteness and abstractness,
and sentence and text structure. Additionally, the discourse features of
coherence and cohesion are critically important. Readers have less difficulty reading a cohesive text such as "the streets were wet because it
had rained" than a less cohesive text such as "The streets were wet. It
had rained" (McNamara, 2001). Yet, the readability of the more cohesive text is higher than that of the less cohesive text (0.8 vs. 0.0 on the
Flesch—Kincaid measure). Thus, a construct central to the comprehensibility of text—its cohesiveness—appears to be orthogonal to traditional
readability measures. Finally, the reader's abilities such as knowledge,
linguistic skills, and cognitive aptitude interact with text characteristics
to challenge any notion of readability that takes into account only the
text itself.

Measurement Error on Specialized Text

Third, readability formulas typically measure specialized documents,
poetry, and primary grade text with a level of error that is unaccept-
able. We will consider the unique characteristics of poetry and primary
grade texts.

Poetry. In the case of poetry, meaning is not conveyed through the
surface features of word frequency and sentence length. Rather, poetry
thrives on the figurative use of language and the unconventional use
of sentence structure and text structure. To take an extreme, consider
a stanza from Lewis Carroll's *Jabberwocky* in Gardner's (1960, p. 191)
Annotated Alice:

> 'Twas brillig, and the slithy toves
> Did gyre and gimble in the wabe;
> All mimsy were the borogoves,
> And the mome raths outgrabe.

We can make sense of this poem because we recognize the words
phonologically and syntactically. We know which words are nouns
and which are verbs and how to pronounce them. In the fifth stanza
the slaying of the Jabberwocky is described, and the seventh and final
stanza repeats the first stanza, quoted above. Alice's reaction to "Jabberwocky" sums up the form-versus-meaning distinction well:

"It seems very pretty," she said when she had finished, but it's rather hard to understand!" (You see she didn't like to confess, even to herself, that she couldn't make it out at all.) "Somehow it seems to fill my head with ideas—only I don't exactly know what they are! However, somebody killed something: that's clear at any rate—." (Gardner, 1960, p. 197)

Primary Grade Text. Beginning reading texts present a challenge to readability formulas because of readers' attention to the sublexical features of words, specifically the phonological, orthographic, and morphological features relevant to computing correct pronunciations in English. The alphabetic orthography of English is opaque and complex (Rayner, Foorman, Perfetti, Pesetsky, & Seidenberg, 2001). In contrast to transparent alphabetic orthographies such as Finnish, Italian, Spanish, German, and Greek, where word reading is highly accurate and efficient by the middle of the first grade (Seymour, Aro, & Erskine, 2003), the mismatch in "grain size" (Ziegler & Goswami, 2005) between phonology and orthography in English leads to much slower development of word reading skill (e.g., an accuracy rate of 40% in first grade in Seymour et al., 2003). In addition to the inconsistency in vowel spellings in English (e.g., the "long *a*" sound in *fate, pain, ray, maybe, freight, vein, great,* and *they*), there is a tendency in English to preserve morphology at the expense of phonology. For example, the *a* in *health* and the *c* in *musician* are preserved in spelling as clues to meaning, but are clearly misleading in pronunciation. Likewise, the past tense marker *-ed* has both /d/ and /t/ pronunciations as in *mobbed* and *pitched*, respectively. Moreover, irregular forms abound in English and promote spelling confusion: *run* (rather than *raned*), *children* (rather than *childs*), *yacht* (rather than *yat*). Thus, decoding instruction in English usually involves the teaching of grapheme—phoneme correspondences (i.e., phonics), spelling rimes (to draw attention to inconsistent vowel patterns), and whole words (that are highly irregular or important to a story's meaning). An important part of decoding instruction often neglected is attention to strategies for pronouncing multisyllabic words. For example, an open syllable has a "long vowel" (e.g., super) versus a closed syllable, which has a "short" vowel (e.g., supper). Additionally, consonant *-le* is typically not accented (e.g., *scrambled*). Finally, it is usually left up to spelling instruction to cover other conventions, such as consonant doubling (e.g., in single words such as *floss* or when adding *-ing* as in *beginning*), changing *y* to *i* when adding *-ed* (e.g., *cried*), homophones (e.g., *bare* vs. *bear*), and contractions (*didn't*). Information about derivations (e.g., *-tion*,

-*ology*) and etymology (e.g., *chimera* is from Greek, meaning fantasy) is also left to spelling instruction (Foorman, Breier, & Fletcher, 2003).

Owing to the opaqueness and complexity of English orthography, readability formulas cannot accurately predict the difficulty of text used for beginning readers. Relational databases have been developed to capture the decodability of beginning reading text (Stein, Johnson, & Gutlohn, 1999; Hiebert, 2002) as well as their semantic and syntactic complexity (Foorman, Francis, Davidson, Harm, & Griffin, 2004). An important finding in Foorman et al. (2004) is that about 70% of words in student anthologies that first graders are exposed to during each 6-week grading period are singletons. This finding suggests that students are not receiving the four or more exposures to a word that research suggests is important for beginning readers to learn the word by sight (Reitsma, 1983). Also, in the most popular of the beginning reading programs, students often encounter words for which the orthographic pattern has not been taught (Foorman et al., 2004). Drawing on this research on the importance of lexical features and word repetition, Hiebert (2005) manipulated text difficulty in a second grade fluency intervention. She found that students reading text that was specifically written to include few low-frequency multisyllabic singletons benefited more from repeated readings than did students reading literature-based text from the basal reading program that did not control text difficulty.

Designing Reading Comprehension Tests

Because reading comprehension is multidetermined (RAND Reading Study Group, 2002), there is no single best way to assess it. One has to consider the format for questions and the way to control for text difficulty.

Question Format

Question formats include multiple choice, oral response (e.g., story retelling or answering questions), written (i.e., constructed response), sentence verification, and cloze. Most high-stakes tests use a multiple-choice format, although NAEP uses a combination of multiple choice and constructed response. In sentence verification (Royer, Hastings, & Hook, 1979), the reader is asked to indicate which of four sentences actually appeared in the text. In addition to the verbatim sentence, there is a sentence that is a paraphrase, one that has a meaning change, and a fourth that is a distracter. The cloze format can be open-ended or multiple-choice. In the open-ended cloze format, the reader is asked to supply a missing word in a paragraph. The Woodcock–Johnson Passage Comprehension is an example of a well-known open-ended cloze (Woodcock, McGrew, & Mather, 2001). An example of a multiple-choice cloze is the maze test, where every seven to nine words is completed by selection of one of three words. All three words are syntactically correct, but only one is semantically correct. MetaMetrics uses the maze format in their *MyReaderWeb* application. Fuchs and colleagues (Fuchs, Fuchs, Hosp, & Jenkins, 2001) assessed reading comprehension with both maze and a question–answer format and showed that mazes tap low-level comprehension at the sentence level and, if time-limited, tap fluency as well. Question–answer formats and multiple-choice formats often tap literal and inferential understanding. We saw from the 2009 NAEP reading framework that these differential cognitive targets interact with text type such that locate/recall is appropriate for literary text and critique/evaluate is appropriate for informational text whereas integrate/interpret is appropriate for both types of text.

Text Equating

The theme of this chapter is that text difficulty interacts with reader characteristics and the purpose of reading in affecting comprehension outcomes. Consequently, the selection of text and the format of questions are the variables that the test developer can control. We have discussed the cognitive and linguistic features that characterize text difficulty and the attempts of readability formulas to capture sentence-level lexical, semantic, and syntactic features. But we have not yet discussed an additional factor relevant to consideration of text difficulty, namely, text equating.

As pointed out earlier, readability formulas can vary widely in their assignment of text to the appropriate grade level. One way to improve on the shortcomings of the formulas is to equate passages for difficulty by putting them on the *same scale*. The importance of passage equating has become apparent in the use of oral reading fluency (ORF) to measure ongoing progress monitoring. In a recent study (Francis et al., 2008), we found that 134 second graders' performance on six passages with identical readability scores from the Dynamic Indicators of Basic Early Literacy Skills (DIBELS; Good & Kaminiski, 2002) differed by 26 words correct per minute (wcpm). The scores ranged from 67.9 to

93.9 wcpm—the difference between being just below the 50th percentile and just below the 75th percentile on the Hasbrouck and Tindal (2006) norms. These passage effects altered growth trajectories and affected estimates of linear growth, thereby jeopardizing the intent of DIBELS ORF to reliably measure growth. We equated the wcpm scores across the six passages by using an equipercentile equating method to account for the fact that the same adjustment could not be made throughout the distribution of the wcpm score range, as is the case in linear equating. We presented a table (Francis et al., 2008, Table 8) that provides equipercentile conversions for the six passages to a common scale score anchored to a base passage, which in this case was the DIBELS passage *Home*. If a student had read the passage *Book*, the teacher could find in Table 8 the student's wcpm score in the *Book* column (53.55) and see that it is associated with a percentile rank of 30 and an equated wcpm score of 73.65. To examine the effectiveness of the equipercentile method, the students' growth over the 7-week period was reanalyzed using the equated scores. A positive average rate of growth was found without differential effects of passage.

Significant educational decisions are made based on the results of progress-monitoring tools. For example, many states report ORF scores as part of their Reading First evaluation, and special education decisions using a response-to-intervention approach are often based on ORF. Thus, the use of appropriate measurement tools such as equipercentile or linear equating to remove the effects of text difficulty and put them on the same scale is crucially important.

Assessing Reading Comprehension for Instructional Decision Making

As we design reading comprehension assessments, we need to keep in mind the purpose of the test. Are we interested in formative or summative assessment—that is, in using the results to inform learning and instruction or to characterize achievement outcomes? In either case, we need to be concerned about the reliability and validity of the assessments so that we reduce error and maximize the utility of the results (Foorman, Fletcher, & Francis, 2004). Careful consideration of text difficulty is important no matter what the purpose of assessment is, and the biggest challenge is characterizing text in terms of grade-level standards. What are the characteristics of 4th-, 8th-, and 12th-grade tests? The 2009 NAEP reading framework provides excellent guidance on text types, cognitive targets, and associated achievement levels. Improved readability formulas such as Lexiles provide a model for assigning reader ability scores to performance on Lexiled text so that readers can subsequently be matched to instructional-level text. Many teachers want students matched to grade-level text, but the typical procedures for doing so, such as the standard readability formulas, are associated with a high degree of error. However, by equating texts horizontally within grade, we can describe a reader's comprehension in terms of average performance for a grade. By horizontally *and* vertically equating text and controlling for reader characteristics, such as decoding, we can place students into instructional-level text where comprehension can be assessed and progress monitored. Decoding can be controlled by empirically linking accuracy in a passage to performance on a word reading list. These kinds of adaptive instructional-level texts can be provided online with automated comprehension questions and online booklists from local libraries matched to readers' abilities and interests. The result is a valuable intervention for increasing text reading that includes embedded formative assessment of reading comprehension with minimal interference from text difficulty.

References

Achieve. (2004). *Executive summary of the American Diploma Project*. Washington, DC: Author.

Carver, R. P., & Leibert, R. E. (1995). The effect of reading library books at different levels of difficulty upon gain in reading ability. *Reading Research Quarterly, 30*, 26–48.

Flesch, R. F. (1955). *Why Johnny can't read*. New York: Harper & Row.

Foorman, B. R., Breier, J. I., & Fletcher, J. M. (2003). Interventions aimed at improving reading success: An evidence-based approach. *Developmental Neuropsychology, 24*(2–3), 613–639.

Foorman, B. R., Fletcher, J. M., & Francis, D. J. (2004). Early reading assessment. In W. M. Evers & H. J. Walberg (Eds.), *Testing student learning, evaluating teaching effectiveness* (pp. 81–125). Stanford, CA: Hoover Institution.

Foorman, B. R., Francis, D. J., Davidson, K., Harm, M., & Griffin, J. (2004). Variability in text features in six grade 1 basal reading programs. *Scientific Studies in Reading, 8*(2), 167–197.

Francis, D. F., Santi, K. L., Barr, C., Fletcher, J. M., Varisco, A., & Foorman, B. R. (2008). Form effects on the estimation of students' oral reading fluency using DIBELS. *Journal of School Psychology, 46*, 315–342.

Fuchs, L. S., Fuchs, D. F., Hosp, M. K., & Jenkins, J. R. (2001). Oral reading fluency as an indicator of reading competence: A theoretical, empirical, and historical analysis. *Scientific Studies of Reading, 5*, 239–256.

Gardner, M. (1960). *The annotated Alice: Alice's Adventures in Wonderland & Through the Looking Glass by Lewis Carroll*. New York: Meridian.

Goldman, S., & Rakestraw, J. (2000). Structural aspects of constructing meaning from text. In R. Barr, M. Kamil, P. Mosenthal, & P. D. Pearson (Eds.), *Handbook of reading research* (Vol. 3, pp. 311–335). New York: Longman.

Good, R. H., & Kaminiski, R. A. (2002). *DIBELS oral reading fluency passages for first through third grades* (Technical Report no. 10). Eugene, OR: University of Oregon.

Graesser, A., Golding, J. M., & Long, D. L. (1991). Narrative representation and comprehension. In R. Barr, M. L. Kamil, P. B. Mosenthal, & P. D. Pearson (Eds.), *Handbook of reading research* (Vol. 2, pp. 171–205). White Plains, NY: Longman.

Guthrie, J. T., & Humenick, N. M. (2004). Motivating students to read: Evidence for classroom practices that increase reading motivation and achievement. In P. McCardle & V. Chhabra (Eds.), *The voice of evidence: Bringing research to classroom educators* (pp. 329–360). Baltimore: Brookes.

Hasbrouck, J., & Tindal, G. A. (2006). Oral reading fluency norms: A valuable assessment tool for reading teachers. *The Reading Teacher, 59,* 636–644.

Hiebert, E. H. (2002). Standards, assessments, and text difficulty. In A. E. Farstrup & S. J. Samuels (Eds.), *What research has to say about reading instruction* (pp. 337–391). Newark, DE: International Reading Association.

Hiebert, E. H. (2005). The effects of text difficulty on second graders' fluency development. *Reading Psychology, 26,* 183–209.

Kintsch, W., & Rawson, K. A. (2005). Comprehension. In M. J. Snowling & C. Hulme (Eds.), *The science of reading: A handbook* (pp. 209–226). New York: Blackwell.

Landauer, T. K. (2001). Single representations of multiple meanings in Latent Semantic Analysis. In D. S. Gorfein (Ed.), *On the consequences of meaning selection* (pp. 217–232). Washington, DC: American Psychological Association.

Landauer, T. K., Laham, D., & Foltz, P. W. (2000). The Intelligent Essay Assessor. *IEEE Intelligent Systems, 15*(5), 27–31.

McNamara, D. S. (2001). Reading both high and low coherence texts: Effects of text sequence and prior knowledge. *Canadian Journal of Experimental Psychology, 55,* 51–62.

National Assessment Governing Board. (2007). *Reading framework for the 2009 National Assessment of Educational Progress*. Washington, DC: Author.

National Center for Education Statistics. (2007). *NAEP 2007 reading: A report card for the nation and the states*. Washington, DC: U.S. Department of Education.

No Child Left Behind Act of 2001. (2001). Public Law No. 107-110, 115 Stat.1425.

Pearson, P. D., & Camperell, K. (1994). Comprehension of text structures. In R. B. Ruddell, M. R. Ruddell, & H. Singer (Eds.), *Theoretical models and processes of reading* (4th ed., pp. 448–468). Newark, DE: International Reading Association.

Porter, A. C. (2007). NCLB lessons learned: Implications for reauthorization. In

A. Gamoran (Ed.), *Standards-based reform and the poverty gap: Lessons from "No Child Left Behind"* (pp. 286–324). Washington, DC: Brookings Institution.

RAND Reading Study Group. (2002). *Reading for understanding.* Santa Monica, CA: RAND Corporation.

Rayner, K., Foorman, B. R., Perfetti, C. A., Pesetsky, D., & Seidenberg, M. S. (2001). How psychological science informs the teaching of reading. *Psychological Science in the Public Interest, 2*(2), 31–74.

Reitsma, P. (1983). Printed word learning in beginning readers. *Journal of Experimental Child Psychology, 36,* 321–339.

Renaissance Learning. (2007, September). *Matching books to students: How to use readability formulas and continuous monitoring to ensure reading success.* Wisconsin Rapids, WI: Author. Available at *research.renlearn.com/research/62. asp.*

Royer, J. M., Hastings, C. N., & Hook, C. (1979). A sentence verification technique for measuring reading comprehension. *Journal of Reading Behavior, 11,* 355–363.

Seymour, P. H. K., Aro, M., & Erskine, J. M. (2003). Foundation literacy acquisition in European orthographies. *British Journal of Psychology, 94,* 143–174.

Shany, M. T., & Biemiller, A. (1995). Assisted reading practice: Effects on performance for poor readers in grades 3 and 4. *Reading Research Quarterly, 30,* 382–395.

Stein, L., & Tobin, T. C. (2007, April 15). Suddenly, 10th graders are FCAT flops. *St. Petersburg Times.* Available at *www.sptimes.com/2007/04/15/news_pf/state/ suddenly_10th_grader.shtml.*

Stein, M., Johnson, B., & Gutlohn, L. (1999). Analyzing beginning reading programs: The relationship between decoding instruction and text. *Remedial and Special Education, 20,* 275–287.

Stenner, A. J., Burdick, H., Sanford, E. E., & Burdick, D. S. (2006). How accurate are Lexile text measures? *Journal of Applied Measurement, 7,* 307–322.

Torgesen, J. K., Miller, D., & Rissman, L. (2008). *Assessment practices to improve instruction in academic literacy for adolescents: A guidance document from the Center on Instruction.* Available at *www.centeroninstruction.org.*

Tuchman, B. (1958). *The Zimmermann Telegram.* New York: Viking Press.

Woodcock, R., McGrew, K., & Mather, N. (2001). *Woodcock–Johnson III.* Itasca, IL: Riverside.

Ziegler, J. C., & Goswami, U. (2005). Reading acquisition, developmental dyslexia, and skilled reading across languages: A psycholinguistic grain size theory. *Psychological Bulletin, 131,* 3–29.

PART IV

SUMMARY

12

CREATING OPPORTUNITIES TO READ MORE SO THAT STUDENTS READ BETTER

LINDA B. GAMBRELL

It is books that are a key to the wide world; if you can't do anything else, read all that you can.
—JANE HAMILTON (1998)

Reading More, Reading Better is an excellent title for this volume. Throughout the chapters in this book, the evidence base supports the belief that the school reading curriculum must incorporate time and opportunity for students to read. Why is the amount of time spent reading a critical consideration in the reading curriculum? First, we know that students who spend more time reading are better readers (Allington & McGill-Franzen, 2003; Anderson, Wilson, & Fielding, 1988; Cunningham & Stanovich, 1998; Taylor, Frye, & Maruyama, 1990). Second, students who have more experiences with books are better prepared for reading success than others (Allington, 1991; Neuman & Celano, 2001). Third, it is clear that supporting and nurturing reading development is crucial to improving the educational prospects for all students, and particularly for who find learning to read difficult (Allington, 1986; Smith-Burke, 1989).

According to Cunningham and Stanovich (1998), reading has cognitive benefits beyond getting meaning from the page. Their research indicates that the very act of reading can help students compensate for modest levels of cognitive ability by increasing their vocabulary and general knowledge. Perhaps the most important finding from the research of Cunningham and Stanovich is that ability is not the only variable that counts in the development of intelligence. Their research supports the notion that students who read a lot will enhance their verbal intelligence. They found that this was true for all students regardless of ability level. Everyone benefited from time spent reading, but struggling readers benefited most. In other words, reading makes a person smarter.

Time to read and *motivation to read* are clearly linked to the notion that the more students read, the better readers they become. Students who are motivated to read will make time for reading, will read more, and as a result are likely to increase in both reading ability and intelligence. Just as we must give attention to making sure that students have sufficient amounts of time to read, we must also promote and support classroom cultures that encourage and nurture motivation to read.

Classroom cultures that foster motivation to read and provide sufficient amounts of reading time create the necessary foundation that is essential for supporting students in developing as competent and proficient readers. Research studies have documented that time spent reading is a primary factor related to intrinsic motivation to reading. For example, observational and interview studies conducted by Heathington (1979), Midgley (1993), and Mizelle (1997) concluded that increased amounts of time for free reading in classrooms were associated with increased motivation to read.

Various constructs have been used throughout this book to describe high-quality and extensive involvement in reading, including reading volume (Allington, Chapter 2, this volume), engaged reading (McRae & Guthrie, Chapter 3, this volume), opportunity to read (Hiebert & Martin, Chapter 1, this volume), and content-area reading (Cervetti, Jaynes, & Hiebert, Chapter 4, this volume). The chapters in this volume attest to the importance of devoting time, on a daily basis, for students to engage in real reading for real purposes, both during instruction and self-selected reading time. In this chapter, I offer yet another dimension of the goal that has been the focus of this book: pleasure reading. Ultimately, we hope that our students will choose to read both narrative and informational text for sheer pleasure. We want all students to be intrinsically motivated to read—reading when no one is looking or offering candy or pizza. We want them to *want* to read because we know that reading is one of the cornerstones—if not *the*, cornerstone—of academic success and good citizenship.

Reading More, Reading Better:
The Role of Pleasure Reading

While pleasure reading is often associated with reading fiction, it can take many forms—reading a scientific magazine, poetry, or the Sunday paper online. In any genre and in any form, pleasure reading enriches our lives in uncountable ways. Through reading we are no longer limited by the confines of our lives, perceptions, and thinking. Through reading we can come to better understand ourselves, others, and the world in which we live.

A 2007 report by the National Endowment for the Arts (NEA; 2007), *To Read or Not to Read: A Question of National Consequence*, sought to gather the best national data available to provide a comprehensive view of American reading habits today. The data sources consisted of large national studies by U.S. federal agencies as well as academic, foundation, and business surveys. Among the many findings reported by the NEA are the following: reading for pleasure correlates strongly with academic achievement; individuals who engage in reading for pleasure are better readers and writers than nonreaders; children and teenagers who read for pleasure on a daily or weekly basis score better on reading tests than infrequent readers; and frequent readers score better on writing texts than infrequent readers. These data sources also yielded three unsettling conclusions: Americans are spending less time reading, comprehension skills are declining, and declines in reading have serious civic, social, cultural, and economic consequences.

Americans Are Spending Less Time Reading

One of the most unsettling statistics is that nearly half of all Americans aged 18–24 read no books for pleasure. From 1984 to 2004, the percentage of 13-year-olds who reported that they "read for fun" on a daily basis declined from 35% to 30%, and for 17-year-olds the decline was from 31% to 22%. Teenagers and young adults read less often and for shorter amounts of time as compared with other age groups and with Americans in the past. Even when reading does occur, it competes with other media (U.S. Department of Education, 2005). Approximately 60% of middle and high school students use other media (i.e., watch TV, play video games, or engage in instant messaging, emailing, or Web surfing) while reading (Henry J. Kaiser Family Foundation, 2006). This multitasking suggests less focused engagement with a text.

Reading Comprehension Skills Are Declining

Reading test scores for 9-year-olds are at an all-time high (U.S. Department of Education, 2005). Beginning in 1992, however, reading scores for 17-year-olds began a slow downward trend. The average reading scores for teenagers and young males have declined. Further, the reading gap between males and females is widening. As young Americans read less, they read less well, resulting in lower levels of academic achievement. Proficient readers with strong comprehension skills accrue personal, professional, and social advantages, while less proficient readers run higher risks of failure in all three of these areas (U.S. Department of Education, 2005).

Declines in Reading Have Civic, Social, and Economic Consequences

Employers now rank reading and writing as top deficiencies in new hires (Higher Education Research Institute, 2007). One in five U.S. workers reads at a lower skill level than their job requires. Approximately 40% of workers reading at the "basic" level reported that their reading level limited their job prospects.

According to a 2006 report, *Reading Next*, approximately 3,000 American students drop out of high school *daily* (Biancarosa & Snow, 2006). Poor reading proficiency correlates with lack of employment, lower wages, and fewer opportunities for advancement. The NEA report indicates that less proficient readers are less likely to become active in civic and cultural life, especially in volunteer activities and voting.

Should We Be Concerned?

Some have criticized the NEA report for its shortcomings. Perhaps the major criticism has been that the report's conclusions are based primarily on correlational data. While the authors of the report caution that none of the data presented should be regarded as drawing a causal relationship between voluntary reading, reading skills, and other variables, the consistent associations between voluntary reading and advanced reading skills and other benefits are compelling.

Another criticism goes to the heart of what it means to read. While the NEA study focused on the reading of books, emerging evidence suggests that much of the pleasure reading that students do today involves the reading of magazines, graphic novels, the Internet, and other forms of text (McGill-Franzen and Botzakis, Chapter 5, this volume). In spite of the possible limitations of the NEA report, the information drawn from a number of large data-based sources tells a consistent and disturbing story about American reading habits. Following the elementary school years, there is a steady decline in reading among teenage and adult Americans. Also of great concern is the finding that both reading ability and the habit of regular reading have greatly declined among college graduates. Whether or not people read, and how much and how often they read, affects their lives in crucial ways. The data from the NEA report suggest how powerfully pleasure reading transforms the lives of individuals—regardless of social and economic circumstances. Simply put, reading changes lives for the better.

Opportunity to Read: Does Practice Make Perfect?

Will reading practice, or time spent reading, make a student a *perfect* reader? Probably not. But I'm convinced that practice helps students become *better* readers. The ancient Assyrian Publilius Syrus (42 B.C.) declared, "Practice is the best of all instructors." Reading has the potential to improve with the right kind of practice.

In their research on experts, Ericsson, Krampe, and Tesch-Römer (1993) explored the role of practice in the development of skill proficiency. They use the term *deliberate practice* to describe the kind of practice that results in the development of expertise. They define deliberate practice as activities designed to improve an individual's performance. In a series of studies of expert musicians, chess players, and athletes, they consistently found that the accumulated amount of deliberate practice was closely related to performance (Charness, Krampe, & Mayr, 1996; Ericsson et al., 1993; Starkes, Deakin, Allard, Hodges, & Hayes, 1996). These researchers concluded that the amount of deliberate practice explains skilled, expert performance rather than innate ability. As Allington (Chapter 2, this volume) notes, this line of research supports Guthrie's (2004) notion of engaged reading and his argument for the importance of extend reading practice. Guthrie and his colleagues (Guthrie & Humenick, 2004; Guthrie, Schafer, & Huang, 2001) characterize engaged reading as purposeful, intrinsically motivated, and socially interactive. Deliberate practice, in this view, would involve intrinsically motivated reading that improves reading performance. Therefore, as the authors of chapters in this book suggest, the productive use of time for independent reading during the school day is critical to the development of both the skill and will to read.

Whatever Happened to Recreational Reading?

As a child in the 1950s, I spent a fair amount of time reading after school. In the part of South Carolina where I grew up, we could get television reception on one channel for about 3 hours a day; so, television was not a huge distraction. Things have changed greatly since the 1950s. Nowadays, students have access to television 24/7, with literally hundreds of channels to choose from. They have computers, the Internet, and video games that compete for their attention. In addition, the after-school time of some students is heavily scheduled. These children have activities such as sports practice, music lessons, and other recreational activities. Whereas students of past generations may have had more time to spend reading for pleasure after school, the competition for those after-school hours has steadily increased over the years. But, as with any skill, reading requires practice. A pressing issue pertains to where students get the opportunities for practice that are necessary for the development of fluent and proficient reading. I suggest that, unless the opportunity to read is provided during the school day, students will not get the practice they need in order to develop to their full literacy potential.

Questions about how to balance teacher-directed reading instruction and independent reading during the school day have intrigued me since my early teaching years. In 1986, I conducted a study to determine the amount of time students spent *actually reading* during teacher-directed reading instruction in grades 1–3. In this particular study, first-grade students spent 3 minutes, second-grade students about 5 minutes, and third graders about 5 minutes engaged in contextual reading during teacher guided instruction (Gambrell, 1984). A recent study by Brenner, Hiebert, and Tompkins (Chapter 6, this volume) revealed that third graders spent an average of 18 minutes reading during the reading/language arts time. These findings, as well as similar findings in other studies (Allington, 1984; Hiebert, 1983, Knapp. 1995; Vaughn, Moody, & Schumm, 1998), suggest that the amount of reading practice that students receive during teacher-directed instruction and the reading/language arts block may not be sufficient to support literacy development. These findings also indicate that providing independent reading time during the school day may be critical to giving students the amount of practice needed for them to develop reading fluency and proficiency.

As Timothy Shanahan, a member of the National Reading Panel (NICHD, 2000), has correctly observed (Shanahan, 2006), the experimental research on sustained silent reading (SSR) and other approaches to independent reading is very slight. The studies that have been done to date have been based on a model of SSR where the teacher sits at the desk and reads during the SSR period. Today, many teachers use SSR in innovative ways that incorporate research-based procedures. For example, some teachers use the SSR period to conference with students and provide individual guidance. Other teachers allow time at the end of the silent reading period for students to talk with a partner about what they've been reading. These adaptations of SSR are based on current research on the value of individualizing strategy instruction and the value of discussing texts. Future research is needed that will explore the dynamics of research-based SSR practices and their effects on reading development.

New Insights about Opportunities to Read and Reading Achievement

Several recent experimental studies cited in chapters throughout this book have provided new insights about the relationship between opportunities to read and reading achievement. In a study that explored the development of fluent and automatic reading with second-graders, Kuhn et al. (2006) reported that increasing the amount of time children spend reading appropriately challenging texts with scaffolds leads to improvement in both word reading and reading comprehension. Samuels and Wu (2003) explored whether differences in independent reading time, when provided in addition to a regular balanced reading program, can affect reading outcomes in third- and fifth-grade classrooms. They found that additional reading practice was beneficial to all students; however, they caution that the amount of time spent in independent reading should match the student's reading ability and capacity to maintain attention. Clearly, there are learning differences that require teacher monitoring in order for independent reading to successfully increase reading achievement. These studies begin to highlight the factors that are important to consider when designing effective independent reading programs.

Creating Opportunities to Read

As a young child, I was very lucky to have a grandmother who was an avid reader and who spent many hours reading aloud to me. Snuggled up on her moss green sofa, we shared many good books. This was pleasure reading at its very best, even though one of my favorite books for these sessions with my grandmother was the *Compton's Encyclopedia*. One could say that my grandmother was ahead of her times—recognizing the importance of informational text! Because my grandmother read to me from the encyclopedia about people from faraway lands, invention and inventors, famous presidents, and many other informational topics, I sought out the encyclopedia and often spent time looking at the pictures and finding things I wanted her to read aloud to me. My grandmother also read aloud to me from the newspaper, magazines, and books that she was reading. I retain vivid memories from my early childhood of my grandmother reading aloud excerpts from what she was reading. When she found a new or unusual word, an interesting description, or a turn of a phrase that she thought was well crafted, those were read aloud to me. She was a great fan of Mickey Spillane. It should be little wonder that I was reading these mystery stories by the time I was a teenager. My grandmother and I had formed our very own Mickey Spillane book club!

Even as a young child, I knew how lucky I was to have a grandmother who was a reading model, mentor, and motivator. My grandmother was followed by numerous others. Throughout my adult life, teachers, friends, and colleagues have played a significant role in my literacy life as models, mentors, and motivators. I always look forward to talking with special friends about good books. How fortunate I am to have such wonderful reading mentors, models, and motivators! And it goes without saying that every child should be blessed with the same. In the section that follows, I share a few practical suggestions that illustrate how teachers can serve as reading mentors, models, and motivators in their classrooms.

Supporting Time to Read in the Classroom

• *Teachers of reading should read themselves.* When teachers read themselves they are better able to serve as active rather than passive *reading models* for their students (Nathanson, Pruslow, & Levitt, 2008). Being a reading model for students goes far beyond sitting at a desk reading so that students "see" the teacher reading. Rather, teachers who are active reading models talk with students about books they are reading. For example, I remember the first time I shared my own reading with my third-grade classroom. I was reading *The Right Stuff* by Tom Wolfe, and I read aloud some of the passages about the astronauts and the rigorous training they received to prepare for space flight. My students showed such great interest that I continued to identify appropriate sections of the book to share with them in the days that followed. While I do acknowledge that not everything that I read is appropriate for sharing with students, in most cases I find ideas, passages, vignettes, and interesting vocabulary that are worthy of sharing with students. I believe that being a reading model for students is tremendously important and I take advantage of opportunities to share my own reading with students, whether they are in an elementary class with which I'm working or in a graduate course that I'm teaching.

• *Teachers of reading should use a broad range of techniques to mentor students into the reading community.* If we know anything about teaching reading, it is that there is no one-size-fits-all formula. Teachers should be encouraged to help individual students and analyze what works for them. Teachers who are effective *reading mentors* support students in developing strategic reading behaviors that help them become proficient and independent readers who read for pleasure.

Teachers also mentor students *into the reading community*. Researchers who have explored the role of mentoring encourage teachers to build and maintain supportive, caring relationships with students through activities such as having teachers and students share appropriate aspects of their personal lives, eat lunch together in small groups, and participate in other activities that communicate to students that teachers are truly interested and concerned about the students' experiences and not just their academic work (Battistich, Solomon, Watson, & Schaps, 1997; Pianta, Stublman, & Hamre, 2002). What better way of forging this type of mentoring relationship than discussing good books with students. Teachers who are reading mentors play an important role in ensuring that their students develop good reading habits and become members of the reading community.

• *Teachers should provide students with adequate opportunities to read.* Students need to have ample opportunities to read, and it is critically important that sufficient time during the school day be devoted to pleasure reading. Devoting time to pleasure reading during the school day demonstrates the value placed on pleasure reading. Pleasure reading means reading whatever brings you pleasure and enjoyment, whether it be fiction, nonfiction, poetry, or any other genre. And today, more than ever before, we must recognize that pleasure reading can take place using many text types, including books, magazines, newspapers, and electronic media.

Teachers can inspire students to read widely as they share books and other texts representing different genres and text types. Children choose to read books that they know something about. As Richard Allington has astutely pointed out, no adult walks into a library or bookstore with the request "Could you help me find a book I know nothing about?" No, what we do is we look for books we know something about—a book a friend has recommended, one by an author we know, or one we've read about in a book review. As teachers we encourage students to read widely; we share lots of books by introducing the book and reading aloud a paragraph or two—and then encourage the students to read the rest of the book. Taking advantage of small bits of time throughout the school day to read a poem from a favorite book of poetry, a fact from the *Guinness Book of World Records*, or an item of interest from the newspaper—these are the ways that teachers support students in choosing to read for pleasure.

While there are many things that can be done to create a classroom culture that supports and nurtures reading development, there has been increasing concern about the decline in reading skills experienced by many struggling readers. In particular, many parents, teachers, and educators voice concern about the substantial loss in reading proficiency that occurs over the summer months for struggling readers.

Supporting Summertime Reading

Most U.S. students go to school for 9 months a year. Most students grow in their knowledge and reading proficiency over the school year. Yet, when the summer comes, many students experience summer learning loss, particularly those from low-socioeconomic-status (SES) families. Research indicates that struggling learners score significantly higher on standardized tests at the beginning of summer vacation than they do at the end of the summer (Allington & McGill-Franzen, 2003; Allington et al., 2007). This loss is particularly evident in reading. While most students show some loss in reading skills over the summer, it is students from low-SES families—who may not have access to books—who experience the greatest reading loss.

A variety of terms have been used to refer to what happens when students are out of school during the summer months—*summer reading gap, summer learning loss, summer setback, summer shortfall,* and *summer slide.* Regardless of the term that is used, the research is clear: summer learning loss contributes to the perpetuation of the reading gap between students from low-SES and high-SES families.

Reading researchers have long been concerned about summer reading loss, with several studies documenting that the most vulnerable literacy learners show a decline in reading proficiency over the summer. In 1978 Barbara Heyns first brought attention to summer learning loss with the publication of her book *Summer Learning and the Effects of Schooling*. The book documented that the achievement of middle grade students from low-SES families regressed over the summer as compared to students from high-SES families. While research consistently shows that struggling readers lose ground over the summer, what is of even greater concern is that these losses are cumulative, adding up each year and creating a wider gap between more proficient and less proficient students. According to Allington and McGill-Franzen (2003), by the time a struggling reader reaches middle school, summer reading loss has accumulated to a 2-year lag in reading achievement.

A 2007 study by Alexander, Entwisle, and Olson reveals that the achievement gap between high-SES and low-SES students at the ninth-grade level traces back to the loss in reading proficiency that occurs over the course of the summer months throughout the elementary grades. The effects are long-lasting in that the summer loss is associated with graduation from high school and transition to college. A surprising finding in this study was the extent to which the *continuing press* of student's summer learning loss contributed to achievement in grade 9: summer learning loss across 5 years of elementary school accounted for more than half the difference in the achievement gap between students from high-SES and low-SES families. This study adds to our knowledge of summer learning loss by isolating the distinctive role of schooling in student's cognitive development. But most importantly, it provides evidence that summer loss is linked to achievement in grade 9 and beyond, separating college track from non-college track students.

According to Luke (1991, 1994), the relationship between poverty and low achievement is clear in an examination of achievement data. Luke, as well as others, argues that it is imperative to address the issue of poverty if the achievement gap is to be alleviated. The relationship between poverty and lack of access to books is also well documented in the literature (Neuman & Celano, 2001). Both educators and policymakers are considering large-scale interventions that overcome the devastating effects of summer learning loss such as modified school year calendars, extended school years, and summer school programs.

At the same time, there are a number of things that classroom teachers can do to encourage reading over the summer. In a study conducted with elementary-age students, Kim (2004) found that reading four to five books during the summer could be enough to prevent a decline in reading achievement from spring to fall. The key to overcoming summer reading loss is finding novel ways to get books into the hands of students during the summer break. Projects such as those of Kim (2004) and Alexander et al. (2007) indicate that there are specific actions that classroom teachers can take to support more reading by their students during the summer.

One such action is to share numerous books with students during teacher read-aloud periods over the course of a school year. Students tend to select books with which they have at least a modicum of familiarity. Therefore, when teachers introduce students to a variety of books rather than focusing on only a small number of books over a school year, students are better able to choose books that fit their interests and skill levels. Including informational books as well as narrative books as part of read-aloud events will ensure that a range of interests and background knowledge is supported (Cervetti, Bravo, Hiebert, Pearson, & Jaynes, in press). Once students have been provided with a rich array of compelling texts, they should be encouraged to generate a list of the books that they intend to read over the summer. For example, if a teacher introduces students to 12–15 books weekly over the last month of school, students will have been exposed to 50–60 books that they can check out of their local library over the summer.

If time for book sharing in classrooms is limited, teachers might consider the "three-a-day" strategy (Gambrell, 2008). In the "three-a-day" format, teachers share at least three books that represent different genres during a sharing period. For example, teachers might share a narrative text, an informational text, and another genre, such as a book of poetry or the *Guinness Book of World Records*. Such an approach—especially if done during the last month of a school year—could introduce students to numerous options for their summertime reading.

Maintaining a high-quality classroom library is similar to maintaining a garden—both need some occasional weeding. As a former classroom teacher, I realize now that I was "guarding" books rather than sharing books. I made certain that each and every book in my classroom library was accounted for. As a result, the number of books in my classroom library grew substantially. While new books were added each year, none ever left my classroom! I've since come to realize that students, like adults, gravitate toward "newer" titles (see McGill-Franzen & Botzakis, Chapter 5, this volume). While there are some classics that we want to retain in our classroom libraries, many of the older out-of-date books are never touched by students' hands. Perhaps it is time to weed out some of the older or never-touched books from your classroom library and give them to your students for summer reading. If the books in the classroom library have been purchased with school funds, first obtain permission from your principal to give these books to students. Giving students books to take home on the last day of class may be an especially powerful way to increase summer reading. The gift of a book might be augmented with a bookplate that students put into the front cover of their new books. A bookplate that says "Happy Summer Reading from your fifth-grade teacher" could be a treasured possession for a student—as well as other members of the student's family. Books given to students by the teacher become favorite books and are likely to be read over the summer.

Educators should explore ways to promote access to books, particularly for students in schools in low-SES communities. Some suggestions include keeping the school library open during the summer months so that students can check books out; or taking students on a class trip to the local library during the last month of school to assure that every student has a library card; or working with local businesses to sponsor the purchase of books for each student to take home on the last day of class.

There is increasing evidence that summer reading loss is one of the most important factors contributing to the reading achievement gap between students from high-SES families and low-SES families. What teachers do during the final month of the school year can increase the odds that students will choose to read over the summer.

Why Opportunity to Read Is Important for Every Student

Throughout this volume, the case is consistently made that providing the opportunities to read in both the classroom and home environments encourages both reading achievement and intrinsic motivation to read. We all want students who are eager to read and who read for both pleasure and information. We all want students who are excited about sharing book experiences and who want to read increasingly challenging text. We all want students who value reading as a source of pleasure, as an avenue for investigating topics of interest, and as a means to solve problems. The most basic goal of any reading curriculum is the development of readers who *can read* and who *choose to read*. In order to reach this goal, instruction in the most essential reading skills is necessary but not sufficient. Only with the practice and expertise that comes from adequate opportunities to engage in reading will students develop their full reading potential.

References

Alexander, K. L., Entwisle, D. R., & Olson, L. S. (2007). Lasting consequences of the summer learning gap. *American Sociological Review, 72*, 167–180.

Allington, R. L. (1984). Content coverage and contextual reading in reading groups. *Journal of Reading Behavior, 16*(1), 85–96.

Allington, R. L. (1986). Policy constraints and effective compensatory reading instruction: A review. In J. V. Hoffman (Ed.), *Effective teaching of reading: Research and practice* (pp. 261–289). Newark, DE: International Reading Association.

Allington, R. L. (1991). The legacy of "slow it down and make it more concrete." In J. Zutell & S. McCormick (Eds.), *Learner factors/teacher factors: Issues in literacy research and instruction* (pp. 19–30). Chicago: National Reading Conference.

Allington, R. L., & McGill-Franzen, A. (2003). The impact of summer loss on the reading achievement gap. *Phi Delta Kappan, 85*(6), 68–75.

Allington, R. L., McGill-Franzen, A., Camilli, G., Williams, L., Zmach, C. C., Love-Zeig, J., et al. (2007, April 11). *Ameliorating summer reading setback among economically disadvantaged children*. Paper presented at the American Educational Research Association Conference, Chicago.

Anderson, R. C., Wilson, P. T., & Fielding, L. G. (1988). Growth in reading and how children spend their time outside of school. *Reading Research Quarterly, 23*, 285–303.

Battistich, V., Solomon, D., Watson, M., & Schaps, E. (1997). Caring school communities. *Educational Psychologist, 32*(3), 425–446.

Biancarosa, C., & Snow, C. E. (2006). *Reading Next—a vision for action and research in middle and high school literacy*. Washington, DC: Alliance for Excellent Education.

Cervetti, G. N., Bravo, M. A., Hiebert, E. H., Pearson, P. D., & Jaynes, C. (in press). Text genre and science content: Ease of reading, comprehension, and reading preference. *Reading Psychology*.

Charness, N. R., Krampe, T., & Mayr, U. (1996). The role of practice and coaching in entrepreneurial skill domains: An international comparison of life-span chess skill acquisition. In K. A. Ericsson (Ed.), *The road to excellence: The acquisition of expert performance in the arts and sciences, sports, and games* (pp. 51–80). Mahwah, NJ: Erlbaum.

Cunningham, A. E., & Stanovich, K. E. (1998, Spring/Summer). What reading does for the mind. *American Educator*, 8–15.

Ericsson, K., Krampe, T., & Tesch-Römer, C. (1993). The role of deliberate practice in the acquisition of expert performance. *Psychological Review, 100,* 363–406.

Gambrell, L. B. (1984). How much time do children spend reading during teacher-directed reading instruction? In J. Niles & L. Harris (Eds.), *Changing perspectives in research in reading/language processing and instruction* (pp. 193–198). Rochester, NY: National Reading Conference.

Gambrell, L. B. (2008, April/May). Closing the summer reading gap: You can make a difference. *Reading Today, 25,* p. 18.

Guthrie, J. T. (2004). Teaching for literacy engagement. *Journal of Literacy Research, 36*(1), 1–28.

Guthrie, J. T., & Humenick, N. M. (2004). Motivating students to read: Evidence for classroom practices that increase motivation and achievement. In P. McCardle & V. Chhabra (Eds.), *The voice of evidence in reading research* (pp. 329–354). Baltimore: Brookes.

Guthrie, J. T., Schafer, W. D., & Huang, C. W. (2001). Benefits of opportunity to read and balanced instruction on the NAEP. *Journal of Educational Research, 94*(3), 145–162.

Hamilton, J. (1998). *The book of Ruth.* New York: Ticknor & Fields.

Heathington, B. S. (1979). What to do about reading motivation in the middle school. *Journal of Reading, 22,* 709–713.

Henry J. Kaiser Family Foundation. (2006). *Media multitasking among youth: Prevalence, predictors and pairings* (#7592). Menlo Park, CA: Author.

Heyns, B. (1978). *Summer learning and the effects of schooling.* San Diego, CA: Academic Press.

Hiebert, E. H. (1983). An examination of ability grouping for reading instruction. *Reading Research Quarterly, 18,* 231–255.

Higher Education Research Institute. (2007). *American Freshmen: Forty-Year Trends 1966–2006.* Los Angeles, CA: UCLA.

Kim, J. (2004). Summer reading and the ethnic achievement gap. *Journal of Education for Students Placed at Risk, 9*(2), 169–189.

Knapp, M. S. (1995). *Teaching for meaning in high-poverty classrooms.* New York: Teachers College Press.

Kuhn, M. R., Schwanenflugel, P. J., Morris, R. D., Morrow, L. M., Woo, D., Meisinger, B., et al. (2006). Teaching children to become fluent and automatic readers. *Journal of Literacy Research, 38,* 357–387.

Luke, A. (1991). The political economy of reading instruction. In C. Baker & A. Luke (Eds.), *Towards a critical sociology of reading pedagogy* (pp. 3–25). Amsterdam and Philadelphia: John Benjamins.

Luke, A. (1994). *The social construction of literacy in the primary school.* South Melbourne, Victoria Macmillan Education Australia.

Midgley, C. (1993). Motivation and middle level schools. *Advances in motivation and achievement* (Vol. 8, pp. 217–274). Greenwich, CT: JAI Press.

Mizelle, N. B. (1997). Enhancing young adolescents' motivation for literacy learning. *Middle School Journal, 24*(2), 5–14.

Nathanson, S., Pruslow, J., & Levitt, R. (2008). The reading habits and literacy attitudes of inservice and prospective teachers. *Journal of Teacher Education, 59,* 313–321.

National Endowment for the Arts. (2007). *To read or not to read: A question of national consequence* (Research Report #47). Washington, DC: Author. Available at *www.arts.gov*.

National Institute of Child Health and Human Development. (2000). *Report of the National Reading Panel. Teaching children to read: An evidence-based assessment of the scientific research literature on reading and its implications for reading instruction* (NIH Publication No. 00-4769). Washington, DC: U.S. Government Printing Office.

Neuman, S. B., & Celano, D. (2001). Access to print in low-income and middle-income communities: An ecological study in four neighborhoods. *Reading Research Quarterly, 36*(1), 8–26.

Pianta, R. C., Stublman, M. W., & Hamre, B. K. (2002). How schools can do better: Fostering stronger connections between teachers and students. In J. E. Rhodes (Ed.), *New directions for youth development: A critical view of youth mentoring* (pp. 91–107). San Francisco: Jossey-Bass.

Samuels, S. J., & Wu, Y. C. (2003). How the amount of time spent on independent reading affects reading achievement: A response to the National Reading Panel. Retrieved April 2007 from *www.tc.umn.edu/~samue001*.

Shanahan, T. (2006, June/July). Does he really think kids shouldn't read? *Reading Today, 24* p. 12.

Smith-Burke, T. M. (1989). Political and economic dimensions of literacy: Challenges for the 1990's. In S. McCormick & J. Zutell (Eds.), *Cognitive and social perspectives for literacy research and instruction* (pp. 1–18). Chicago: National Reading Conference.

Starkes, J. L., Deakin, J., Allard, F., Hodges, N. J., & Hayes, A. (1996). Deliberate practice in sports: What is it anyway? In K. A. Ericsson (Ed.), *The road to excellence: The acquisition of expert performance in the arts and sciences, sports, and games* (pp. 81–106). Mahwah, NJ: Erlbaum.

Taylor, B. M., Frye, B. J., & Maruyama, G. M. (1990). Time spent reading and reading growth. *American Educational Research Journal, 27*(2), 351–362.

U.S. Department of Education. (2005). *NAEP 2004 trends in academic progress: Three decades of student performance in reading and mathematics.* Washington, DC: National Center for Education Statistics.

Vaughn, S., Moody, S. W., & Schumm, J. S. (1998). Broken promises: Reading instruction in the resource room. *Exceptional Children, 64*, 211–225.

INDEX